T0257729

Encyclopedia of MATLAB: Science and Engineering

Volume IV

Encyclopedia of MATLAB: Science and Engineering Volume IV

Edited by **Louis Young**

CLANRYE
INTERNATIONAL

New Jersey

Published by Clanrye International,
55 Van Reypen Street,
Jersey City, NJ 07306, USA
www.clanryeinternational.com

Encyclopedia of MATLAB: Science and Engineering
Volume IV
Edited by Louis Young

International Standard Book Number: 978-1-63240-192-2 (Hardback)

Printed in the United States of America.

Contents

Permissions

List of Contributors

Preface

This book discusses MATLAB based applications in nearly every branch of science. The collection of insightful chapters will provide beneficial results to the readers in their spheres of work. It deals with the use of MATLAB for formulation of mathematical methods in applied sciences. This compilation of valued chapters covers a wide range of professional fields and can be used for applications in science as well as for engineering.

After months of intensive research and writing, this book is the end result of all who devoted their time and efforts in the initiation and progress of this book. It will surely be a source of reference in enhancing the required knowledge of the new developments in the area. During the course of developing this book, certain measures such as accuracy, authenticity and research focused analytical studies were given preference in order to produce a comprehensive book in the area of study.

This book would not have been possible without the efforts of the authors and the publisher. I extend my sincere thanks to them. Secondly, I express my gratitude to my family and well-wishers. And most importantly, I thank my students for constantly expressing their willingness and curiosity in enhancing their knowledge in the field, which encourages me to take up further research projects for the advancement of the area.

Editor

Mathematical Methods in the Applied Sciences

Simulation of Piecewise Hybrid Dynamical Systems in Matlab

Fatima El Guezar and Hassane Bouzahir

Additional information is available at the end of the chapter

1. Introduction

A hybrid dynamical system is a system containing on the same time continuous state variables and event variables in interaction. We find hybrid systems in different fields. We cite robotic systems, chemical systems controlled by vans and pumps, biological systems (growth and division) and nonlinear electronics systems.

Because of interaction between continuous and discrete aspects, the behavior of hybrid systems can be seen as extremely complex. However, this behavior becomes relatively simple for piece-wise affine hybrid dynamical systems that can, in contrast, generate bifurcation and chaos. There are many examples such as power electronics DC-DC converters.

The common power electronics DC-DC converters are the buck converter and the boost converter. They are switching systems with time variant structure [9].

DC-DC converters are widely used in industrial, commercial, residential and aerospace environments. These circuits are typically controlled by PWM (Piece Wise Modulation) or other similar techniques to regulate the tension and the current given to the charges. The controller decides to pass from one configuration to another by considering that transitions occur cyclically or in discrete time. In order to make the analysis possible, most of mathematical treatments use some techniques that are based on averaging or discretization. Averaging can mean to wrong conclusions on operation of a system. Discrete models do not give any information on the state of the system between the sampled instants. In addition, they are difficult to obtain. In fact, in most cases, a pure analytic study is not possible. Another possible approach to analyze these converters can be done via some models of hybrid dynamical systems. DC-DC converters are particularly good candidates for this type of analysis because of their natural hybrid structure. The nature of commutations of these systems makes them strongly nonlinear. They present specific complex phenomena such as fractals structures of bifurcation and chaos.

The study of nonlinear dynamics of DC-DC converters started in 1984 by works of Brockett and Wood [4]. Since then, chaos and nonlinear dynamics in power electronics circuits have attracted different research groups around the world. Different nonlinear phenomena have been observed such as routes to chaos following the period doubling cascade [16], [5], [19], [20] and [23] or quasi-periodic phenomena [6], [7] and [8], besides border collision bifurcations [23] and [2].

Switched circuits behavior is mostly simulated by pure numerical methods where precision step is increased when the system is near a switching condition. Those numerical tools are widely used mainly because of their ease-of-use and their ability to simulate a wide range of circuits including nonlinear, time–variant, and non–autonomous systems.

Even if those simulators can reach the desired relative precision for a continuous trajectory, they can miss a switching condition and then diverge drastically from the trajectory as in figure 1. This could be annoying when one is interested by border collision bifurcations, or when local behavior is needed with a good accuracy. In those applications, an alternative is to write down analytical, or semi–analytical, trajectories and switching conditions to obtain a recurrence which is very accurate and fast to run. Building and adapting such *ad'hoc* simulators represent a lot of efforts and a risk of mistakes.

Generic and accurate simulators can be proposed if we are restricted to a certain class of systems. A simulation tool with no loss of events is proposed in [14] and [15] for PWAHSs defined on polytopes (finite regions that are bounded by hyperplanes). This class of PWA differential systems has been widely studied as a standard technique to approximate a range of nonlinear systems.

But closed polytopic partition of the state space does not allow simulation of most switching circuits where switching frontiers are mostly single affine constraints or time–dependent periodical events.

This chapter follows our previous study in [13], [12] and [11].

We focus on planar PWAHSs with such simple switching conditions which can model a family of switched planar circuits: bang–bang regulators, the Boost converter, the Charge-Pump Phase Locked Loop (CP-PLL), . . .

This class of systems has analytical trajectories that help to build fast algorithms with no loss of events. We propose a semi-analytical solver for hybrid systems which provides:

- A pure numerical method when the system is nonlinear or non-planar;

- A pure analytic method when all continuous parts of the system and switching conditions can be solved symbolically. This can be the case for the boost converter [3], [21], the second order charge-pump phase locked loop [17], [22].

- A mixed method using analytical trajectories and numerical computation of the switching instant when those solutions are transcendent. This has been used for the third order CP-PLL [17]. It can also be the case for the Buck converter [10], [21], . . .

This chapter is organized as follows. Section 2 contains our main results. We describe the problem to be deal with, we introduce a general algorithm to solve planar HSs, we present the algorithm that detects events' occurrence and devote a subsection to our approach efficiency. Section 3 Illustrates the current-mode controlled Boost converter example. Finally, a conclusion is stated in Section 4.

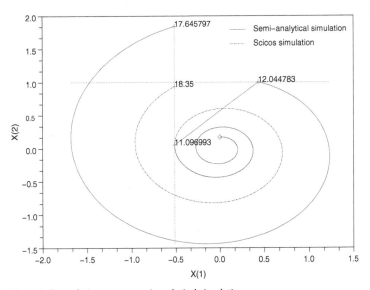

Figure 1. Numerical simulation versus semi–analytical simulation.

2. Main results

2.1. A HS (X, E, t): general definition

A general definition of HSs is presented here. This type of dynamical systems is characterized by the coexistence of two kinds of state vectors: continuous state vector $X(t)$ of real values, and discrete state vector $E(t)$ belonging to a countable discrete set $\mathcal{M}$.

Definition 1. *A continuous-time, autonomous HS is a system of the form:*

$$\dot{X}(t) = F(X(t), E(t)), \; F : \mathcal{H} \to \mathbb{R}^n$$
$$E^+(t) = \phi(X(t), E(t)), \; \phi : \mathcal{H} \to \mathcal{M} \tag{1}$$

$\mathcal{H} = \mathbb{R}^n \times \mathcal{M}$ *is called the hybrid state space.* $X(t) \in \mathbb{R}^n$ *is the continuous state vector of the HS at time instant t and* $E(t) \in \mathcal{M} := \{1, \dots, N\}$ *is its discrete state.* $E^+(t)$ *denotes the updated discrete state right after time instant t.* $\phi : \mathcal{H} \to \mathcal{M}$ *describes the discrete dynamic, it is usually modeled by Petri Nets. A transition from* $E(t) = i$ *to* $E^+(t) = j$ *is valid when the state X reaches a switching set called* $\mathcal{S}_{E_i, E_j}$. *Such transitions are called state dependent events. A HS is called piece-wise affine if for each* $E \in \mathcal{M}$, $F(X, E)$ *can be defined by* $F(X, E) = A_E X + B_E, \forall X$.

Remark — For non–autonomous HSs, the function ϕ can also depend on time $\phi(X, E, t)$: $\mathbb{R}^n \times \mathcal{M} \times \mathbb{R} \rightarrow \mathcal{M}$. Then time dependent events can occur and validate a transition, such as periodic events.

2.2. HSs class of interest

We consider a two dimensional PWAHS ($X(t) \in \mathbb{R}^2$). F has then the affine piece-wise form, $F(.,.)$ is defined for each $E \in \mathcal{M}$ and $X \in \mathbb{R}^2$ by $F(X(t), E(t)) = A_{E(t)}X + B_{E(t)}$, where $A_{E(t)} \in \mathbb{R}^{2 \times 2}$ and $B_{E(t)} \in \mathbb{R}^2$ are two matrices that depend on the discrete state $E(t)$. Hence, a two dimensional PWAHS is a HS that take the form:

$$\dot{X}(t) = A_{E(t)}X + B_{E(t)},$$
$$E(t) \in \mathcal{M} = \{1, 2, \ldots, N\} \tag{2}$$

We consider two kinds of events: state dependent events and periodic events.

The state dependent event transition $\mathcal{S}_{E_i E_j}$ is defined by an affine state border of the form $N'_{ij}.X < l_{ij}$. In this case an event can occur when the continuous state reaches the border of the set $\mathcal{S}_{E_i E_j} = \left\{ X(t) \in \mathbb{R}^2 : N'_{ij}.X \leq l_{ij} \right\}$.

Note that the set $\mathcal{S}_{E_i E_j}$ is not polytopic in the sense that the domain is not the interior of a closed bounded polytope.

Remark — We consider, without loss of generality, the case where a transition occurs at time $d\mathcal{S}_{E_i E_j}$ if and only if the state $X(d\mathcal{S}_{E_i E_j})$ reaches a border of the set $\mathcal{S}_{E_i E_j}$ from outside. Figure 2 defines a transition with the complimentary set $\bar{\mathcal{S}}$, which allows to detect the event in both directions. Both transitions can be met with the set $B = \mathcal{S} \cup \bar{\mathcal{S}}$. Periodic

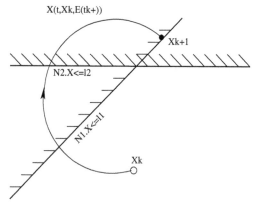

Figure 2. Oriented polytopic state dependent transitions.

events are simply defined by time instants $t = d\mathcal{P}_{E_i E_j}$, where $d\mathcal{P}_{E_i E_j}$ belongs to the set $\mathcal{P}_{E_i E_j} = \{t : t = kT + \varphi, \ k \in \mathbb{N}\}$. T is the period and φ is the phase of such periodic events.

2.3. Event–driven simulation of PWAHSs

The simulation will compute the hybrid state from event to event. Knowing the states $X(t_k)$ and $E(t_k^+)$, one can compute the trajectory $X(t > t_k) = \int_{t_k}^{t} f\left(X(t_k), E(t_k^+)\right) dt + X(t_k)$, assuming that the discrete state is constant $E(t > t_k^+) = E(t_k^+)$. Then the following algorithm runs the simulation determining the date at the next event as the smallest:

Data: t_k, X_k, E_k.
while $t < t_{fin}$ **do**
    Compute all events' dates $d\mathcal{S}_{E_i E_j}$ and $d\mathcal{P}_{E_i E_j}$;
    $t_{k+1} = \min(d\mathcal{S}_{E_i E_j}, d\mathcal{P}_{E_i E_j})$;
    $X_{k+1} = f(X_k, E_k, t_{k+1})$;
    $E_{k+1} = \phi(X_k, E_k, t_{k+1})$;
end

Algorithm 1: Algorithm computing the hybrid state at t_{k+1}.

2.4. Event detection occurrence: description and algorithm

We consider the affine Cauchy problem in $\mathbb{R}^2$:

$$\begin{cases} \dot{X}(t) = AX(t) + B, \; t > t_0 \\ X(t_0) = X_0 \end{cases} \tag{3}$$

where X_0 is the initial value. We compute the smallest strictly positive time t_i^* so that the trajectory of $X(t)$ intersects the fixed border B_i arriving from the part of the plan where $N_i'.X < l_i$. The function $f_i(t) = N_i'.X(t) - l_i$ defines the guard condition for a border B_i. Thus, the problem can be formulated as follows:

$$\text{Find the smallest } t_i^* \text{ such that} \begin{cases} f_i(t_i^*) = 0 \\ \exists\, \delta > 0, \forall t \in \,]t_i^* - \delta, t_i^*[\,, \; f_i(t) < 0 \end{cases} \tag{4}$$

If f_i does not have any strictly positive root or the last condition is not satisfied, t_i^* is given the infinite value.

2.4.1. Analytical trajectories

Definition 2. *For any square matrix A of order n and t in $\mathbb{R}$, the exponential matrix e^{tA} is defined by*

$$e^{tA} = \sum_{k=0}^{\infty} \frac{t^k A^k}{k!} = \mathbb{I} + tA + \frac{t^2 A^2}{2!} + \frac{t^3 A^3}{3!} + \dots \tag{5}$$

where $\mathbb{I}$ is the identity matrix.

It is well known that the analytical trajectory $X(t)$ of the initial value matrix differential equation (3) is given in terms of the exponential matrix and the variation of constants formula by the general integral form:

$$X(t) = e^{(t-t_0)A}X_0 + \int_{t_0}^{t} e^{(t-s)A}B ds. \tag{6}$$

When A is invertible, the above expression becomes linear:

$$X(t) + A^{-1}B = e^{(t-t_0)A}(X_0 + A^{-1}B) \tag{7}$$

The analytical expression of the exponential matrix e^{At} takes two forms depending on whether the eigenvalues p_1 and p_2 of the matrix A are equal or not:

If $p_1 \neq p_2$, then

$$e^{tA} = \frac{(p_1\mathbb{I} - A^\circ)}{p_1 - p_2} e^{p_1 t} - \frac{(p_2\mathbb{I} - A^\circ)}{p_1 - p_2} e^{p_2 t} \tag{8}$$

If $p_1 = p_2 = p$, then

$$e^{tA} = (\mathbb{I} + (p\,\mathbb{I} - A^\circ)\, t)\, e^{pt} \tag{9}$$

where $A = \begin{pmatrix} a_{11} & a_{12} \\ a_{21} & a_{22} \end{pmatrix}$, $A^\circ = \begin{pmatrix} a_{22} & -a_{12} \\ -a_{21} & a_{11} \end{pmatrix}$ and $\mathbb{I} = \begin{pmatrix} 1 & 0 \\ 0 & 1 \end{pmatrix}$.

Using these expressions, we can determine the function $f(t)$ of the problem (4) as follows:

$$f(t) = a_1 + a_2 t + a_3 t^2 + (a_4 + a_5 t) e^{p_1 t} + a_6 e^{p_2 t}$$

where a_i are real scalars.

Depending on the eigenvalues p_1 and p_2, there are five cases that determine the values of the coefficients a_i as shown in Table 1. **Remark** — Coefficients a_i are real scalars that depend on

$f(t) = a_1 + \dots$	$p_1 \in \mathbb{R}^*$	$p_1 = 0$
$p_2 \in \mathbb{R}^*$	$a_4 e^{p_1 t} + a_6 e^{p_2 t}$	$a_2 t + a_6 e^{p_2 t}$
$p_2 = 0$	$a_2 t + a_4 e^{p_1 t}$	$a_2 t + a_3 t^2$
$p_1 = \overline{p_2} \in \mathbb{C}^*$	$a_4 e^{p_1 t} + a_5 e^{p_2 t}$, with $a_5 = \overline{a_4} \in \mathbb{C}^*$	
$p_1 = p_2 \in \mathbb{R}^*$	$(a_4 + a_5 t) e^{p_1 t}$	

Table 1. Expressions of $f(t)$ depending on the eigenvalues p_1 and p_2.

the eigenvalues p_1 and p_2, the initial point X_k and the border parameters are N_i and l_i.

In some cases, ($p_1 = p_2 = 0$, gray cell in Table 1) roots of $f(t)$ can be found analytically and the problem is solved with machine precision.

In other cases, the solution can not be found with classical functions and then a numeric algorithm should be used. Using classical methods like Newton does not guaranty existence or convergence of the smallest positive root. To meet these conditions, let us use analytical roots of the derivative function $f'(t)$ expressed in Table 2. We can then compute analytically

$f'(t) = \dots$	$p_1 \in \mathbb{R}^*$	$p_1 = 0$
$p_2 \in \mathbb{R}^*$	$a_4\, p_1\, e^{p_1 t} + a_6\, p_2\, e^{p_2 t}$	$a_2 + a_6\, p_2\, e^{p_2 t}$
$p_2 = 0$	$a_2 + a_4\, p_1\, e^{p_1 t}$	$a_2 + 2\, a_3\, t$
$p_1 = \overline{p_2} \in \mathbb{C}^*$	$a_4\, p_1\, e^{p_1 t} + \overline{a_4 p_1}\, e^{\overline{p_1} t}$, with $a_4 \in \mathbb{C}^*$	
$p_1 = p_2 \in \mathbb{R}^*$	$(a_4\, p_1 + a_5 + a_5\, p_1\, t)\, e^{p_1 t}$	

Table 2. Expressions of $f'(t)$ depending on the eigenvalues p_1 and p_2

the set L of ordered roots of $f'(t)$, those roots determines monotone intervals of $f(t)$. The following algorithm is used to return the solution t^* when it exists or the value ∞ if not.

Remark — When $(p_1, p_2) \in \mathbb{C}^* \times \mathbb{C}^*$ the set L is infinite: when the real part of p_i is positive, the algorithm

---

Data: N_i, l_i, A, B, X_k
Result: construct the set L, compute t^*
$T \leftarrow \{0, L, \infty\}$;
$t^* \leftarrow \infty$;
for $i \leftarrow 1$ **to** $(card(T) - 1)$ **do**
    if $f(T(i)) < 0 \,\&\, f(T(i+1)) > 0$ **then**
        $t^* \leftarrow solve\,[T(i), T(i+1)]$;
        Break;
    end
end

Algorithm 2: Algorithm computing t^* when a solution is transcendent.

---

will end by finding a root. In the other case, the set L should be reduced to its three first elements, to find a crossing point when it exists.

3. Matlab modelling

Our semi-analytical solver is composed of different main programs that define the studied affine system. First, we create the affine system given with a specifically chosen name. Then, we define the matrices A_i and B_i. After that, we give the switching borders with the sign of transitions and all necessary elements or we give the period if it is about a periodic event. Finally, we execute the simulation by specifying the initial state and the time of simulation.

3.1. Application: Current-mode controlled Boost converter

A current-mode controlled Boost converter in open loop consists of two parts: a converter and a switching controller. The basic circuit is given in figure 3.

This converter is a second-order circuit comprising an inductor, a capacitor, a diode, a switch and a load resistance connected in parallel with the capacitor.

The general circuit operation is driven by the switching controller. It compares the inductor current i_L with the reference current I_{ref} and generates the on/off driving signal for the switch S. When S is on, the current builds up in the inductor.

When the inductor current i_L reaches a reference value, the switch opens and the inductor current flows through the load and the diode. The switch is again closed at the arrival of the next clock pulse from a free running clock of period T.

The Boost converter controlled in current mode is modeled by an affine piece-wise hybrid system defined by the same sub-systems given in equation as follows:

$$S_1 : \dot{X}(t) = \begin{bmatrix} \frac{-1}{RC} & 0 \\ 0 & 0 \end{bmatrix} X(t) + \begin{bmatrix} 0 \\ \frac{V_{in}}{L} \end{bmatrix}$$

(10)

$$S_2 : \dot{X}(t) = \begin{bmatrix} \frac{-1}{RC} & \frac{1}{C} \\ \frac{-1}{L} & 0 \end{bmatrix} X(t) + \begin{bmatrix} 0 \\ \frac{V_{in}}{L} \end{bmatrix},$$

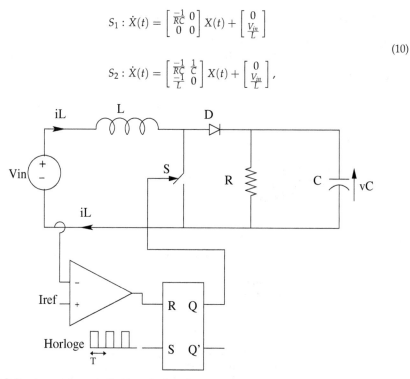

Figure 3. Boost converter controlled in current mode.

In the case of the Boost converter controlled in current mode, there are two types of events:

A state event defined by a fixed border of the set $\mathcal{S}_{E_1 E_2}$:

$$\mathcal{S}_{E_1 E_2} = \left\{ X \in \mathbb{R}^2 : [0\ 1]\, X < I_{ref} \right\}$$

(11)

and another periodic event defined by the dates $t = d\mathcal{P}_{E_i E_j}$, where $d\mathcal{P}_{E_i E_j}$ belongs to the set:

$$\mathcal{P}_{E_2 E_1} = \{ t \in \mathbb{R} : t = nT,\ n \in \mathbb{N} \}$$

(12)

where T is the period of this periodic event. The different simulations are obtained using our planar PWA solver.

Before performing any study of the observed bifurcations in this circuit, a numerical simulation in the parametric plane is needed.

The following program calcule_balayage_mod.m is used to obtain the parametric plane:

```
%%%%-------------------------------calcule_balayage_mod.m---------------
%
%
clear all;
close all;
%
%% File calculating points to display a figure of parametric plane
% Example of boost
% Save data in...
%
monfich=('data_balais');
% You should specify the path of hybrid_solver_matlab
%
addpath('.\hybrid_solver_matlab');
%
eps=1E-6;
ordre_max=15;
x_eps = 1e-5;
Xmax=100;
nb_trans=500;
nb_inits=1;
ta= 0.5:1.1/200:1.6;
tb= 5:15/200:20;
a=ta(1);
b=tb(1);
%% Definition of BOOST
%Iref changes and noted a
%Vin changes and noted b
%
L=1.5e-3;
T=100e-6;
R=40;
Vin=b;
C=5e-6;
Iref=a;
AE1=[
    -1/R/C  0 ;
    0    0
    ];
```

```
AE2=[
    -1/R/C   1/C ;
    -1/L     0
    ];
B1=[0;
    b/L];
B2=B1;
N1 = [0 1];
S1 = '<';
[p1,p2]=racines(AE1);
H=create_hybrid_system('affine');
H=add_state(H,1,'On',AE1,B1);
H=add_state(H,2,'Off',AE2,B2);
H=add_event(H,1,'Iref',N1,a,S1);
H=add_periodic_event(H,1,'Clock',T,0);
H=add_transition(H,1,2,1);
H=add_periodic_transition(H,2,1,1);
%
%% initial state
Xi.t=T/1000;
Xi.E=1;
Xi.Xc=[16.5;0.47];
mape=colormap(ma_color);
na=length(ta)
tic
for ia = 1 : na
    a=ta(ia);
    for ib= 1 : length(tb)
        b=tb(ib);
        %% update of the equation with a new a
        % here only Iref that changes and modifies a border
        B1=[0;
            b/L];
        H=add_state(H,1,'On',AE1,B1);
        H=add_state(H,2,'Off',AE2,B2);
        H=add_event(H,1,'Iref',N1,a,S1);
        H=update_transition(H,1,2,1);
        ordres(ib,ia)=-2;
        for init = 1:nb_inits
            X=Xi;
             or = ordre_max;
            for i = 1 : nb_trans
                [X]=recu(H,X); %1->2;
                [X]=recu(H,X); %2->1;
                if (X.t==Inf)
                    or=-1;
```

```
                        break;
                    end
                    if (max(abs(X.Xc))>Xmax)
                        or=0;
                        break;
                    end
                end
                if (or==ordre_max)
        %% check if we have periodic event state E=1
                    if (X.E ~= 1)
                      [X]=recu(H,X);
                    end
                     it=1;
                     X0 = X;
                     tt0=X.t;
                     while (it<ordre_max) & (or == ordre_max)
                        [X]=recu(H,X); %1->2;
                                tt=X.t-tt0;
                                ii=1;
                                while (ii*T<tt)
                                    it=it+1;
                                    ii=ii+1;
                                end
                        [X]=recu(H,X);
                        tt0=X.t;
                        if (max(abs(X.Xc-X0.Xc))<x_eps)
                            or=it;
                            break;
                        else
                            it = it + 1;
                        end
                    end
                end
                or;
                ordres(ib,ia)=max(or,ordres(ib,ia));
            end
        end
        fprintf('About %2.1f %% done, still about %5.0f secondes to be...
            %3.0f minutes\n',ia/na*100,toc/ia*(na-ia),toc/ia*(na-ia)/60)
end
temps=toc
save(monfich)
affiche_balayage
```

After calculating the necessary points of the parametric plane saved in the file named dat_balais, the next program affiche_balayage.m plots the figure given in Fig.4

```
%%%%------------------------------affiche_balayage_mod.m-------------
% Used in general after calcule_balayage

%% Charge the saved 2-D bifurcation scan
%if the file was not executed
if (exist('ordres')==1)
    disp('use the points matrix of the workspace');
elseif (exist('data_balais.mat')==2)
    disp('charge the points that are in data_balais.mat');
    load data_balais.mat
else
    disp('There are no points or files of points: try ordres.mat...
          insha ALLAH! It may be long...')
    load ordres.mat
end
%
%% Display the bifurcation scan diagram
da=(ta(2)-ta(1))/2;
db=(tb(2)-tb(1))/2;
colormap(mape)
for ia = 1 : length(ta)
    a=ta(ia);
    for ib= 1 : length(tb)
        b=tb(ib);
        if (ordres(ib,ia)<0)
            %plot(a,b,'.w');
            fill([a-da a-da a+da a+da],[b-db b+db b+db b-db],...
            'w','EdgeColor','none')
        elseif (ordres(ib,ia)==0)
            %plot(a,b,'+w');
            fill([a-da a-da a+da a+da],[b-db b+db b+db b-db],...
            'w','EdgeColor','none')
        else
            %plot(a,b,'s','color',mape(ordres(ib,ia),:),...
            'MarkerFaceColor',mape(ordres(ib,ia),:),'MarkerSize');
            fill([a-da a-da a+da a+da],[b-db b+db b+db b-db],...
            mape(ordres(ib,ia),:),'EdgeColor','none')
        end
        hold on
    end
end
colormap(mape)
colorbar %(mape)
colorbar('YTickLabel',...
        {'01','02','03','04','05','06','07',...
         '08','09','10','11','12','13','14','0+'})
```

The figure 4 of the parametric plane allows to emphasize the parameters values for which there exists at least one attractor (fixed point, cycle of order k, strange attractor).

Figure 5 shows a bifurcation diagram (Feigenbaum type) in the plane (I_{ref}, i_L). However, figure 6 shows the bifurcation diagram in the space plane (I, i_L, v_C).

To draw these two figures we use programs: calcule_figuier.m and affiche_figuier.m

```
%%%%--------------------------calcule_figuier.m---------------
%
clear all;
close all;
%
%% Code that calculates then displays the points of a bifurcation
tree
% Boost converter example
% Save the data in ...
monfich=('data_points');
%
addpath('../hybrid_solver_matlab');
%
eps=1E-6; % precision of the solver
nb_trans=400;%400 %Number of iterations to pass the transient phase
ordre_max=100; %100% nombre de points affichés après le transitoire
ta= 0.5:0.0025:1.6; % values of the parameter a to be calculated
%ta= 1.22:0.001:1.4;%0.5:0.001:1.6;
points=zeros(2,length(ta),ordre_max);
% points (x or y, index a, the ordre_max of the last trajectory
points)
a=ta(1);
%
%% Definition of the Boost converter
%Iref is a variable denoted a
L=1.5e-3;
T=100e-6;
R=40;
Vin=10;
C=5e-6;
Iref=a;
AE1=[
    -1/R/C   0 ;
       0     0
    ];
AE2=[
    -1/R/C  1/C ;
    -1/L     0
    ];
```

```
B1=[0;
    Vin/L];
B2=B1;
N1 = [0 1];
S1 = '<';
[p1,p2]=racines(AE1)
H=create_hybrid_system('affine');
H=add_state(H,1,'On',AE1,B1);
H=add_state(H,2,'Off',AE2,B2);
H=add_event(H,1,'Iref',N1,a,S1);
H=add_periodic_event(H,2,'Clock',T,0);
H=add_transition(H,1,2,1);
H=add_periodic_transition(H,2,1,2);
%
%% Initial condition
X0.t=T/1000;
X0.E=1;
X0.Xc=[16.4549;0.4648];
%
%% Vary a and memorize the points for the bifurcation tree
na=length(ta);
tic;
for ia = 1 : na
    a=ta(ia);
    if a==1.3
    end
    %% Update of the equation with a new a
     vi=X.Xc;
     cc=ia;
    % Here only Iref varies and the corresponding border is then
    modified
    H=add_event(H,1,'Iref',N1,a,S1);
    H=update_transition(H,1,2,1);
    X=X0;
    %
    %% transient zone
    for i = 1: nb_trans
        [X]=recu(H,X);
          [X]=recu(H,X);
    end
    %% Assure that we are on a periodic event, state E=1
    %
     if (X.E ~= 1)
         [X]=recu(H,X);
     end
     %
```

```
      Xin=X.Xc;
        tt0=X.t;
        it=1;
    %% memorize ordremax points issued from the periodic transition
    2-> 1
    %
      while (it<(ordre_max+1))
          [X]=recu(H,X);%1->2
          tt=X.t-tt0;
          ii=1;
          while (ii*T<tt)
              points(:,ia,it)=traj_ni(AE1,B1,p1,p2,Xin,ii*T);
              Xin=traj_ni(AE1,B1,p1,p2,Xin,ii*T);
              it=it+1;
              ii=ii+1;
          end
        %
        [X]=recu(H,X);%2->1

        points(:,ia,it)=X.Xc;
        Xin=X.Xc;
        tt0=X.t;
        it=it+1;
      end
    %
    fprintf('Approximately %2.1f %% are done, yet approximately %5.0f
    seconds...
            that is %3.0f minutes\n',ia/na*100,toc/ia*(na-ia),toc/ia*
            (na-ia)/60)
end
%scan the values of 'a'
temps_ecoule=toc
save(monfich)
%%
cc
vi
affiche_figuier

%%%%---------------------------affiche_figuier.m---------------
%% Charges the file containing the saved points
% if the file "figuier" is not executed
if (exist('points')==1)
   disp('use the points matrix of the workspace');
elseif (exist('data_points.mat')==2)
   disp('charge the points that are in data_points.mat');
   load data_points
```

```
else
  disp('There are no points or files of points: try points.mat insh
  ALLAH!')
  load points
end
%% bifurcation tree depending on the dimensions x then y
% % for dim=1:2
% %
% %      plot(points(dim,1,1));
% %      hold on;
% %      for ia=1:length(ta)
% %          for io=2:ordre_max
% %              plot(ta(ia),points(dim,ia,io));
% %          end
% %      end
% %      xlabel('a');
% %      figure
% % end
%   figure
%
%      plot(points(1,1,1));
%      hold on;
%      for ia=1:length(ta)
%          for io=2:ordre_max
%              plot(ta(ia),points(1,ia,io));
%          end
%      end
%      xlabel('Vin(V)');
%      ylabel('vC(V)');
     plot(points(2,1,1));
     hold on;
     for ia=1:length(ta)
         for io=2:ordre_max
             plot(ta(ia),points(2,ia,io));
         end
     end
     xlabel('Iref(A)');
     ylabel('iL(A)');
%% bifurcation tree in 3D
% z = variable parameter denoted a
% x the dimension x
% y the dimension y of the point

  plot3(points(1,1,1),points(2,1,1),ta(1));
  plot3(ta(1),points(2,1,1),points(1,1,1));
  hold on;
```

```
for ia=1:length(ta)
    for io=1:ordre_max
        plot3(ta(ia),points(2,ia,io),points(1,ia,io));
    end
end
xlabel('Iref(A)');
ylabel('iL(A)');
zlabel('vC(V)');
```

In these two figures, the voltage V_{in} is fixed to 10V and the current I_{ref} varies in the interval $[0.5, 1.6]$. We observe a period cascade doubling leading to a chaotic regime, interrupted by a border collision bifurcation at $I_{ref} = 1.23A$ (see figure 7). In this figure, a distinction is given between the attractors of attractive cycle type of the order 1 to 14. Each cycle of order k is associated with one color.

For example, the blue area O1 represents the parameters' values for which there exists an attractive fixed point (fundamental periodic regime). The red area O2 represents the existence of an attractive cycle of order 2. The yellow area O4 represents the existence of an attractive cycle of order 4 and so on until getting the cycles O14 of order $k = 14$. The black area O+ corresponds to parameters values (I_{ref}, V_{in}) for which there exist cycles of order $k \geq 15$ or other types of attractors. In this last area, a chaotic phenomenon could be observed. This bi-dimensional diagram shows some bifurcation curves. In fact, for the rectangle defined by the interval of parameter $V_{in} \in [7, 15]$ and the parameter $I_{ref} \in [0.5, 1.6]$, we observe an area of blue color (existence of attractive fixed point) followed by an area of red color (existence of cycle of order 2), an area of yellow color (existence of cycle of order 4) and another area of black color (existence of cycle of order $k \geq 15$ or another attractor type); this succession of zones corresponds to the existence of period doubling cascade.

This representation of the parametric plane is not enough to establish a bifurcation structure of the hybrid model of the Boost converter, but it is useful for the initialization of programs to draw bifurcation curves.

The simulation results (temporal domain and voltage-current plane (v_C, i_L)) are obtained using the planar PWH solver in the case of the Boost converter controlled in current mode for periods: 1T (figure 8) for $I_{ref} = 0.7A$, 2T (figure 9) for $I_{ref} = 1A$, 4T (figure 10) for $I_{ref} = 1.3A$ and the chaotic regime (figure 11) for $I_{ref} = 1.5A$. For these plots we used the code below by choosing the bifurcation parameter I_{ref} corresponding to each period case.

```
%%
% Define an affine system ii at random and simulate it
% by use of our Matlab toolbox solver
%
%detection of errors manually
%
% Warning
% In the affine case '=' is not supported yet !
addpath('.\hybrid_solver');
%
```

```
L=1.5E-3;
T=100E-6;
R=40;
E=10;
C=5E-6;
%Bifurcation parameter
Iref=0.7; %1;%1.3;%1.5;
% X = [vc ; iL]
%
%System 1 On
A1=[ -1/R/C,  0 ;
       0       0 ];
B1=[0 ; E/L];
N1 = [0 1];
Lim1= Iref;

% System 2 Off
A2=[ -1/R/C,  1/C ;
      -1/L      0 ];
B2=[0 ; E/L];
%
%% Initial condition
X0.t=0;
X0.E=1;
X0.Xc=[16.4549;0.4648];%[13.6097 ;0.3435];
%
%% Boost converter
clear H;
H=create_hybrid_system('Boost Converter');
H=add_state(H,1,'On',A1,B1);
H=add_state(H,2,'Off',A2,B2);
%
H=add_event(H,1,'Iref',N1,Lim1,'<');
H=add_transition(H,1,2,1);
H=add_periodic_event(H,2,'Clock',T,0);
H=add_periodic_transition(H,2,1,2);
Han=H;
%
Xan = hsim(Han,X0,4*T);
%
[XcAn,EAn,tAn]=split_state(Xan);
%
 trajplane(Xan,Han)
     figure;
    subplot(211);
    trajplot(Xan,Han,1);
    subplot(212);
    trajplot(Xan,Han,2);
```

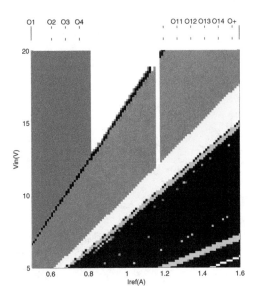

Figure 4. Parametric diagram of the Boost converter in the plane (I_{ref}, V_{in}) for $I_{ref} \in [0.5, 1.6]$A and $V_{in} \in [5, 20]$V.

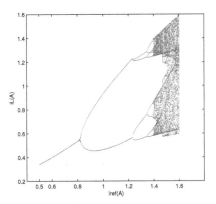

Figure 5. Bifurcation diagram of the Boost in the plane (I_{ref}, i_L) for $I_{ref} \in [0.5, 1.6]$A and $V_{in} = 10$V fixed.

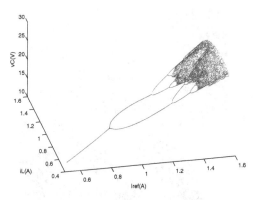

Figure 6. Bifurcation diagram of the Boost in the space (I_{ref}, i_L, v_c) for $I_{ref} \in [0.5, 1.6]$A and $V_{in} = 10$V fixed.

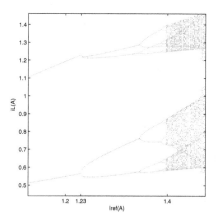

Figure 7. Zoom of figure 5: Border collision for $I_{ref} = 1.23$A.

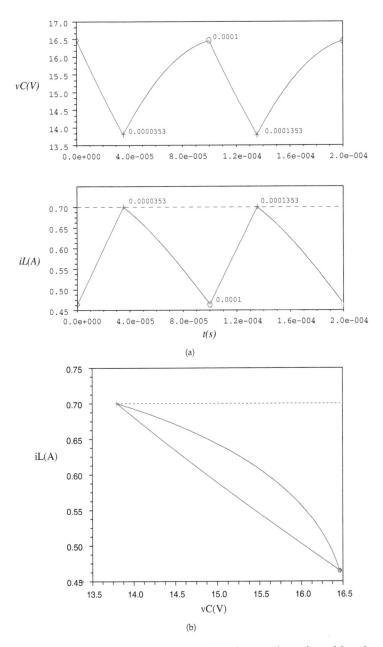

Figure 8. Fundamental periodic regime for $I_{ref} = 0.7$A: (a) (up) temporal waveform of the voltage v_C, (down) temporal waveform of the current i_L; (b) phase plane (v_C, i_L).

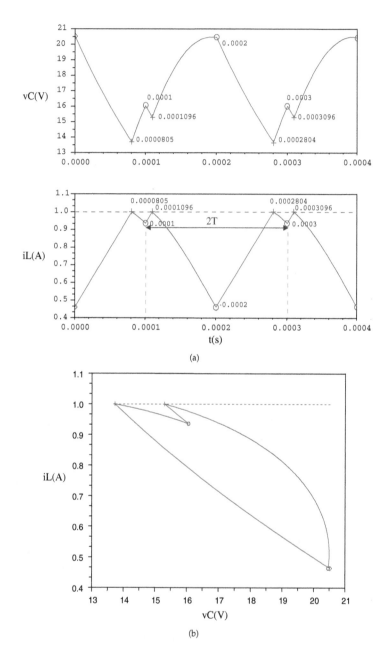

Figure 9. Cycle of order 2 for $I_{ref} = 1$A:(a) (up) temporal waveform of the voltage v_C, (down) temporal waveform of the current i_L; (b) phase plane (v_C, i_L).

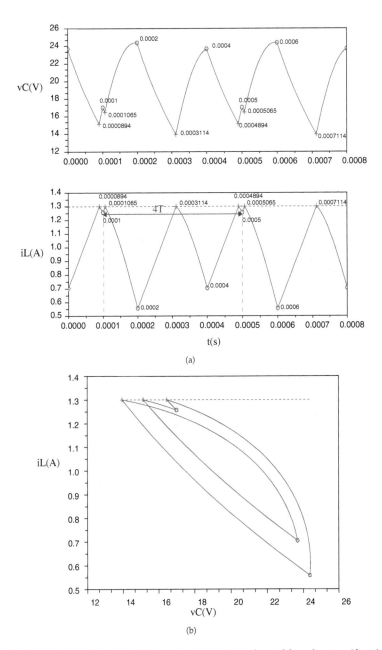

Figure 10. Cycle of order 4 for $I_{ref} = 1.3A$: (a) (up) temporal waveform of the voltage v_C, (down) temporal waveform of the current i_L; (b) phase plane (v_C, i_L).

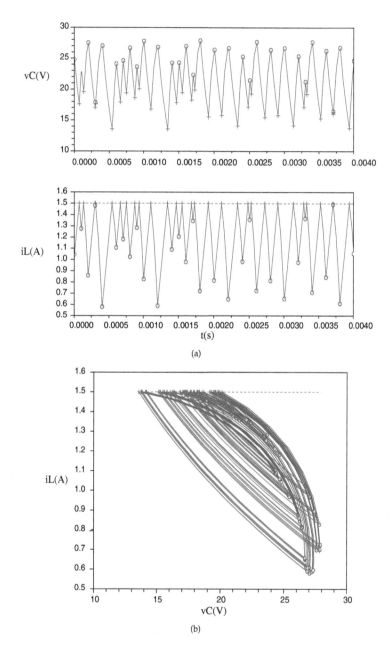

Figure 11. Chaotic regime for $I_{ref} = 1.5$A: (a) (up) temporal waveform of the voltage v_C, (down) temporal waveform of the current i_L; (b) phase plane (v_C, i_L).

4. Conclusion

In this chapter, we have showed an accurate and fast method to determine events' occurrence for planar piece-wise affine hybrid systems. As a result, we have implemented our algorithm in Matlab toolbox version (free downloadable on http://felguezar.000space.com/).

This toolbox has also been completed by analysis tools such as displaying the bifurcation and parametric diagrams. The algorithm takes the advantage of the analytical form that appears in the planar case. Our approach can not be extended to a higher dimension. DC-DC converters like Boost converter are known to be simple switched circuits but very rich in nonlinear dynamics. As application, we have chosen the example of Boost converter controlled in current mode.

Acknowledgments

The authors would like to thank Pascal Acco and Danièle Fournier–Prunaret for crucial discussions on the original version of our work on this subject.

Author details

Fatima El Guezar
ESSI & ERMAGIM, Ibn Zohr University, EST, PO Box 32/S, Agadir, Morocco

Hassane Bouzahir
ESSI & ERMAGIM, Ibn Zohr University, EST, PO Box 32/S, Agadir, Morocco
Faculty of Engineering, AlHosn University, PO Box 38772, Abu Dhabi, United Arab Emirates

5. References

[1] Acco, P. (December 2003). Etude de la boucle à verrouillage de phase par impulsions de charge: Prise en compte des aspects hybrides. *Ph D thesis*, Institut National des Sciences Appliquées de Toulouse, France.

[2] Banerjee, S. (2000). Bifurcations in two-dimensional piecewise smooth maps - theory and applications in switching circuits, *IEEE Trans. on Circuits and Systems-I*, Vol.47, pp. 633-647.

[3] Bouzahir H.; El Guezar, F. & Ueta, T. (2007). On Scicos simulation of a hybrid dynamical system. *Proceedings of the 15th IEEE International Workshop on Nonlinear Dynamics of Electronic Systems*, Tokushima, Japan, pp. 62–65.

[4] Brockett R. W. & Wood J. R. (1984). Understanding power converter chaotic behavior mechanisms in protective and abnormal modes. *Proceedings of POWERCON 11*, pp. E–14.

[5] Deane, J. H. B. & Hamill D. C. (1990). Instability, subharmonics, and chaos in power electronic systems. *IEEE Trans. Power Electronics*, Volume 5, pp. 260–268, 1990.

[6] El Aroudi, A.; Benadero, L.; Toribio, E. & Machiche, S. (2000). Quasiperiodicty and chaos in the DC-DC buck-boost converter. *International Journal of Bifurcation and Chaos*, Vol. 10, pp. 359-371.

[7] El Aroudi, A. (February 2000). Study of nonlinear phenomena and quasiperiodicity route to chaos in PWM DC/DC converters. *Ph D thesis*, Universitat Politécnica de Catalunya, Spain.

[8] El Aroudi, A. & Leyva, R. (2001). Quasi-periodic route to chaos in a PWM voltage-controlled DC-DC boost converter. *IEEE Trans. on Circuits and Systems*, Vol. 48, No. 8, pp. 967-978.

[9] El Aroudi, A.; Debbat, M.; Giral, R.; Olivar, G.; Benadero, L.& Toribio, E. (2005). Bifurcations in DC-DC switching converters: review of methods and applications. *International Journal of Bifurcation and Chaos*, Vol. 5, pp. 1549–1578.

[10] El Guezar, F. & Bouzahir, H. (2008). Chaotic behavior in a switched dynamical system. *Modelling and Simulation in Engineering*, Vol. 2008, Article ID 798395, 6 pages.

[11] El Guezar, F.; Acco, P.; Bouzahir, H. & Fournier-Prunaret, D. (2008). Accurate and Fast Event Detection Occurrence in Planar Piecewise Affine Hybrid Systems. *Proceedings of the International Symposium NOLTA (NOn Linear Theory and its Applications)*, September 7-10, Budapest-Hungary, pp. 341–344.

[12] El Guezar, F. (December 2009). Modélisation et simulation des systèmes dynamiques hybrides affines par morceaux. Exemples en électronique de puissance. *Ph D thesis*, Institut National des Sciences Appliquées de Toulouse, France.

[13] El Guezar, F.; Bouzahir, H. & Fournier-Prunaret, D. (2011). Event Detection Occurrence For Planar Piecewise Affine Hybrid Systems. *Nonlinear Analysis: Hybrid Systems*, Vol. 5, pp. 626–638.

[14] Girard, A. (2002). Detection of event occurrence in piece-wise linear hybrid systems. *Proceedings of the 4th International Conference on Recent Advances in Soft Computing*, Nottingham, United Kingdom, December, pp. 19–25.

[15] Girard, A. (September 2004). Analyse algorithmique des systèmes hybrides. *Ph D thesis*, Institut National Polytechnique de Grenoble, France.

[16] Hamill , D. C. & Jeffries, D. J. (1988). Subharmonics and chaos in a controlled switched-mode power converter. *IEEE Trans. Circuits Syst. I*, Vol. 35, No. 8, pp. 1059–1060.

[17] Hedayat, C. D.; Hachem, A.; Leduc, Y. & Benbassat, G. (March–April 1997). High-level modeling applied to the second-order charge-pump PLL circuit. *Technical report, Texas Instrument Technical Journal*. Vol. 14, No. 2.

[18] Mira, C. (1987). Chaotic dynamics. *World scientific Publishing*.

[19] Tse, C.K. (1994). Chaos from a Buck switching regulator operating in discontinuous mode. *IEEE Transactions on International Journal of Circuit Theory and Application*. Vol. 22, No. 7, pp. 262–278.

[20] Tse, C.K. (1994). Flip bifurcation and chaos in three–state boost switching regulators. *IEEE Transactions on Circuits and Systems I: Theory and Applications*, Vol. 41, No. 1, pp. 16–23.

[21] Tse, C.K. (2003). *Complex behavior of switching Power converters*, CRC Press.

[22] Van Paemel, M. (July 1994). Analysis of a charge pump PLL: a new model. *IEEE Transactions on Communications*, Vol. 42, No. 7, pp. 2490-2498.

[23] Yuan, G. H.; Banerjee, S.; Ott, E. & Yorke, J. A. (1998). Border-collision bifurcations in the buck converter, *IEEE Trans. on Circuits and Systems-I*, Vol. 45, pp. 707–715.

Chapter 2

Fouling in Heat Exchangers

Hassan Al-Haj Ibrahim

Additional information is available at the end of the chapter

1. Introduction

Fouling is generally defined as the deposition and accumulation of unwanted materials such as scale, algae, suspended solids and insoluble salts on the internal or external surfaces of processing equipment including boilers and heat exchangers (Fig 1). Heat exchangers are process equipment in which heat is continuously or semi-continuously transferred from a hot to a cold fluid directly or indirectly through a heat transfer surface that separates the two fluids. Heat exchangers consist primarily of bundles of pipes, tubes or plate coils.

Figure 1. Fouling of heat exchangers.

Fouling on process equipment surfaces can have a significant, negative impact on the operational efficiency of the unit. On most industries today, a major economic drain may be caused by fouling. The total fouling related costs for major industrialised nations is estimated to exceed US$4.4 milliard annually. One estimate puts the losses due to fouling of heat exchangers in industrialised nations to be about 0.25% to 30% of their GDP [1, 2]. According to Pritchard and Thackery (Harwell Laboratories), about 15% of the maintenance costs of a process plant can be attributed to heat exchangers and boilers, and of this, half is probably caused by fouling. Costs associated with heat exchanger fouling include production losses due to efficiency deterioration and to loss of production during planned or unplanned shutdowns due to fouling, and maintenance costs resulting from the removal of fouling deposits with chemicals and/or mechanical antifouling devices or the replacement of corroded or plugged equipment. Typically, cleaning costs are in the range of $40,000 to $50,000 per heat exchanger per cleaning.

Fouling in heat exchangers is not a new problem. In fact, fouling has been recognised for a long time, and research on heat exchanger fouling was conducted as early as 1910 and the first practical application of this research was implemented in the 1920's. Technological progress in prevention, mitigation and removal techniques in industrial fouling was investigated in a study conducted at the Battelle Pacific Northwest Laboratories for the U.S. Department of Energy. Two hundred and thirty one patents relevant to fouling were analysed [3]. Furthermore, great technical advance in the design and manufacture of heat exchangers has in the meantime been achieved. Nonetheless, heat exchanger fouling remains today one of the major unresolved problems in Thermal Science, and prevention or mitigation of the fouling problem is still an ongoing process. Further research on the problem of fouling in heat exchangers and practical methods for predicting the fouling factor, making use in particular of modern digital techniques, are still called for. One significant and clear indication of the relevance and urgency of the problem may be seen in the current international patent activity on fouling (Table 1).

Country	No. of Patents	% of Patents
U.S.A.	147	63.6
Germany	22	9.5
Japan	21	9.1
Sweden	9	3.9
Switzerland	8	3.5
Other	24	10.4
Total	231	100.0

Table 1. International Patent Activity [4]

Major detrimental effects of fouling include loss of heat transfer as indicated by charge outlet temperature decrease and pressure drop increase. Other detrimental effects of fouling may also include blocked process pipes, under-deposit corrosion and pollution. Where the heat flux is high, as in steam generators, fouling can lead to local hot spots resulting ultimately in mechanical failure of the heat transfer surface. Such effects lead in most cases to production losses and increased maintenance costs.

Loss of heat transfer and subsequent charge outlet temperature decrease is a result of the low thermal conductivity of the fouling layer or layers which is generally lower than the thermal conductivity of the fluids or conduction wall. As a result of this lower thermal conductivity, the overall thermal resistance to heat transfer is increased and the effectiveness and thermal efficiency of heat exchangers are reduced. A simple way to monitor a heat transfer system is to plot the outlet temperature versus time. In one unit at an oil refinery, in Homs, Syria, fouling led to a feed temperature decrease from 210°C to 170°C. In order to bring the feed to the required temperature, the heat duty of the furnace may have to be increased with additional fuel required and resulting increased fuel cost. Alternatively, the heat exchanger surface area may have to be increased with consequent additional installation and maintenance costs. The required excess surface area may vary between 10-50%, with an average around 35%, and the additional extra costs involved may add up to a staggering 2.5 to 3.0 times the initial purchase price of the heat exchangers.

With the onset of fouling and the consequent build up of fouling layer or layers, the cross sectional area of tubes or flow channels is reduced. In addition, increased surface roughness due to fouling will increase frictional resistance to flow. Such effects inevitably lead to an increase in the pressure drop across the heat exchanger, which is required to maintain the flow rate through the exchanger, and may even lead to flow blocks. Experience with pressure drop monitoring has shown, however, that it is not usually as sensitive an indicator of the early onset of fouling when compared to heat transfer data; thus pressure drop is not commonly used for crude preheat monitoring. In situations where significant swings in flow rates are experienced, flow correction can be applied to both pressure drop and to heat transfer calculations to normalise the data to a standard flow.

Different fouling deposit structures can lead to under-deposit corrosion of the substrate material such as localised fouling, deposit tubercles and sludge piles. The factors that are most likely to influence the probability of under-deposit corrosion include deposit composition and its porosity and permeability. Even minor components of the deposits can sometimes cause severe corrosion of the underlying metal such as the hot corrosion caused by vanadium in the deposits of fired boilers [5].

Fouling is responsible for the emission of many millions of tonnes of carbon dioxide as well as the use and disposal of hazardous cleaning chemicals. Data from oil refineries suggest that crude oil fouling accounts for about 10% of the total CO_2 emission of these plants. Wastes generated from the cleaning of heat exchangers may contain hazardous wastes such as lead and chromium, although some refineries which do not produce leaded gasoline and which use non-chrome corrosion inhibitors typically do not generate sludge that contains these constituents. Oily wastewater is also generated during heat exchanger cleaning.

The factors that govern fouling in heat exchangers are many and varied. Of such factors some may be related to the feed properties such as its chemical nature, density, viscosity, diffusivity, pour and cloud points, interfacial properties and colloidal stability factors. The chemical nature of the feed in particular can be an important factor affecting to a large degree the rate and extent of fouling. This includes the chemical composition of the feed and the stability of its components and their compatibility with one another and with heat exchanger surfaces as well as the presence in the feed of unsaturated and unstable compounds, inorganic salts and trace elements such as sulphur, nitrogen and oxygen. The feed storage conditions and its exposure to oxygen on storage in particular can in most cases also affect materially the rate and nature of fouling.

Other factors of equal importance to the feed properties may be related to operating conditions and equipment design, such as feed temperature, bulk fluid velocity or flow rate, heat exchanger geometry, nature of alloy used and wettability of surfaces where fouling occurs. The rate of fouling is feed temperature dependent with different rates of fouling between the feed inlet and outlet sides of the heat exchanger. In a shell and tube heat exchanger, the conventional segment baffle geometry is largely responsible for higher fouling rates. Uneven velocity profiles, back-flows and eddies generated on the shell side of a segmentally-baffled heat exchanger results in higher fouling and shorter run lengths between periodic cleaning and maintenance of tube bundles.

All these and other factors that may affect fouling need to be considered and taken into account in order to be able to prevent fouling if possible or to predict the rate of fouling or fouling factor prior to taking the necessary steps for fouling mitigation, control and removal.

2. Fouling mechanisms and stages

Fouling can be divided into a number of distinctively different mechanisms. Generally speaking, several of these fouling mechanisms occur at the same time and each requires a different prevention technique. Of these different mechanisms some represent different stages in the process of fouling. The chief fouling mechanisms or stages include:

1. Initiation or delay period. This is the clean surface period before dirt accumulation. The accumulation of relatively small amounts of deposit can even lead to improved heat transfer, relative to clean surface, and give an appearance of "negative" fouling rate and negative total fouling amount.
2. Particulate fouling and particle formation, aggregation and flocculation.
3. Mass transport and migration of foulants to the fouling sites.
4. Phase separation and deposition involving nucleation or initiation of fouling sites and attachment leading to deposit formation.
5. Growth, aging and hardening and the increase of deposits strength or auto-retardation, erosion and removal.

Detailed analysis of deposits from the heat exchanger may provide an excellent clue to fouling mechanisms. It can be used to identify and provide valuable information about such mechanisms. The deposits consist primarily of organic material that is predominantly asphaltenic in nature, with some inorganic deposits, mainly iron salts such as iron sulphide. The inorganic content of the deposits is relatively consistent in most cases at 22-26% [6].

Deposit analysis is performed by taking a sample and extracting any degraded hydrocarbon oil by using a solvent, such as methyl chloride, that is effective at removing hydrocarbon oils and low molecular weight polymers that may have been trapped in the deposit.

The remaining material from this extraction will consist of any organic polymers, coke, and inorganic components. The basic analysis of the non-extractable material involves ashing in which organic and volatile inorganic compounds are lost. By this means, volatile inorganics such as chlorides and sulphur compounds which are lost on ashing, may be determined. The detection of iron sulphide or other volatile inorganic materials determines the cause of inorganic fouling. These values can be compared throughout the exchanger train [6]. The non-volatile material or ash will include all oxidised metallic salt–type materials or corrosion products. The presence of iron in the ash may indicate corrosion in tankage in an upstream unit or in the exchanger train itself. This basic analysis indicates if the deposits are primarily organic or inorganic.

Special techniques and tools such as the use of optical microscopy and solubility in solvents may be used for the analysis of the non-extractable material. Infrared analysis can identify various functional groups present in the deposit which may include nitrogen, carbonyls, and unsaturated paraffinic or aromatic compounds which are polymerisation precursors, identified in feed stream characterisation [6]. The carbon and hydrogen content of the non-extractable deposit can be determined by elemental analysis. If the carbon to hydrogen ratio is very high, it may indicate that the majority of the organic portion of the deposit is coke. The coke may have been particles entrained in the stream or material which has been thermally dehydrogenated in the heat exchangers. The carbon to hydrogen ratio also indicates whether the deposit is more paraffinic or aromatic. This information helps identify the polymers formed [6].

In Table 2 analytical results are shown from deposits obtained from the four chain feed/effluent heat exchangers in which the hot product effluent is used for pre-heating the cold naphtha feedstock for a naphtha hydrotreater plant at the Homs Oil Refinery [7]. This plant is one of the most important units at the Homs Refinery, with an annual capacity of 480,000 tons/yr. It is used to remove impurities such as sulphur, nitrogen, oxygen, halides and trace metal impurities that may deactivate reforming catalysts. Furthermore, the quality of the naphtha fractions is also upgraded by reducing potential gum formation as a result of the conversion of olefins and diolefins into paraffins. The process utilises a catalyst (Hydrobon) in the presence of substantial amounts of hydrogen under high pressures (50 bars) and temperatures (320°C) (Fig. 2). A major fouling problem was encountered early on in the heat exchangers, indicated by an increased pressure drop, decreased flow rate and lower temperatures at the heat exchangers outlet.

Particulate fouling

Particulate fouling, which is the most common form of fouling, can be defined as the process in which particles in the process stream deposit onto heat exchanger surfaces. These particles include particles originally carried by the feed stream before entering the heat exchanger and particles formed in the heat exchanger itself as a result of various reactions, aggregation and flocculation. Particulate fouling increases with particle concentration, and typically particles greater than 1 ppm lead to significant fouling problems.

Heat exchanger	A	B1	B2	C	D
Loss at 105°C (wt %)	1.17	1.03	1.05	1.15	1.14
Loss at 550°C (wt %)	79.70	95.10	90.17	94.42	57.17
Loss at 840°C (wt %)	80.00	95.29	90.19	94.48	57.99
Ash (wt %)	20.00	4.71	9.81	5.52	42.01
Chloride (wt %)	170	435	0	664	508
Sulphur (wt %)	17.00	13.50	13.80	10.20	13.00
Ammonium (ppm)	42	1184	43	134	4969
Iron (wt % of ash)	19.30	2.83	1.70	2.80	15.58
Sodium (ppm of ash)	1473	1047	825	3301	914
Calcium (ppm of ash)	459	179	78	377	1431
Magnesium(ppm of ash)	90	41	19	102	1341
Chromium (ppm of ash)	231	107	1166	196	1096
Copper (ppm of ash)	511	319	74	443	126
Nickel (ppm of ash)	378	129	63	90	52

Table 2. Analysis of deposits on heat exchanger surfaces [7].

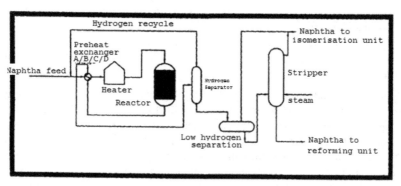

Figure 2. Naphtha hydrotreating unit

2.1. Particles in the feed stream

Particles in the fluid feed stream are solid particles which are entrained or contained in the feed stream before entering the heat exchanger and which can settle out upon the heat exchanger surfaces. These solid particles are for the most part insoluble inorganic particles such as corrosion products (iron sulphide and rust), catalyst particles or fines, dirt, silt and sand particles, and other inorganic salts such as sodium chloride, calcium chloride and magnesium chloride. The feed streams may also contain some organic particles that may have been formed during their storage or transport.

Many streams including cooling water and other product streams from different units or plants may contain solid particles. In particular, streams from such oil refinery units as vacuum units, visbreakers, and cokers may have more particulates and metals than straight-run products due to the heavier nature of the feeds processed. Streams can also be purchased from other refiners. Due to the increased transit time and exposure to oxygen before being fed to the unit these feeds may have higher particulate levels as a result of polymerisation reactions and corrosion [6].

Particles in the fluid stream, regardless of whether they are organic or inorganic in nature, fall in general into tow classes: basic sediment and filterable solids.

Typically, particles in the fluid stream greater than 1 ptb (pounds per thousand barrels) lead to significant fouling problems in the unit. Their effect on fouling can be avoided however if these particles are removed by solid-liquid filtration, sedimentation, centrifugation or by any of various fluid cleaning devices. The only particles that need to be considered in this regard are those that are not filterable or those particles that are left to proceed to the heat exchanger.

The amount of filterable solids in the stream, reported in ptb or wt% (weight percent), may be determined by filtration of the unit feed. Filterable solids analysis can evaluate a stream deposition potential by indicating the type of materials that could contribute to fouling if allowed to pass through to the heat exchanger.

Table 3 shows the analysis of filterable solids in the naphtha feed stream to the heat exchangers of the hydrotreater unit at the Homs oil refinery. The feedstock for this unit is a blend of light and heavy straight-run naphtha fractions from four different topping units. The resulting blend is left in a blending tank for a sufficient period of time to allow for equilibrium conditions to be established [8]. To evaluate the quantity of particulate solids which are entrained with the naphtha stream before entering the heat exchangers, a number of samples of the naphtha feed were filtered and the amount of entrained particles determined. Two samples of the filterable solids were taken, one sample was taken from the feed entering a macrofilter on the unit boundary and the other from a second macrofilter on the feed pump suction. The nature of the materials entrained was then determined by ashing and analysing these two samples (Table 3). The size distribution of the filterable solid particles was also determined (Table 4).

Examination of the deposit analysis for heat exchanger D (Table 2), where the deposits are a mixture of inorganic (42%) and organic (58%) deposits, indicate particulate and polymerisation fouling. The nature of particulate fouling in D is confirmed by the variation of fouling factor with time, with no induction time or delay period indicated (Fig. 3). The fouling factor curve is linear with saw-tooth shape, where both the fouling factor and the deposition rate increase with time. This means continuous build up of the fouling layer followed by break off periods [9].

2.2. Particle formation

Chemical particle formation is the basic mechanism of particle formation in heat exchangers fluid streams, although organic material growth and biological particle formation, or biofouling, may occur in sea water systems and in types of waste treatment systems. Biofouling may be of two kinds: microbial fouling, due to microorganisms (bacteria, algae, and fungi) and their products, and macrobial fouling, due to the growth of macroorganisms such as barnacles, sponges, seaweeds or mussels. On contact with heat-transfer surfaces, these organisms can attach and breed, reducing thereby both flow and heat transfer to an absolute minimum and sometimes completely clogging the fluid passages. Such organisms may also entrap silt or other suspended solids and give rise to deposit corrosion. Corrosion due to biological attachment to heat transfer surfaces is known as microbiologically influenced corrosion. For open recirculating systems, bacteria concentrations of the order of 1×10^5 cells/ml and fungi of 1×10^3 cells/ml may be regarded as limiting values [10].

	Feed filter	Pump filter
Loss at 105°C (wt. %)	10.0	0.1
Loss at 550°C (wt. %)	28.3	25.3
Loss at 840°C (wt. %)	30.4	26.7
Ash (wt. %)	69.5	73.2
Carbon (wt. %)	2.6	6.4
Sulphur (wt. %)	36.9	19.7
Sulphates (wt. %)	55.8	50.7
Chloride (ppm)	-	281
Ammonium (ppm)	-	52
Iron (wt. % of ash)	45	58
Sodium (ppm of ash)	-	9
Calcium (ppm of ash)	-	161

Table 3. Analysis of two samples of the filterable solids.

Mesh size (μm)	< 90	90	125	355
Particle distribution (%)	24	8	36	32

Table 4. Size distribution of the filterable solid particles

Chemical particle formation can be the result of either corrosion or decomposition and polymerisation reactions. Trace contaminants present in the fluid stream can have a significant effect on the fouling encountered in certain chemical processes. Such contaminants may include oxygen, nitrogen, NH_3, H_2S, CN, HCN, Hg, unsaturates, organic sulphides and chlorides, and heavy hydrocarbon compounds such as paraffin wax, resins, asphaltenes, and organometallic compounds. Individual metals, which may exist as metal salts in the feed stream, can catalyse different polymerisation reactions. The concentrations of such metals are typically very low, not exceeding few ppms. However, small concentrations of certain metals can have a significant effect on catalysing different fouling-related polymerisation reactions. Metal detectors on unit feed samples can detect individual metals in the stream at less than 1 ppm.

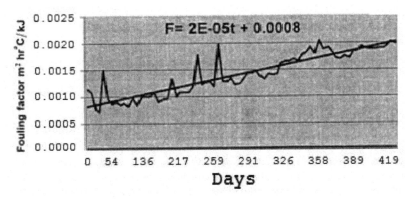

Figure 3. Variation of fouling factor in exchanger D in 2001.

Corrosion fouling is fouling deposit formation as a result of the corrosion of the substrate metal of heat transfer surfaces. This type of corrosion should not be confused, however, with the under-deposit corrosion, referred to earlier, which is one of the aftereffects of fouling.

Corrosion fouling is a mechanism which is dependent on several factors such as thermal resistance, surface roughness and composition of the substrate and fluid stream. In particular, impurities present in the fluid stream can greatly contribute to the onset of corrosion. Such impurities include hydrogen sulphide, ammonia and hydrogen chloride. In crude oil, for example, sulphur and nitrogen compounds are two very common contaminants which are mostly decomposed in certain situations to hydrogen sulphide and ammonia respectively. Chlorides which may be found in oil streams are converted to hydrogen chloride by the following reaction.

$$R\text{-}Cl + H_2 \rightarrow HCl + R$$

The chlorides may enter the refinery as salt with the crude. Chlorides in the oil stream may also be derived from various chemicals used in the oil industry which can contain high levels of chloride. Such chemicals include tertiary oil recovery enhancement chemicals and solvents used to clean tankers, barges, trucks and pipelines. As the crude oil is processed, some of these chemicals and solvents, which are thermally stable and not soluble in water, pass overhead in the main tower of the atmospheric distillation unit along with the naphtha.

In the hydrotreater feed stream, chloride levels as high as 50 wt. ppm have been reported. High levels of chloride were detected with the filterable solids in the naphtha feed stream to the heat exchangers of the hydrotreater unit at the Homs refinery (Table 3) and in the deposits obtained from the heat exchangers (Table 2). Furthermore, the makeup hydrogen from the platforming unit will always contain trace quantities of hydrogen chloride. In order to maintain catalyst performance, modern platforming catalysts require a small, but continuous dosage of chloride, some of which is always stripped and leaves the platforming unit in the net gas stream that supplies the hydrotreater with makeup hydrogen.

In a hydrogen sulphide environment the sulphur reacts with the exposed iron to form iron sulphide compounds. This happens in both the hot and cooler sections of the unit. The sulphur effectively corrodes the plant. However, once reacted, the iron sulphide forms a complex protective scale or lattice on the base metal, which inhibits further corrosion. The sulphide lattice would remain in equilibrium with its surroundings and the corrosion rate would be minimal if no other impurities were present in the system. The presence of other impurities, however, can accelerate corrosion as these impurities interact with the sulphide lattice.

Of the impurities that contribute to corrosion and fouling, hydrogen chloride may be the most important. By itself hydrogen chloride does not cause a problem. It will not foul equipment or corrode the carbon steel in the unit. Chloride corrosion and fouling, however, take place when hydrogen chloride, ammonia, and water all interact in the colder sections of the unit to defeat the protective sulphide lattice. The extent of the damage depends on their concentration and is directly dependent on pH, with the corrosion rate increasing rapidly with pH decrease.

Hydrogen chloride will become corrosive when it comes in contact with free water, i.e. water that is not in the vapour phase or is not saturated in the liquid hydrocarbon. Oil products are almost always saturated with water, and entrained water, even if it is less of a problem, does occur in most cases. Furthermore, continuous water wash at key locations is recommended as part of the solution to minimise the effects of chloride corrosion and fouling and this further contributes to the total water in the system.

Hydrogen chloride is highly soluble in water, and in a free water environment, any hydrogen chloride present in the vapour or hydrocarbon liquid will be quickly absorbed by the water, thus driving the pH down to approximately 1.

If the iron sulphide lattice is intact this chloride competes with the bisulphate ion (SH⁻) for the iron ions in the lattice:

$$S\text{-}Fe\text{-}S\text{-}Fe\text{-}SH + Cl^- \rightleftarrows Fe\text{-}S\text{-}S\text{-}Fe\text{-}Cl + SH^-$$

With a high concentration of hydrogen chloride present the reaction shifts to the right. As more and more bisulphate is released from the sulphide lattice, it eventually dissolves leaving the base metal exposed. The reaction rate is then only limited by the chloride ion concentration in the solution at low pH. Loss of wall metal takes place very rapidly.

In water the chloride ions react directly with any exposed iron to form $FeCl_2$.

$$Fe^{++} + 2Cl^- \rightarrow FeCl_2$$

$$2e^- + 2H^+ \rightarrow H_2$$

As the chloride concentration in water is reduced by removing the source, diluting with additional water or neutralising with a base, the pH will increase. Hydrogen sulphide will begin to react with the exposed iron and start building a new protective layer. This sulphide lattice gets stronger as the pH increases to 6 and above. The corrosion rate falls off to a minimum.

Hydrogen chloride will also cause serious fouling problems if ammonia is present in the system. The ammonia reacts with hydrogen chloride to form ammonium chloride which may cause fouling and plugging problems. In the cooler parts of the unit, the ammonium chloride will condense from the vapour phase and solidify and deposit directly and accumulate on the walls. The salt can also break away from the walls and be carried downstream to eventually deposit somewhere else. If free water is present, ammonium chloride will be absorbed directly from the vapour phase into the water and no solid salts will form on the equipment. Another problem associated with ammonium chloride salt deposits is under deposit pitting corrosion as the hygroscopic nature of the salt will result in a wet environment at the wall under the deposit. The chloride ions will react with the iron to form iron chloride causing serious localised corrosion, the reaction rate accelerating in the presence of hydrogen sulphide. The sulphide ion as part of an ammonium sulphide salt will react with the iron chloride to form iron sulphide, thus releasing the chloride ion to start over.

Any excess ammonia available may react with the disulphide ions present in the solution to form ammonium sulphide salts, but only after most of the chloride has been neutralised. While hydrogen sulphide is only slightly soluble in the water, its salt is highly soluble. Therefore, as the pH is raised to 6 and higher the free ammonia present reacts with the small quantity of hydrogen sulphide in solution, making more ammonium sulphide salts. The rich hydrogen sulphide vapour above the water will continuously replace the consumed hydrogen sulphide. The overall sulphide concentration in the water increases making it difficult to raise the pH much further.

The sharp increase in corrosion rate in the 6.8 to 7.3 pH range is related to the concentration of the ammonium chloride and sulphide salts present. In large quantities these salts can become aggressive, especially the sulphide salts. If the pH is raised further the corrosion rate again falls off to a very low value. This is because the sulphide lattice has formed into a very strong hard film that cannot easily be broken.

The iron content in the deposits obtained from the heat exchangers may be an indication of fouling by corrosion. Although polymerisation may account for about 80% of the total fouling associated with the "A" heat exchanger, in the Homs hydrotreating plant, fouling by corrosion is not negligible, with about 19% of the total fouling may be due to corrosion, as is clearly indicated by the iron content of the deposits obtained from this exchanger (Table 2).

Coking and Polymerisation are major causes of fouling in heat exchangers. Decomposition of organic products can lead to the formation of very viscous tar or solid coke particles at high temperatures and polymerisation involves the formation of undesirable organic sediments or polymers. The coke particles and polymers formed in the heat exchanger may grow to such a large size that they drop out of solution and deposit on the process equipment. Such deposits can be extremely tenacious and may require burning off the deposit to return the heat exchanger to satisfactory operation.

There are two major polymerisation mechanisms which can occur in the feed stream: free radical and non-free radical polymerisation.

Free radical polymerisation occurs when a free radical is formed and continues to react with other molecules. The free radicals continue to propagate in the feed stream producing longer chain polymers which will continue to be produced as long as free radicals are being formed. Free radical polymerisation is easily initiated in the presence of light and heat and its rate for polymer formation increases exponentially with temperature. A general rule is that for every 10ºC increase in temperature the rate of polymer formation doubles. Free radical polymerisation readily takes place in heat exchanger tubes and storage tanks [6].

The formation of free radicals has been investigated extensively and it is known that numerous types of free radicals can be formed in a feed stream. These include alkyl radicals produced by the breaking of double or unsaturated bonds as well as other types of precursors such as nitrogen and sulphur radicals which arc easily formed at the temperatures found in the heat exchanger train. Organic sulphur, nitrogen and oxygen compounds increase the potential for various polymerisation reactions, depending on the form in which they exist. Acidic compounds can promote free radical polymerisation by initiating free radicals through the formation of a positive ion or cation. Additional polymerisation precursors include carbonyls, mercaptans, and pyrrole nitrogen.

Oxygen may also react with hydrocarbons to form peroxide free radicals, a step that could occur in the storage tank. When the temperature is increased in the heat exchangers, the peroxides start fast polymerisation reactions leading to the formation of polymers which increase in chain length as more hydrocarbons are attached. The oxygen source is typically from air in non-blanketed storage tanks or oxygenated compounds in the feed stream, which become more reactive as the feed stream is heated [6, 11].

At lower temperatures, free radicals may be formed when a ligand is broken from a metal complex or salt. The unshared electrons resulting from this break react with an unsaturated hydrocarbon or oxygen to form a free radical [5]. There are numerous transition metals which, in very low concentrations, can act as a catalyst and initiate polymerisation reactions.

Some of these catalytically reactive metals are iron, copper, nickel, vanadium, chromium, calcium, and magnesium [6]

In non-free radical polymerisation, polymer formation results from the reaction of two different molecules under the right conditions. One of the reactive molecules may be a radical, or a compound from a free radical-initiated polymerisation step. Basic compounds can react with other compounds or with themselves to form polymers by several different polymerisation mechanisms. In condensation polymerisation, two large radicals or compounds react together to form an even larger compound, but in their reaction also generate a smaller compound, such as water. This new larger compound can continue to react with other reactive species in the feed stream to make higher molecular weight polymers. At some point, the polymer will either get so large in size that it is no longer able to stay entrained or soluble in the fluid stream and deposit, or all the different compounds that can react with it are consumed, and no further polymer is formed [6].

Various laboratory tests can provide an indication of a stream's polymerisation potential. These include laboratory simulations and analytical characterisation, to identify specific compounds in the feed which are known to contribute to polymerisation mechanisms. Such polymerisation precursors may include unsaturated hydrocarbons, acidic compounds, amines, carbonyls, mercaptans and pyrrole nitrogen.

The presence of unsaturated components in the feed stream contributes significantly to polymerisation reactions, particularly at high temperatures. The bromine number is a method of measuring the degree of unsaturation in a feed stream. The unsaturated bonds react with bromine, and the amount of bromine reacted is an indication of the degree of unsaturation [12].

The neutralisation, or acid, number measures the acidity of the fluid as it is titrated with a base. This number can be an indication of fouling tendency, where the more acidic the feed stream, the greater is its tendency to foul. This is most likely due to the fact that acidic compounds, as mentioned above, can promote free radical polymerisation.

The basic nitrogen test determines the amount of basic compounds in a sample, assumed to be mostly amines, by titrating with a mixture of organic acids. This method can, however, overestimate the basic nitrogen content.

A method of determining a sample's oxidative polymerisation potential is to run a potential gums test. This test is a method of determining a sample's oxidative polymerisation potential. In this test, the fluid is subjected to 100% oxygen for four hours, at 100ºC, in a pressurised sample bomb. The measured gum content, as compared to an initial gum value, will indicate the impact of oxygen on the stream's polymerisation potential.

Detailed deposit analysis, as mentioned earlier, can also indicate the occurrence of polymerisation. It is apparent from examination of the deposit analysis results shown in Table 2 that most deposits are organic in nature, as the loss reported on heating the deposit samples to 840°C was greater than 80% in both the "B" and "C" heat exchangers, where working temperatures are rather high. Since organic deposits result mainly from polymerisation reactions, the high organic content observed in the deposit analysis could be taken as an indication that the fouling in these two heat exchangers is due mainly to polymerisation, which could take place in the heat exchangers themselves or it could occur prior to the heat exchangers either during storage or in transport. Analysis for metals in the deposits indicates the presence of individual metals in the stream. Although, some of these metals are only found in very low concentrations, this may be sufficient for catalysing different polymerisation mechanisms [7].

2.3. Aggregation and flocculation

Some of the heavy organics, especially asphaltenes, will separate from the oil phase into large particles or aggregates. These aggregates may then remain in the oil by some peptising agents, like resins, which will be adsorbed on their surface and keep them afloat, but the stability of such steric colloids is a function of concentration of the peptising agent in the solution. When this concentration drops to a point at which its adsorbed amount is not high enough to cover the entire surface of heavy organic particles, these particles coalesce together, grow in size and flocculate. Flocculation of asphaltene in paraffinic crude oils is known to be irreversible. Due to their large size and their adsorption affinity to solid surfaces flocculated asphaltenes can cause irreversible deposition. Segments of the separated particles which contain S, N and/or H bonds could also start to flocculate and as a result produce the irreversible heavy organic deposits which may be insoluble in solvents.

Inorganic particles may also act as nuclei on which agglomeration of organic particles proceed until the particles become eventually large enough to drop out.

2.4. Transport and migration to the fouling sites

Starting with submicron particles, three transport mechanisms progressively predominate in turbulent flow as the particle size increases. After Gudmunsson [13], the corresponding regimes are designated simply as diffusion, inertia and impaction, respectively.

2.4.1. Diffusion

In the diffusion regime, suspended colloidal particles i.e., particles smaller than about 1 μm in at least one dimension, move with the fluid and are carried to the wall by the Brownian motion of the fluid molecules and through the viscous sublayer in the case of a turbulent flow. The submicron particles can then be treated like large molecules, so that the transport coefficient becomes equivalent to the conventional mass transfer coefficient, which can be obtained from the relevant empirical correlations or theoretical equations for forced convection mass transfer in the literature [14].

In the diffusion regime, the smaller the particle size, the greater is its propensity to be deposited. Thus, it is precisely the very fine submicron particles that are most difficult to remove by filtration or other means which have the greatest propensity to foul a surface.

2.4.2. Inertia

The transition from diffusional to inertial control of transport occurs at particle diameter in the order of 1–2 μm. In the inertia regime the particles are sufficiently large that turbulent eddies give some of them a transverse (Free flight) velocity which is not completely dissipated in the viscous sublayer. These particles then possess sufficient momentum to reach the wall. Some of the particles also experience a more gradual movement towards the wall by migration down the turbulence intensity gradient, i.e. by "turbophoresis" [15]. Much work has been done by a large number of investigators on predicting the results of this free flight excursion or inertial coasting in a turbulent field [16].

In the inertial regime a more desirable situation prevails. Here the larger particles, which are relatively easy to remove, are those which have the greater propensity to be deposited.

2.4.3. Impaction

In this regime, which starts at particle diameter $d_P \cong$ 10–20 μm, the particle velocity towards the wall approaches the friction velocity and the particle stopping distance becomes of the same order as the pipe diameter. The response of such large particles to turbulent fluctuations becomes limited and the transport coefficient therefore levels off. As the particles get still larger they get even more sluggish in their response to turbulent eddies and the transport coefficient actually starts to fall gradually [14].

In the impaction regime, transport-controlled deposition would be virtually independent of particle size.

There is considerable experimental evidence to indicate that the effect of surface roughness is usually to enhance the transport of particles to the surface. The enhancement occurs because of the decrease of viscous sublayer thickness and corresponding increase in turbulence level above the roughness elements, because of the smaller stopping distance required for the particles to arrive at the outer asperities of the roughness elements, and because of the additional mechanism of particle interception by those elements along flow lines parallel to the macrosurface [15].

On the other hand, turbulent particle transport may be retarded as a result of deposition of very fine particles which tends to smooth initially rough surfaces. Transport-retardation is, however, far less common than transport-enhancement by surface roughness. The importance of clean and, where feasible also, polished surfaces for mitigating particle deposition under transport-controlled conditions is thus apparent [15].

2.5. Phase separation

Separation of solid particles from fluid stream and their eventual deposition onto heat exchanger surfaces may be a result of many physical processes including condensation from gas phase, gravitational settling, crystallisation and electro-kinetic effect.

Suspended particles such as sand, silt, clay, and non-oxides may become too large to remain entrained in the flowing fluid stream. If the particles are sufficiently large and/or heavy that gravity controls the deposition process, we then have what is known as sedimentation fouling, which can often be prevented with relative ease by pre-filtration or pre-sedimentation of the offending particles. Sedimentation fouling is strongly affected by fluid velocity, and suspended particles in the process fluids will deposit in low-velocity regions, particularly where the velocity changes quickly, as in heat exchanger water boxes and on the shell side [17]. Wall temperature, on the other hand, may have less effect in general on sedimentation fouling, although a hot wall may cause a deposit to "bake on" and become very hard to remove.

Dissolved inorganic salts in a polydisperse fluid may become supersaturated if any change in temperature, pressure, composition (such as solvent evaporation or degasification or addition of a miscible solvent) or other factors destabilises the fluid. The heavy and/or polar fractions may then separate from the fluid into steric colloids, micelles (= charged groups of molecules), another liquid phase or into a solid precipitate.

The dependence of salt solubility on temperature is often the driving force for precipitation fouling. This temperature dependence may be different for different salts, with salt solubility increasing or decreasing with increasing temperature so that different salts may foul the cooling or heating surfaces depending on their solubility temperature dependence. While for most salts the solubility gets higher with increasing temperatures, there are salts such as calcium sulphate which have retrograde solubility dependence and are therefore less soluble in warm streams. Such salts will crystallise on heat transfer surfaces if the streams encounter a surface at a temperature higher than the saturation temperature of these salts. The calcium sulphate scale is hard and adherent and usually requires vigorous mechanical or chemical treatment to remove it. Other typical scaling problems are calcium and magnesium carbonates and silica deposits.

Crystallisation normally begins at specially-active nucleation sites such as scratches and pits, whereas a scratch-free or a smooth surface can flush salt crystals. Subsequently particle deposit will start and continue to build up as long as the surface in contact with the fluid has a temperature above or below saturation. High fluid velocity, by increasing the attrition, can however reduce the rate of particle deposition and fouling.

The solubility of certain heavy hydrocarbons with high melting points such as paraffin wax and diamondoids depends strongly on temperature. If the temperature is decreased, the heavy hydrocarbons may precipitate in the form of solid crystals. Deposition of paraffin wax in cooled heat exchanger tubes showed an asymptotic behaviour due to decreasing heat flux and increasing shear stress [18]. When various heavy organic compounds are present in a petroleum fluid, their interactive effects largely determine their collective deposition especially when one of the interacting heavy organic compounds is asphaltene.

Changes in the nature of oil fluids may lead to the precipitation of some heavy hydrocarbons, mainly asphaltenes, exceeding their solubility limits. Asphaltenes precipitation, which may be a major cause of crude unit fouling, is affected by many factors including variations of temperature, pressure, composition, flow regime, and wall and electrokinetic effect.

The deposition of heavy hydrocarbons is an example of what is known as solidification fouling, another example of which is the solidification of molten ash carried in a furnace exhaust gas onto a heat exchanger surface.

Precipitation fouling can also occur as a result of pressure changes, where the solubility of salts such as calcium sulphate decreases with decreasing pressure. Laboratory tests have further indicated that variations of pressure exerted on a petroleum fluid can cause the deposition of some of its heavy organic contents.

Motion of charged particles in a conduit may lead to the development of electrical potential differences along the conduit. This electrical potential difference could then cause a change in charges of the colloidal particles further down in the conduit, the ultimate result of which is their untimely deposition. The factors influencing this effect are the electrical and thermal characteristics of the conduit, flow regime, flowing oil properties, characteristics of the polar heavy organics and colloidal particles.

2.6. Particle deposition

Deposition and attachment of solid particles on heat exchanger surfaces is a function of several different operating variables which include particle size and concentration, bulk fluid density and bulk fluid velocity through the heat exchanger [4, 19]. Furthermore, the stickiness and attractive or repulsive forces between particles can significantly contribute to the deposition of particles [3]. Organic deposits may also be the result of heavy hydrocarbon particles bound to the metal surfaces by inorganic deposition. Attachment is also a function of the interfacial properties of the fouling material and the roughness and wettability of the surface where the fouling is going to occur. Whereas smooth and nonwetting surfaces may delay fouling, rough surfaces provide "nucleation sites" that encourage the laying down of the initial fouling deposits. Most initially smooth walls would tend to roughen as particle deposition occurred, so that roughness would then have to be taken into account. On the other hand, deposition of very fine particles onto initially rough surfaces can conceivably result in filling the roughness cavities, thereby smoothing the surface [15].

Recent studies have shown that particle size and concentration have great impact on every type of particle deposition. The average diameter of particles entrained in the fluid stream may vary widely, between a maximum of over 350 μm and a minimum of less than 90 μm (Table 4). Solid particles which foul heat exchangers range in size from submicron to several hundred microns. Investigation revealed that shell and tube exchangers are generally plugged by particles above 20 microns. On the other hand, plate fin exchangers, having much narrower slots, can be plugged by particles as small as 2 microns [3]. The deposition mechanism for the smaller particles is Brownian diffusion while for the larger particles (10-100 μm) it is mainly gravitational settling. At areas of minimum flow velocities, the larger particles in the stream deposit first followed by the smaller particles and the fouling layer starts to build up as a consequence.

2.7. Deposit growth, aging and hardening

Following particle deposition, deposit growth and consolidation or alternatively auto-retardation and erosion, re-entrainment or removal may take place.

The rate of deposition growth and the accumulation of particles on heat exchanger surfaces is a function of the nature of the fouling material, the composition of the fluid stream and other variables such as temperature and flow rate.

With time, the surface deposit strength may increase and the deposit hardens through various processes collectively known as aging such as, for example, polymerisation, recrystallisation and dehydration. Some types of particles can bake on the surface and will become more difficult to remove over time. The toughness of the deposits may be further affected by the presence of asphaltenes, which are highly polar compounds, and which could act as glue and mortar in hardening the deposits. Biological deposits, on the other hand, may weaken with time due to contamination of organisms.

2.8. Auto-retardation and erosion or removal

The decline of particle deposition rate is commonly referred to as auto-retardation. This is a desirable but spontaneous process that is in the main not under the control of the designer or operator. Several mechanisms may account for auto-retardation and the progressive decrease in adherence of particles to the surface including the already referred to possibility of slowing down particle transport in cases where very fine particles fill the roughness cavities of a surface.

Depending on the strength of the deposit, erosion occurs immediately after the first deposit has been laid down. In saw-tooth fouling part of the deposit is detached after a critical residence time or once a critical deposit thickness has been reached. The fouling layer then builds up and breaks off again. Sometimes impurities such as sand or other suspended particles in fluid streams may have a scouring action, which will reduce or remove deposits [13].

3. Fouling mitigation, control and removal

In order to prevent or mitigate the impact of fouling problems, various steps can be taken during plant design and construction and also during plant operation and maintenance.

However, fouling mitigation and control is a very complex process and anticipating the likely extent of fouling problems to be encountered with different flow streams is a major difficulty faced alike by designers and operators of heat exchangers. In most cases, optimisation of the design and operational conditions is not possible or at least would not be realistic without a comprehensive modelling of the process backed up by practical observations. Modelling, however, is not an easy process, and the different models available in the literature are generally of limited value and application.

The use of multiple regression analysis (MRA), which is an extension of simple least squares regression analysis on a set of data, is an excellent means of modelling heat exchanger fouling. A dependent variable, such as the heat exchanger outlet temperature, is regressed against a set of independent variables, temperatures, pressures, and flows, which directly impact the dependent variable. Regression analysis results in a model equation of independent variables that combine to yield the dependent response. Variability in data and the interaction between independent variables is taken into account in the model equation which can be used to predict future performance. The impact of a change, such as antifoulant addition, can then be compared to the predicted response from the model to determine how effective the treatment programme is.

3.1. Plant design and construction

Fouling mitigation and control require scientific considerations in design and construction. In general, high turbulence, absence of stagnant areas, uniform fluid flow and smooth surfaces reduce fouling and the need for frequent cleaning. In addition, designers of heat exchangers must consider the effects of fouling upon heat exchanger performance during the desired operational lifetime of the heat exchangers. The factors that need to be considered in the designs include the extra surface required to ensure that the heat exchangers will meet process specifications up to shutdown for cleaning, the additional pressure drop expected due to fouling, and the choice of appropriate construction materials. The designers must also consider the mechanical arrangements that may be necessary for fouling inspection or fouling removal and cleaning.

Fouling resistances are different in different designs of heat exchangers. More than 35-40% of heat exchangers employed in global heat transfer processes are of the shell and tube type of heat exchangers. In process industries, more than 90% of heat exchangers used are of the shell and tube type [20]. This is primarily due to the robust construction geometry as well as ease of maintenance and upgrades possible with the shell and tube heat exchangers [1]. Well established procedures for their design and manufacture from a wide variety of materials, as well as availability of codes and standards for design and fabrication and many years of satisfactory service make them first choice in most process industries. However, fouling resistance in the shell and tube heat exchangers are usually much greater than in other types of heat exchangers (Table 5). In the shell side in particular lower fluid flow velocities and low-velocity or stagnant regions, for example in the vicinity of baffles, encourage the accumulation of foulants. Furthermore, segmental baffles have the tendency for poor flow distribution if spacing or baffle cut ratio is not in the correct proportions. Fouling resistance in plate heat exchangers, on the other hand, can be much smaller. This may be due to the high degree of turbulence even at low velocities which keeps solids in suspension. Also, in plate exchangers there are no dead spaces where fluids can stagnate and solids deposit. Furthermore, heat transfer surfaces are generally smooth and plates are built with higher-quality materials with no corrosion products to which fouling may adhere. Finally, cleaning of plate heat exchangers is a very simple operation and the interval between cleanings is usually smaller [21]. Hence, the fouling factors required in plate heat exchangers are normally 20-25% of those used in shell and tube exchangers [22]. In certain applications, spiral plate exchangers may be chosen for fouling services, where the scrubbing action of the fluids on the curved surfaces minimises fouling. On the other hand, fouling is one of the major problems in compact heat exchangers, particularly with various fin geometries and fine flow passages that cannot be cleaned mechanically [23].

Type	Shell and tube	Plate	Spiral plate	Air cooled	Lamella	Plate fin	Coiled tube	Double pipe	Graphite	Scraped surface
Fouling risk	Very poor	Very good	Good	Poor	Fair	Poor	Fair	Fair	Fair	Very good
Fouling effect	Poor	Good	Good	Very poor	Poor	Very poor	Poor	Fair	Poor	Good

Table 5. Fouling risk and effects for different types of heat exchangers [24, 25]

Over the years, there has been much advance in the design and manufacture of shell and tube heat exchangers with resultant improvements in their fouling behaviour in operation. A striking example of a new design is the Helixchanger heat exchanger (Fig. 4) where the conventional segmental baffle plates are replaced by quadrant shaped baffles arranged at an angle to the tube axis creating a uniform velocity helical flow through the tube bundle. Near plug flow conditions are achieved in a Helixchanger heat exchanger with little back-flow and eddies, often responsible for fouling and corrosion. Low fouling characteristics are provided offering much longer exchanger run lengths between scheduled cleaning of tube bundles. Such run lengths are increased by 2 to 3 times those achieved using the conventionally baffled shell and tube heat exchangers. Heat exchanger performance is maintained at a higher level for longer periods of time with consequent savings in total life cycle costs of owning and operating Helixchanger heat exchanger banks [1].

If fouling is expected on the tube side, some engineers recommend using larger diameter tubes (a minimum of 25 mm OD) [26]. The use of corrugated tubes has been shown to be beneficial in minimising the effects of at least two of the common types of fouling mechanisms, *viz. deposition fouling* because of an enhanced level of turbulence generated at lower velocities, and *chemical fouling* because the enhanced heat transfer coefficients produced by the corrugated tube result in tube wall temperatures closer to the bulk fluid temperature of the working fluids.

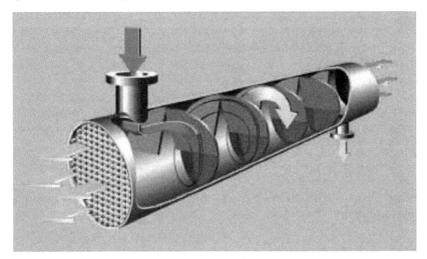

Figure 4. Helixchanger heat exchanger.

Mounting the heat exchanger vertically can minimise the effect of deposition fouling as gravity would tend to pull the particles out of the heat exchanger away from the heat transfer surface even at low velocity levels. Appropriate orientation of heat exchangers may also make cleaning easier [27]. In fluid allocation, it is usually preferred to allocate the most fouling fluid to the tube side as it is easier to clean the tube interiors than the exteriors and the probability of low-velocity or stagnant regions is less on the tube side. Placing the fouling fluid in the tube side tends also to minimise fouling by allowing better velocity control. The use of concurrent flow instead of counterflow is a strategy that may be resorted to sometimes in order to control solidification fouling [23].

Appropriate choice of construction materials for heat transfer surfaces may be necessary to alleviate fouling problems. For example, the use of low-fouling surfaces such as surfaces implanted with ions, very smooth surfaces or surfaces of low surface energy may be an option for some applications. Surface coatings and treatment, ultraviolet, acoustic, electric and radiation treatment, may further help to alleviate fouling problems. Surface treatment by plastics, vitreous enamel, glass, and some polymers can also minimise the accumulation of deposits [13]. Similarly, if biofouling is expected or encountered, the use of non-ferrous high copper alloys, which are poisonous to some organisms, can discourage the settling of these organisms on the heat transfer surfaces. Alloys containing copper in quantities greater than 70% are effective in preventing or minimising biological fouling, and generally 70% to 90% copper and 30% to 10% nickel are used for this purpose. Copper alloys are however prohibited in high-pressure steam power plant heat exchangers, since the corrosion deposits of copper alloys are transported and deposited in high-pressure steam generators and subsequently block the turbine blades. Environmental protection also limits the use of copper in river, lake, and ocean waters, since copper is poisonous to aquatic life [23].

Corrosion-type fouling can also be minimised by the choice of a construction material which does not readily corrode or produce voluminous deposits of corrosion products. A wide range of corrosion resistant materials based on stainless steel is now available to the heat exchanger manufacturer. Noncorrosive but expensive materials such as titanium and nickel based alloys may be used sometimes to prevent corrosion. If one of the fluids is more corrosive, it may be convenient to send it through the tube side because the shell can then be built with a lower-quality and cheaper material.

The construction material selected must also be resistant to attack by the cleaning solutions in situations where chemical removal of the fouling deposit is planned. For fluid allocation, it is usually preferred to allocate the most fouling fluid to the tube side as it is easier to clean the tube interiors than the exteriors.

3.2. Plant operation and maintenance

In many cases, even the right design of a heat exchanger will not prevent fouling problems that may not be predictable at the design stage. For the control and mitigation of fouling it is generally necessary to take into account the different plant operational conditions such as temperature range, fluid flow rate and chemical composition, and, where possible, make such changes as are required by the severity and type of the fouling problems. For example, some types of fouling can be minimised by using high flow velocities, with due consideration of the possibility of metal erosion as it may be necessary to restrict the velocity to values consistent with satisfactory tube life.

Several techniques may be used for the control of fouling as part of plant maintenance. Some of these techniques are designed to prevent or mitigate fouling. These include avoidance of feed contact with air or oxygen by nitrogen blanketing, elimination or reduction of unsaturates, prior treatment of feed, the use of anti-foulants and application of mechanical on-line mitigation strategies. Cathodic protection and surface treatment such as passivation of stainless steel will minimise corrosion fouling [23].

Prior treatment of feed includes caustic scrubbing, desalting, filtration or sedimentation of feed. Caustic scrubbing removes sulphur compounds and desalting reduces trace metal contamination, both of which reduce polymerisation fouling [10]. Depending on system parameters, including fluid temperature, viscosity, pressure, solid concentration, particle size distribution, and fluid compatibility with the filter media, a filter can be designed to remove solid particles from the fluid. Filtration, however, can only remove the larger-sized particles leaving the smaller-sized particles in the feed stream. Filters used on the feed line require also regular maintenance. At the filter design stage, the most important question to be answered is, whether the cost of filtration is higher than the fouling cost [3].

Antifoulants or chemical fouling inhibitors may be used to reduce fouling in many systems mainly by preventing reactions causing fouling, and minimising or interfering with the different steps of the fouling process such as crystallisation, agglomeration of small insoluble polymeric or coke-like particles, sticking or attachment of particles to tube walls and deposit consolidation [28]. Such antifoulants include antioxidation additives used to inhibit polymerisation reactions, metal coordinators which react with the trace elements and prevent them from functioning as fouling catalysts, corrosion inhibitors and dispersion agents. Other antifoulants may be used to control crystallisation such as distortion and dispersion agents, sequestering agents and threshold chemicals [28].

Various strategies and devices for the continuous mitigation and reduction of fouling have been proposed such as periodical reversal of flow direction for the removal of weakly adherent deposits, intermittent air injection and/or increasing wall shear stress by raising flow velocity or by increasing turbulence level. In order to enhance the removal of the fouling deposits, velocities in tubes should in general be above 2 m/s and about 1 m/s on the shell side [10]. In several patents, tubular heat exchangers equipped with fouling reduction devices mounted inside the exchanger tubes are described [29]. Such fouling reducers may comprise a mobile turbulence generating element that consists of a metallic winding in the form of a solenoid. The solenoid can be held in position by a hanging system in such a manner that the turbulence generating element can be driven in rotation by the liquid that circulates in the exchanger. The mobile components can be made of spring steel to make them unstretchable. Alternatively, an elastic solenoid may be used that extends over the entire length of the tubes and is agitated by the liquid that circulates in the exchanger [19]. In some heat-transfer applications, mechanical mitigation with dynamic scraped surface heat exchangers is an option. In self-cleaning fluidised-bed exchangers, a fluidised bed of particles is used to control fouling on the outside or inside of tubular exchangers. The self-cleaning exchanger consists of a large number of parallel vertical tubes, in which small solid particles are kept in a fluidised condition by the liquid velocities. The particles have a slightly abrasive effect on the tube walls, so that they remove the deposits [30].

Finally, different mechanical strategies for continuous on-stream cleaning of the interior surfaces of the tubes have been proposed including such strategies as circulation of cleaning balls such as sponge rubber or grit coated balls and pushing of brushes through tubes. In the sponge rubber ball cleaning system, the balls used for normal operation should have the right surface roughness to gently clean the tubes without scoring the tube surface. To remove heavy deposits, special abrasive balls that have a coating of carborundum are available [31]. In the Amertap System, slightly oversized sponge rubber balls are continuously recirculated through the tubes in order to remove the accumulation of scale or corrosion products. The M.A.N. System provides for on-stream cleaning by passage of brushes through the tubes.

Notwithstanding the various control and maintenance techniques which can minimise fouling problems and reduce their severity, fouling may still occur and fouling removal and process equipment cleaning may be necessary. A review of the patent activities related to fouling indicates in fact that most of the work deals with fouling removal and process equipment cleaning techniques. This could also mean that many process equipment manufacturers face problems after they appear rather than proactively prevent them from occurring [3].

There are several different techniques that can be employed for the removal of fouling. All such techniques require, however, costly system shutdown after a longer period of low efficiency heat transfer. The chief techniques normally utilised are either chemical or mechanical cleaning, but other procedures may sometimes be employed for some specific applications such as ultrasonic cleaning, which is a more recent procedure, and abrasive cleaning.

Mechanical cleaning is generally preferred over chemical cleaning because it can be a more environmentally-friendly alternative, whereas chemical cleaning causes environmental problems through the handling, application, storage and disposal of chemicals. However, mechanical cleaning may damage the equipment, particularly tubes, and it does not produce a chemically clean surface. Furthermore, chemical cleaning may be the only alternative if uniform or complete cleaning is required and for cleaning inaccessible areas. The shell side in particular can only be chemically cleaned. The tubes on the other hand can be mechanically cleaned provided that the tube pattern and pitch provide sufficient space and access to the inside of the bundle, and if mechanical cleaning is required for one of the fluids, the usual practice is to put that fluid in the tube side.

For the chemical removal of fouling material, weak acids and special solvents or detergents are normally used. Chlorination may be used for the removal of carbonate deposits. Mechanical techniques for the removal of fouling include scraping and air bumping. Air bumping is a technique that involves the creation of slugs of air, thereby creating localised turbulence as slugs pass through the equipment.

For tightly plugged tubes drilling, generally known as bulleting, may be employed and for lightly plugged tubes roding is employed. Particularly weakly adherent deposits may be mechanically removed by applying high velocity water jets or a mixture of sand and water. Jet cleaning can be used mostly on external surfaces where there is an easy accessibility for passing the high pressure jet [23].

In cases where biofouling occurs it may be removed by either chemical treatment or mechanical brushing processes. In chemical cleaning techniques biocides are employed such as chlorine, chlorine dioxide, bromine, ozone and surfactants. A more usual practice, however, is by continuous or intermittent "shock" chlorination which kills off the responsible organisms. Other cleaning techniques that can be effective in controlling biological fouling include thermal shock treatment by application of heat or deslugging with steam or hot water, and some less well-known techniques like ultraviolet radiation [23].

4. Rate of fouling

The rate of fouling is normally defined as the average deposit surface loading per unit of surface area in a unit of time. Deposit thickness (μm) and porosity (%) are also often used for description of the amount of fouling.

Depending on the fouling mechanism and conditions, the rate of fouling may be linear, falling, accelerating, asymptotic or saw-tooth as the case may be.

1. Linear fouling is the type of fouling where the fouling rate can be steady with time with increasing fouling resistance and deposit thickness. This is perhaps the most common type of fouling. It occurs in general where the temperature of the deposit in contact with the flowing fluid remains constant.

Ebert and Panchal [32] have presented a fouling model that expressed the average (linear) fouling rate under given conditions as a result of two competing terms, namely, a deposition term and a mitigation term.

Fouling Rate = (deposition term) - (anti-deposition term)

$$\frac{dR_f}{dt} = \alpha \, \mathrm{Re}^\beta \, \mathrm{Pr}^\delta \, \exp\left(\frac{-E}{RT_{film}} \right) - \gamma \tau_w \tag{1}$$

where α, β, γ and δ are parameters determined by regression, τ_w is the shear stress at the tube wall and T_{film} is the fluid film temperature (average of the local bulk fluid and local wall temperatures). The relationship in Eq. (1) points to the possibility of identifying combinations of temperature and velocity below which the fouling rates will be negligible. Ebert and Panchal [32] present this as the "threshold condition". The model in Eq. (1) suggests that the heat exchanger geometry which affects the surface and film temperatures, velocities and shear stresses can be effectively applied to maintain the conditions below the "threshold conditions" in a given heat exchanger.

2. Falling fouling is the type of fouling where the fouling rate decreases with time, and the deposit thickness does not achieve a constant value, although the fouling rate never drops below a certain minimum value. Falling fouling in general is due to an increase of removal rate with time. Its progress can often be described by two numbers: the initial fouling rate and the fouling rate after a long period of time.
3. Accelerating fouling is the type of fouling where the fouling rate increases with time. It is the result of hard and adherent deposit where removal and aging can be ignored. It can develop when fouling increases the surface roughness, or when the deposit surface exhibits higher chemical propensity to fouling than the pure underlying metal.
4. Asymptotic fouling rate is where rate decreases with time until it becomes negligible after a period of time when the deposition rate becomes equal to the deposit removal rate and the deposit thickness remains constant. In general, this type of fouling occurs

where the tube surface temperature remains constant while the temperature of the flowing fluid drops as a result of increased resistance of fouling material to heat transfer. Asymptotic fouling may also be the result of soft or poorly adherent suspended solid deposits upon heat transfer surfaces in areas of fast flow where they do not adhere strongly to the surface with the result that the thicker the deposit becomes, the more likely it is to wash off in patches and thus attain some average asymptotic value over a period of time.

The asymptotic fouling resistance increases with increasing particle concentration and decreasing fluid bulk temperature, flow velocity, and particle diameter. The asymptotic fouling model was first described by Kern and Seaton [33]. In this model, the competing fouling mechanisms lead to an asymptotic fouling resistance beyond which no further increase in fouling occurs. The Tubular Heat Exchanger Manufacturers Association (TEMA) standards suggest fouling factors for several fluids based upon the asymptotic values. This approach, however, does not address all fouling phenomena as it does not, for example, address fouling at the "hot" end of a crude oil preheat train, since fouling there does not exhibit the asymptotic behaviour.

5.   Saw-tooth fouling occurs where part of the deposit is detached after a critical residence time or once a critical deposit thickness has been reached. The fouling layer then builds up and breaks off again. This periodic variation could be due to pressure pulses, spalling, trapping of air inside the surface deposits during shutdowns or other reasons. It often corresponds to the moments of system shutdowns, startups or other transients in operation.

5. Prediction of fouling factor

The effect of fouling, as has been noted above, is to form an essentially solid deposit of low thermal conductivity upon the heat transfer surface, through which heat must be transferred by conduction. But since the thermal conductivity of the fouling layer and its thickness are not generally known, the only possible solution to the heat transfer problem is by the introduction of a fouling factor in order to take into account the additional resistance to heat transfer and make possible the calculation of the overall heat transfer coefficient. A fouling coefficient also is sometimes specified, which is the reciprocal value of the fouling factor.

In carrying out heat transfer calculations, caution needs to be exerted in selecting fouling factors, particularly where fouling resistances completely dominate the thermal design. The influence of uncertainties inherent in fouling factors is generally greater than that of uncertainties in other design parameters such as fluid properties, flow rates and temperatures [34]. A large fouling factor is sometimes adopted as a safety margin to cover uncertainties in fluid properties and even in process knowledge but the use of an excessively large fouling factor will result in an oversized heat exchanger with two or three times more area than is really necessary. Although there are many experience-based tabulations available that provide typical fouling factors such as TEMA Table RGP-T-2.4 [35], acceptable evaluation of the effects of fouling needs to be judged and evaluated for each particular application. Such tabulations, however, can be used as a guide in the absence of more specific information.

A number of methods empirical or otherwise have been proposed over the years for the prediction of the rate of fouling in heat exchangers or for estimating a fouling factor to be used in heat transfer calculations. With the advent and development of digital computers with their ability to provide rapid means of performing calculations, new and accurate methods became possible. Matlab being a programming language widely used in all scientific fields and in engineering sciences in particular may be used in conjunction with the artificial neural network (ANN) approach to provide an accurate and reliable method for predicting the fouling rate and rate of heat transfer in heat exchangers. The development of high speed digital computers has provided a rapid means of performing the many calculations involved in the ANN method, and has had a stimulating effect on the current expansion of the ANN method which is progressing at an impressive rate.

In recent years, the ANN method has been applied in many disciplines of engineering and has produced promising results. The main feature of this method is its ability to learn and generalise the relationships in a data set and to provide quick and satisfactory estimations, which make it attractive for many different applications.

The artificial neural network method is a computational structure inspired by a biological neural system. An ANN consists of very simple and highly interconnected processors called neurons. The neurons are connected to each other by weighted links over which signals can pass. Each neuron receives multiple inputs from other neurons in proportion to their connection weights and generates a single output, which may be propagated to several other neurons [36]. The inputs (X) into a neuron are multiplied by their corresponding connection weights (W) and summed together, a threshold (θ), acting at a bias, is added also to the sum. This sum is transformed through a transfer function (f) to produce a single output (Y), which may be passed on to other neurons. The function of a neuron can be mathematically expressed as

$$Y = f\left(\sum wx - \theta\right) \qquad (2)$$

Where the transfer function (f) of the neuron is the linear activation function, being in the present work given as:

$$f(x) = purelin(x) \qquad (3)$$

for the output layer and the tansing function

$$f(x) = tansig(x) \qquad (4)$$

for the hidden layers

Among the various existing kinds of ANNS, the back propagation (BP) learning algorithm has become the most popular in engineering applications [37]. The BP algorithm is designed to solve the problem of determining weight values for a multi-layer ANN with feed forward connections from the input layer to the hidden layers and then to the output layer. The algorithm is an iterative gradient algorithm, designed to minimise the mean square error between the predicted output and the desired output. Fig. 5 shows a scheme of a simple example for BP algorithm, and Fig. 6 is a flow chart for the back propagation (BP) learning algorithm.

Results of the application of the ANN approach show that it can be used to develop the best configuration in the training period. In general, this approach may however be time consuming; it is nonetheless feasible due to its ability to learn and generalise the complex data set with a wide range of experimental conditions. For exhaustive and fundamental treatment of the ANN technique, the reader is referred to any of the textbooks [38, 39].

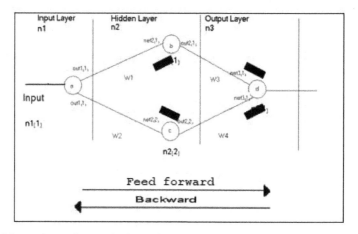

Figure 5. Scheme of a simple example of a BP algorithm.

Some of the recent applications for energy systems include modelling of appliances, light and space cooling energy consumption [40], solar radiation estimation [41], modelling gasoline consumption [42], modelling of heat pumps [43], performance prediction of solar domestic water heating systems [44], prediction of energy consumption of a passive solar building [45], prediction of temperature profiles in producing oil wells [46] and developing heating, ventilating and air conditioning systems for automobiles [47]. In addition, various applications of artificial neural networks in energy problems have been presented thematically [48−50].

In the field of heat exchangers, the Ann approach has been widely used, particularly in the design and control of heat exchangers [51, 52], and in the simulation of heat exchanger performance [14] and heat transfer analysis for different systems such as air−water spray cooling [53].

The ANN approach has also been used as an alternative and practical technique to evaluate the rate of heat exchange and heat transfer coefficient for tubular heat exchangers [34], fin tube heat exchangers [37], fluid−particle systems [54], heat rate predictions in humid air−water heat exchangers [55], and in other applications [22] including in particular the prediction of the rate of fouling and fouling factor in a shell-and-tube heat exchanger [56].

For predicting the rate of fouling and fouling factor in heat exchangers an ANN model can be developed and the available data set used for training the network and verifying its generalisation capability. The rates of heat transfer are then calculated and the input−output pairs presented to the network, and the weights adjusted to minimise the error between the network output and the actual value. Once training is complete, predictions from a new set of data may be done using the already trained network. The proposed algorithm is solved by a Matlab computer programme. After the rate of heat transfer is calculated, it can be used to estimate the fouling factor.

In order to test the applicability of the ANN model using the back propagation learning algorithm to predict the rate of heat transfer and fouling factor for heat exchangers, it was applied on a tube-shell heat exchanger used as a preheat device for the naphtha feed to the reactor in the naphtha hydrotreating unit at the Homs oil refinery.

Operation data of the heat exchanger are collected for this purpose [8]. A total of 73 readings tabulated in Table 6 are used for the ANN method. Empirical correlations for the rate of heat transfer (Q) is determined [57] as given below by Eq.5:

$$Q = m \, Cp \, (t1d\text{-}t2d) \text{ kJ/hr} \qquad (5)$$

$Q = q1+q2$
$q1 = m \cdot 1 \times Cp1 \times (t1d\text{-}t2d) \text{ (liquid)}$
$q2 = m \cdot 2 \times Cp2 \times (t1d\text{-}t2d) \text{ (gas)}$
$Cp1 = 0.0045 \times t + 2.0687$
$Cp2 = Cp \text{ (hydrogen)} + Cp \text{ (hydrocarbons)}$
$Cp \text{ (hydrogen)} = 4.19 \, (6.8 + 0.0006 \times t) \, y$
$Cp \text{ (hydrocarbons)} = (0.00428 \times t + 1.5606) \, (1\text{-}y)$
$y = 2.016 \times N/(100 \times M)$

In developing an ANN model, the available data set is used for training the network and the same data are used to verify the generalisation capability of the network [58]. The input parameters were liquid naphtha feed quantity (m·1), gas reaction quantity (m·2), inlet temperature (t1d), outlet temperature (t2d), hydrogen purity (N), gas molecular weight (M), naphtha specific heat (Cp1), gas specific heat (Cp2) and the output parameter is heat transfer rate (Q).

The rates of heat transfer (Q) for the same data are calculated using Excel programme (actual values). Input−output pairs are presented to the network, and the weights are adjusted to minimise the error between the network output and the actual value (this is done at the training step on a number of data (n = 73)). Once training is complete, predictions from a new set of data may be done using the already trained network. The proposed algorithm in this study was solved by a computer programme developed using the Matlab programming language, and all computations were performed with a personal computer. After the rate of heat transfer is calculated, it can be used to estimate the fouling factor.

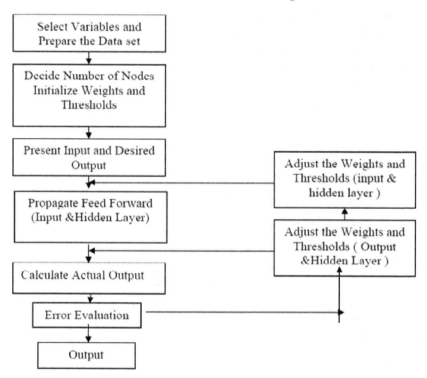

Figure 6. Flow chart for the back propagation (BP) learning algorithm.

The same steps used to calculate the rate of heat transfer by neural network (design, training) are used to calculate fouling factor for different data (Input-output pairs). The empirical correlations for the fouling factor are determined [57] as given below in Eq. 6:

$$f = Uc\text{-}Ud/Uc \times Ud \ m2hr°C/kJ \tag{6}$$

$Uc = ho \times hi/ho + hi$
$Ud = Q/A \times LMTD$
$ho = Jh \times k/De \times pr0.33$
$hi = Jh \times k/D \times pr0.33$
$LMTD = (T1\text{-}t2)\text{--}(T2\text{-}t1)/\ln(T1\text{-}t2)/(T2\text{-}t1)$

$Gs = m\cdot/as$ where $as = ID \times C \times B/Pt$
$Res = Gs \times De/\mu$ (shell)
$Prs = Cp \times \mu /K$ (shell)
$Gt = m\cdot/at$ where $at = Nt \times at'/z$
$Ret = D \times Gt/ \mu$ (tube)
$Prt = Cp \times \mu /k$ (tube)

A total of 73 values of input date tabulated in Table 7 are used for the ANN method, which were the rate of heat transfer (Q) obtained from the neural network, log mean temperature difference (LMTD), shell volumetric flow Gs, tube volumetric flow Gt, shell Reynolds Res and Prandtl Prs numbers, tube Reynolds Ret and Prandtl Prt numbers, and the output is the fouling factor (f).

The Fouling factor (f) for the same data is calculated using Excel programme (actual value). Input—output pairs are presented to the network, and the weights are adjusted to minimise the error between the network output and the actual value (this is done at the training step on a number of data (n=73). Once training is complete, predictions from a new set of data may be done using the already trained network. The proposed algorithm in this study was solved by a computer programme developed using Matlab programming language; also all computations were performed with a personal computer.

The purpose of using the ANN model with the considered BP learning algorithm as a practical approach is to test the ability to predict the rate of heat transfer and fouling factor of heat exchanger. For the heat transfer function a network is designed with eight input parameters, namely liquid naphtha feed quantity (m·1), gas reaction quantity (m·2), inlet temperature (t1d), outlet temperature (t2d), hydrogen purity (N), gas molecular weight (M), naphtha specific heat (Cp1) and gas specific heat (Cp2), and one output parameter, the rate of heat exchange (Q). Model sensitivity was examined for different numbers of hidden layer nodes in the range of (1-5). There is no general rule for selecting the number of a hidden layer. The choice of hidden layer size is a specific problem and, to some extent, depends on the number and the quality of training patterns. The number of neurons in a neural network must be sufficient for correct modelling of the problem, and also, it should be low to ensure generalisation.

The number of neurons in a hidden layer drastically affects the outcome of the network training. If too few neurons are included, then the network may not be able to learn properly. On the other band, if too many neurons were included, the network would encourage over fitting. Some researchers mentioned that the upper bound for the required number of neurons in the hidden layer should be greater than twice the number of input units. This rule does not guarantee generalisation of the network [59]. Every stage of an ANN problem requires a little trial and error to establish a suitable and stable network for the problem; so many networks are built by changing their parameters in order to reach a suitable result in these statements:

```
net_q=newff(minmax(input),[8,10,1],{'tansig','tansig','purelin'},'trainlm');
net_q.trainParam.show = 5;
```

```
net_q.trainParam.lr = 0.05;
net_q.trainParam.epochs = 1000;
net_q.trainParam.goal = 1e-13;
[net_q,tr]=train(net_q,input,q);
```

Q	Cp_2	Cp_1	M	N	t_2d	t_1d	m'_2	m'_1
7420754	5.62	2.43	5.9	88.1	113	50	30	1097
7897551	4.93	2.43	7.0	85.3	112	50	37	1173
10427147	4.50	2.42	7.9	82.2	111	48	53	1529
10937005	5.48	2.43	6.2	89.7	113	49	65	1548
6782209	4.47	2.43	7.9	81.6	112	50	69	945
9735495	4.71	2.42	7.3	82.5	111	48	46	1430
10815713	4.50	2.43	7.9	82.2	111	49	80	1564
10467559	5.07	2.42	6.7	85.4	111	47	41	1525
10544419	5.49	2.44	6.2	89.7	114	53	85	1512
9775821	6.32	2.453	5.1	90.2	116	55	75	1380
10508073	5.79	2.443	5.7	88.9	113	53	91	1491
9889096	5.87	2.454	5.6	88.9	115	56	94	1409
10594878	6.12	2.447	5.3	89.9	114	54	88	1507
10333419	6.19	2.436	5.2	89.5	112	51	85	1450
10032838	5.58	2.446	6.0	87.9	114	54	90	1449
9756511	6.05	2.452	5.4	89.6	114	56	83	1435
93056465	5.43	2.433	6.2	88	111	51	86	1342
10170994	5.29	2.433	6.5	88.6	112	50	79	1444
9552569	5.56	2.440	5.9	87	113	52	78	1368
10403199	6.52	2.427	4.9	90,9	110	49	86	1443
7971085	6.03	2.425	5.3	88.6	110	48	64	1105
10522022	5.17	2.418	6.5	85.7	109	46	73	1492
10463870	5.65	2.412	5.8	88.1	107	45	78	1486
10277598	5.18	2.407	6.5	86	106	44	88	1453
10288698	5.56	2.412	5.9	87	107	45	82	1452
9849226	5.36	2.408	6.2	86.5	107	44	77	1394
6762596	4.83	2.415	7.1	84.4	109	45	80	890
9817752	4.36	2.412	8.3	82.6	107	45	73	1488
9993798	5.10	2.400	6.6	85.5	105	42	81	1490
9955236	5.27	2.400	6.3	85.9	105	42	76	1492
9836656	5.38	2.423	6.2	86.9	109	48	82	1497
7035618	5.28	2.392	6.34	86.8	104	40	73	1060
10432795	5.26	2.381	6.2	84.7	102	37	81	1528
9787933	5.25	2.403	6.36	86.2	106	43	76	1471
9465628	5.27	2.415	6.3	85.7	108	46	82	1467

Table 6. Operation data for heat transfer.

f	Tube Pr	Tube Re	Gt	Shell Pr	Shell Re	Gs	LMTD	Q
0.0011	1.48	21626.83	602030	1.62	21123	757392	66.59	7420754
0.0011	1.47	23438.94	646368	1.62	22744	813172	67.64	7897551
0.0008	1.48	30387.8	845085	1.62	29534	1063172	67.38	10427147
0.0007	1.47	31538.99	361645	1.62	30543	1084005	67.95	10937005
0.0015	1.45	21187.03	541667	1.61	19793	681452	73.76	6782209
0.0010	1.46	29257.62	788462	1.62	27492	991935	72.36	9735495
0.0009	1.46	33515.82	878205	1.62	31264	1104839	73.89	10815713
0.0009	1.46	31068.49	836538	1.63	28929	1052419	73.99	10467559
0.0008	1.45	32702.56	853098	1.61	31140	1073253	70.74	10544419
0.0009	1.45	29913.23	777244	1.60	28687	977823	69.61	9775821
0.0008	1.46	32350.07	845085	1.61	30950	1063172	70.04	10508073
0.0010	1.44	32120.8	802885	1.60	30004	1010081	73.84	9889096
0.0008	1.45	32907.62	852030	1.60	31298	1071909	70.96	10594878
0.0010	1.44	32575.66	819979	1.61	29646	1031586	77.83	10333419
0.0010	1.44	32759.62	822115	1.60	30239	1034274	75.68	10032838
0.0010	1.44	32013.2	810897	1.60	29970	1020161	73.48	9756511
0.0011	1.45	29774.46	762821	1.61	27603	959677	75.02	93056465
0.0009	1.46	30972.04	813568	1.61	29213	1023522	72.19	10170994
0.0010	1.45	29631.19	772436	1.61	28037	971774	71.75	9552569
0.0009	1.45	31756.42	816774	1.62	29211	1027554	76.16	10403199
0.0013	1.45	24243.94	624466	1.62	22226	785618	76.65	7971085
0.0010	1.45	32383.05	836004	1.63	29227	1051747	79.01	10522022
0.0011	1.44	32829.65	835470	1.63	29028	1051075	82.29	10463870
0.0011	1.45	32212.47	823184	1.63	28628	1035618	81.54	10277598
0.0011	1.44	32131.64	819444	1.63	28575	1030914	81.41	10288698
0.0012	1.44	32125.61	785791	1.63	27224	988575	83.99	9849226
0.0018	1.43	21261.79	518162	1.62	18711	651882	83.17	6762596
0.0012	1.44	31827.77	817842	1.64	27804	1028898	84.03	9817752
0.0012	1.44	31967.45	817842	1.64	27325	1028898	87.40	9993798
0.0013	1.44	13937.11	816239	1.64	27185	1026882	88.28	9955236
0.0012	1.44	32069.81	821047	1.63	28309	1032930	82.41	9836656
0.0020	1.44	22709.1	577991	1.65	18965	727151	90.99	7035618
0.0013	1.44	32925.24	838141	1.66	27244	1054435	92.43	10432795
0.0013	1.44	31540.68	807158	1.64	27077	1015457	86.75	9787933
0.0013	1.43	31264.22	795406	1.64	26834	1000672	86.70	9465628
0.0012	1.44	31845.35	814637	1.63	27932	1024866	83.42	9780958
0.0012	1.44	31368.23	795940	1.63	27658	1001344	82.63	9517534
0.0013	1.43	32173.46	804487	1.63	27566	1012097	87,09	9509371
0.0014	1.44	29723.24	756410	1.64	25225	951613	88.49	9116431

f	Tube Pr	Tube Re	Gt	Shell Pr	Shell Re	Gs	LMTD	Q
0.0014	1.43	30476.46	760684	1.63	26214	956989	86,47	8893684
0.0015	1.42	33656.34	831197	1.65	27457	1045699	94.73	9748671
0.0014	1.43	33818.59	840812	1.64	28607	1057796	89.17	9601441
0.0013	1.43	32548.29	815171	1.62	28482	1025538	83.92	9280739
0.0014	1.43	34152.85	848825	1.65	28277	1067876	92.50	9834141

Table 7. Operation data for fouling factor.

After 211 training cycles the goal set was achieved, the level of error was satisfactory, and further cycles had no significant effect on error reduction. The network configuration with ten nodes in the hidden layer, a learning rate of 0.05 resulted in the fastest convergence and a low level of error during the training period. To be able to design a stable ANN, it would be more appropriate to conduct a parametric study by changing the number of neurons in the hidden layer in order to test the stability of the network. Fig. 7 shows the performance of the network with the numbers of neurons in the hidden layer (training step); in Fig. 8 the experimental values (actual value) of heat transfer rate (Q) are compared with the results predicted using the best ANN configuration.

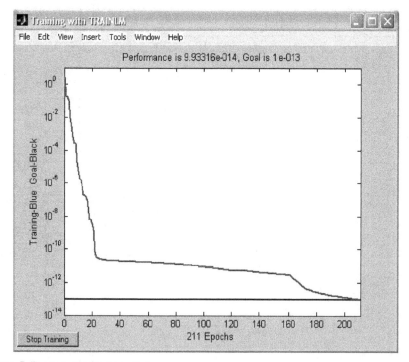

Figure 7. Training step (Heat transfer)

For fouling factor determination a network is designed with eight input parameters, the rate of heat transfer (Q) obtained from the neural network, log mean temperature difference LMTD, shell volumetric flow Gs, tube volumetric flow Gt, shell Reynolds number Res, shell Prandtl number Prs, tube Prandtl number Prt, tube Reynolds Number Ret, and one output parameter, fouling factor (f), all physical properties are estimated at average values of the inlet and outlet temperatures for both sides of the heat exchanger. As before, every stage of an ANN problem requires a little trial and error to establish a suitable and stable network for the problem; so many networks are built by changing their parameters in order to reach a suitable result in these statements:

```
net_f=newff(minmax(input),[8,10,1],{'tansig','tansig','purelin'},'trainlm');
net_f.trainParam.show = 5;
net_f.trainParam.lr = 0.05;
net_f.trainParam.epochs = 1000;
net_f.trainParam.goal = 1e-13;
[net_f,tr]=train(net_f,input,f);
```

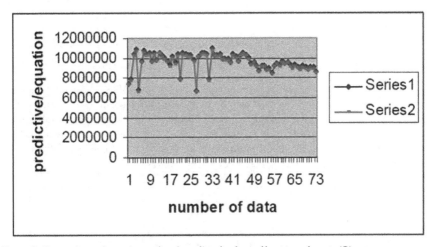

Figure 8. Comparison of experimental and predicted values of heat transfer rate (Q)

After 623 training cycles, the goal set was achieved, the level of error is satisfactory, and further cycles had no significant effect on error reduction. The network configuration with ten nodes in the hidden layer, a learning rate of 0.05 resulted in the fastest convergence and a low level of error during the training period. To be able to design a stable ANN, it would be more appropriate to conduct a parametric study by changing the number of neurons in the hidden layer in order to test the stability of the network. Fig. 9 shows the performance of the network with the numbers of neurons in the hidden layer (training step). In Fig. 10 the experimental values of fouling factor (f) are compared with the results predicted using the best ANN configuration.

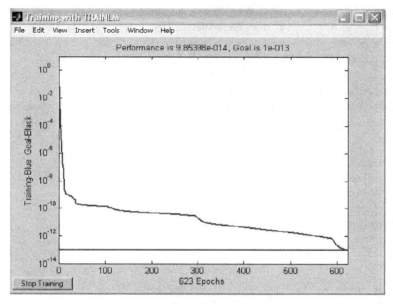

Figure 9. Training step (Fouling factor)

The results obtained and the comparisons made using both the ANN model and empirical correlations show conclusively that the proposed ANN approach could be used successfully to predict both the rate of heat transfer and fouling factor for heat exchangers. The accuracy and reliability of this approach for predicting the fouling factor can go a long way towards mitigating the detrimental effects of fouling in heat exchangers in particular and in other process equipment in which fouling may be of a major concern.

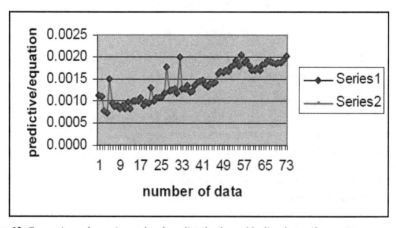

Figure 10. Comparison of experimental and predicted values of fouling factor (f)

Nomenclature

C_p	Specific heat, kJ/kg.°C
C_{p1}	Liquid specific heat, kJ/kg.°C
C_{p2}	Gas specific heat, kJ/kg.°C
D	Flow area per tube, m^2
D_e	Equivalent diameter, m
E	Activation energy, J/mol K
f	Fouling factor, $hr.m^2.°C/kJ$
G_s	Shell mass flow, $kg/hr.m^2$
G_t	Tube mass flow, $kg/hr.m^2$
h_i	Heat transfer coefficient inside tube, $kJ/hr.m^2.°C$
h_o	Heat transfer coefficient outside tube, $kJ/hr.m^2.°C$
k	Thermal conductivity, $kJ/hr.m.°C$
LMTD	Log mean temperature difference, °C
M	Gas molecular weight
m	Mass flow of gas and naphtha, kg/hr
m_1	Liquid mass flow, kg/hr
m_2	Gas mass flow, kg/hr
N	Hydrogen purity, %
n	Number of data
Pr	Prandtl number
Pr_s	Shell Prandtl number
Pr_t	Tube Prandtl number
Q	Total heat transfer, kJ/hr
q_1	Liquid heat transfer, kJ/hr
q_2	Gas heat transfer, kJ/hr
R	Gas constant, J/mol K
Re	Reynolds number
Re_s	Shell Reynolds number
Re_t	Tube Reynolds number
R_f	Fouling resistance, $m^2 K/kW$
T_{1d}	Tube inlet temperature, °C
T_{2d}	Tube outlet temperature, °C
T_{film}	Fluid film temperature, K
t	Time, s
t_{1d}	Shell inlet temperature, °C
t_{2d}	Shell outlet temperature, °C
U_c	Clean overall coefficient, $kJ/hr.m^2.°C$
U_d	Dirt overall coefficient, $kJ/hr.m^2.°C$
W	Weight
x	Input
y	Output
θ	Threshold

μ   Viscosity, kg/m. hr
τw   Shear stress at the tube wall

Author details

Hassan Al-Haj Ibrahim
Department of Chemical Engineering, Al-Baath University, Homs, Syria

6. References

[1] Master BI, Chunangad KS, Pushpanathan V. Fouling mitigation using helixchanger heat exchangers.

[2] Mueller-Steinhagen H, Malayeri MR, Watkinson AP. Fouling of heat exchanger-New approaches to solve old problem. Heat Transfer Engineering, 2005;26(2).

[3] Hashemi R and R. L. Brown, Jr. RL. Heat exchanger fouling causes problems in gas and liquid systems. American Filtration Society Seminar, Chicago, Illinois, May 11, 1992.

[4] Muller-Stehinhagen H, Reif F, Epstein N, Watkinson AP. Influence of operating conditions on particulate fouling. Canadian Journal of Chemical Engineering, 1988: 66, 42-50.

[5] Herro HM. Deposit-Related Corrosion in Industrial Cooling Water Systems, Presented at the National Association of Corrosion Engineers Corrosion '89 meeting, New Orleans, Louisiana, April 17–21, 1989.

[6] Bernard C and Groce PE. Controlling hydrotreater fouling problem identification is key to cost-effective solutions. Betz process Chemicals, Oil and Gas Journal, January 1996.

[7] Al-haj Ibrahim H, Safwat A, Hussamy N. Investigation of the fouling mechanisms in the heat exchangers of a hydrotreater. Engineering Journal of the University of Qatar, 2005: 18, 9-14.

[8] Process and operating manual of naphtha hydrotreating unit, Homs Oil Refinery, 1989, 15-20.

[9] Al-haj Ibrahim H, Safwat A, Hussamy N. Particulate fouling evaluation in the preheat exchangers of a hydrotreater, Yemeni Journal of science, 2006: 7(1), 15-20.

[10] Bott TR. Fouling Notebook, Institution of Chemical Engineers, London, 1990.

[11] Fouling problems on Homs refinery naphtha hydrotreater, Technical note, Betzdearborn, 2000, 1-4.

[12] Vanhove A. Fouling Control in Refinery, Hydrocarbon Engineering, July/august 1998, 50-6.

[13] Gudmundsson JS. Particulate fouling, fouling of heat transfer equipment, E.F.C. Somerscales and J.G. Knudsen (eds.), Proceedings of the International Conference on the Fouling of Heat Transfer Equipment, Hemisphere, Washington, D.C., 1981, 357-388.

[14] Din G, Sen M, Yang KT, McClain RL. Simulation of heat exchanger performance by artificial neural networks, IVAC Res 5, 1999, 195−208.

[15] Epstein N. Particle deposition and mitigation, Dept Of Chemical engineering, The University of British Columbia.

[16] Papavergos PG and Hedley AB. Particle deposition behaviour from turbulent flows, Chem. Eng. Res. Des. 1984: 62, 275-295.

[17] Puckorius PR. Contolling deposits in cooling water systems, Mater. Protect. Perform., November, 1972, 19-22.

[18] Bott TR and Gudmunson JS. Operation of paraffin wax from flowing system, Institute of petroleum, IP77-007, London, 1978.

[19] Muller-Steinhagen H and Blochl R. Particulate fouling in heat exchangers, Transcripts of Institute of Professional Engineers, New Zealand, EMC Eng-Sec., 1988: 15(3), 109-118.

[20] Chisholm D (ed.). Developments in heat exchanger technology-I, Applied Science Publishers, London, 1980.

[21] Marriot J. Where and how to use plate heat exchangers, Chem Eng, May 4, 1971, p. 127.

[22] Marriott J. Where and how to use plate heat exchangers, in Process Heat Exchange, Chemical Engineering Magazine (V. Cavaseno, ed.), McGraw-Hill, New York, 1979, 156-162.

[23] Kuppan T. Heat exchanger design handbook, Marcel Dekker, Inc., New York, 2000.

[24] Larowski A and M.A. Taylor MA. Systematic procedures for selection of heat exchangers, C58/82, Institution of Mechanical Engineers, London, 1982, 32-56.

[25] Larowski A and Taylor MA. Systematic procedures for selection of heat exchangers, Proc. Instn. Mech. Eng., 1983: 197A, 51-69.

[26] Mukherjee R. Conquer heat exchanger fouling, Hydrocarbon Processing, January, 1996, 121-127.

[27] Chenoweth JM. Final Report of the HTRVTEMA Joint Committee to Review the Fouling Section of the TEMA Standards, Heat Transfer Research, Inc., Alhambra, Calif., 1988.

[28] Cowan JC and Weintritt DJ. Water-formed scale deposits. A comprehensive study of the prevention, control, removal and use of mineral scale, Gulf Publishing Company, Houston, Texas, 1976.

[29] Fouling reduction device for a tubular heat exchanger, Patents FR 2479964 dated Apr. 8, 1980; EP 0174254 dated Nov. 9, 1986; US Patent 6782943 dated Aug. 31, 2004.

[30] Klaren DG. Fluid bed heat exchangers-A new approach in severe fouling heat transfer, Resources and Conservation, 1981, 301-314.

[31] Stegelman AF, Renfftlen R. On line mechanical cleaning of heat exchangers, Hydrocarbon Processing, 1983, 95-97.

[32] Ebert WA and Panchal CB. Analysis of Exxon crude-oil slip stream coking data, Fouling Mitigation of Industrial Heat-Exchange Equipment, Begell House, New York, 1997, 451-460.

[33] D. Q. Kern DQ and Seaton RE. A Theoretical Analysis of Thermal Fouling, Br. Chem. Eng., 1959: 4(5), 258-269.

[34] Riverol C, Napolitano V. Estimation of the overall heat transfer coefficient in a tubular heat exchanger under fouling using neural networks, Appl Flash Pasteurizer Int Comm Heat Mass Transfer, 2002: 29, 453—7.

[35] Standards of Tubular Exchanger Manufacturers Associaton, seventh edition, Tubular Exchanger Manufacturers Association, Tarrytown, NY, 1988.

[36] Sreekanth S, Ramaswamy US, Sablani SS, Prasher SO. A neural network approach for evaluation of surface heat transfer coefficient, J Food Process Reser, 1999: 23, 329—48.

[37] Pacheco-Vega A, Sen M, Yang KT, MeClain RL. Neural network analysis of fin-tube refrigerating heat exchanger with limited experimental data, Int J Heat Mass Transfer, 2001: 44, 763—70.

[38] S. Haykin. Neural networks: a comprehensive foundation, New York, McMillan College Publishing Company, 1994.

[39] Fauselt L. Fundamentals of neural networks, New York, Prentice-Hall, 1994.

[40] Aydinalp M, Ugursal VI, Fung AS. Modelling of the appliance, lighting, and space cooling to energy consumptions in the residential sector using neural networks. Appl Energy, 2002: 71, 87-100.

[41] Dorylo ASS, J.A. Jervase JA, AI-Lawati A. Solar radiation estimation using artificial neural network. Appl Energy; 2002: 71, 307−19.

[42] Masr GE, Hadr EA, Joun C. Back propagation neural networks for modelling gasoline consumption, Energy Conver Manage, 2002: 44, 893−905.

[43] Bechtler H, Browne MW, Bansal PK, Kecman V. Neural networks−a new approach to model vapour-compression heat pumps, Int J Energy Res, 2001: 25, 591−9.

[44] Kalogirou SA. Long-term performance prediction of forced circulation solar domestic water heating systems using artificial neural networks, Appl Energy, 2000: 6663−74.

[45] Kalogirou SA, Bojic M. Artificial neural networks for the prediction of the energy consumption of a passive solar building, Energy, 2000: 1(5), 419−91.

[46] Farshad FE, Garber SD, Lorde IN. Predicting temperature profiles in producing oil wells using artificial neural networks, Eng Comput, 2000: 17, 735−54.

[47] Ueda M, Taniguchi Y, Asano A, Mochizuki M, Ikegarni T, Kawai T. An automobile heating, ventilating and air conditioning (HVAC) system with a neural network for controlling the thermal sensations felt by a passenger, ISME Ins J Series B-Fluid Thermal Eng, 1997: 40, 469−77.

[48] Kalogiron SA. Artificial neural networks in renewable energy systems applications: a review, ken Sustain Energy Rev, 2001: 5, 373−401.

[49] Kalogiron SA. Applications of artificial neural-networks for energy systems, Appl Energy, 2000: 67, 17−35.

[50] Kalogiron SA. Applications of artificial neural networks in energy systems: a review, Energy Conver Manage, 1999: 40, 1073−91.

[51] Diaz G, Sen M, Yang KT, McClain RL. Dynamic prediction and control of heat exchangers using artificial neural networks, Int Heat Mass Transfer, 2001: 44, 1671−9.

[52] Lavric D, Lavric L, Woinaroschy A, Danciu AE. Designing tin heat exchanger with a neural network, Rev Roumaine De Chim, 1995: 40, 561−5.

[53] Oliveira MSA, Sousa ACM. Neural network analysis of experimental data for air/water spray cooling, S Mater Process Technol, 2001: 113, 439−45.

[54] Sablani SS. A neural network approach for non-iterative calculation of heat transfer coefficient in fluid−particle systems, Chem Eng Process, 2001: 40, 363−9.

[55] Pacheco-Vega A, Diax G, Sen M, Yang KT, McClain RL. Heat rate predictions air-water beat exchangers using correlations and neural networks, S Heat Transfer−Trans ASME, 2001: 123, 348−54.

[56] Al-haj Ibrahim H, Safwat A, Hussamy N. Prediction of the rate of heat transfer and fouling factor by using artificial neural network approach, Bassel Al-Assad Journal for engineering sciences, 2007: 23, 9-27.

[57] Kern DQ. Process Heat Transfer, McGraw-Hill Book Co., 1950, 151-153.

[58] Aydinalp M, Ugursal VI, Fung AS. Predicting residential appliance, lighting, and space cooling energy consumption using neural networks, Proc. the Fourth International Thermal Energy Congress, Cesme, Turkey, 2001, 417-22.

[59] Rafig MY, Bugmann G, Easterbrook DI. Neural network design for engineering applications, Comput Struct, 2001: 79, 1541-52.

Chapter 3

Robust Control of Distributed Parameter Systems with Demonstration in Casting Technology and MATLAB/Simulink/DPS Blockset Software Support

Cyril Belavý, Gabriel Hulkó and Karol Ondrejkovič

Additional information is available at the end of the chapter

1. Introduction

Most of the dynamical systems analysed in engineering practice have the dynamics, which depends on both position and time. Such systems are classified as distributed parameter systems (DPS). The time-space coupled nature of the DPS is usually mathematically described by partial differential equations (PDE) as infinite-dimensional systems. However, from point of view of implementation of DPS control in technological practice, where a finite number of sensors and actuators for practical sensing and control is at disposal, such infinite-dimensional systems need to be approximated by finite-dimensional systems. There are many dimension reduction methods, which can be used to solve this problem.

In the first mathematical foundations of DPS control, analytical solutions of the underlying PDE have been used (Butkovskij, 1965; Lions, 1971; Wang, 1964). That is the decomposition of dynamics into time and space components based on the eigenfunctions of the PDE. Continuous and approximation theories aimed to control of parabolic systems presents monograph (Lasiecka & Triggiani, 2000). Methodical approach from the view of time-space separation with model reduction is presented in (Li & Qi, 2010). Variety of transfer functions for systems described by PDE are illustrated by means of several examples in (Curtain & Morris, 2009). Well-known reduction methods based on finite difference method (FDM), or finite element method (FEM), spectral method require an accurate nominal PDE model and usually lead to a high-order model, which requires unpractical high-order controller.

An engineering approach for the control of DPS is being developed since the eighties of the last century (Hulkó et al., 1981, 1987, 1998, 2009a, 2009b). In the field of lumped parameters system (LPS) control, where the state/output quantities $x(t)/y(t)$ – parameters are given as finite dimensional vectors, the actuator together with the controlled plant make up a controlled LPS. In this sense the actuators and the controlled plant as a DPS create a controlled lumped-input and distributed-parameter-output system (LDS).

In this chapter the decomposition of dynamics of controlled LDS into time and space components is introduced. Based on this decomposition a methodical framework of control synthesis decomposition into space and time tasks will be presented. In the space domain, approximation problems are solved. In the time domain, synthesis of control is performed by lumped parameter control loops, where robust controllers are used.

The casting technology is a typical case of the DPS. There in order to obtain the desired solidification structure, the casting process requires a specific temperature field of the mould, which is defined on complex-shape 3D definition domain. Modelling, simulation and evaluation of real-time experiments in this area is now widely accepted as an important tool in product design and process development to improve productivity and casting quality. For analysis of the casting process dynamics as DPS, especially temperature fields in the casting mould and control synthesis purposes, the benchmark casting plant with steel mould of complex-shape was designed at Faculty of Mechanical Engineering STU in Bratislava.

The main emphasis of this chapter is to present an engineering approach for the robust control of DPS with demonstration in the casting technology along with software support in the MATLAB & Simulink programming environment. This approach opens a wide space for novel applications of the toolboxes and blocksets of the MATLAB & Simulink software environment. For the software support of modelling, control and design of DPS, given on 1D-3D definition domains, the **Distributed Parameter Systems Blockset for MATLAB & Simulink (DPS Blockset),** a Third-Party Product of The MathWorks Company - www.mathworks.com/products/connections/ has been developed at the Institute of Automation, Measurement and Applied Informatics, Faculty of Mechanical Engineering STU, (Hulkó et al. 2003-2010). Also a web portal named **Distributed Parameter Systems Control** - www.dpscontrol.sk has been created for those, who are interested in solving problems of DPS control (Hulkó et al., 2003-2007). This web portal contains application examples from different areas of engineering practice, such as the control of technological and manufacturing processes, mechatronic structures, groundwater remediation, etc. In addition, this web portal offers the demo version of the **DPS Blockset** with the **Tutorial, Show, Demos** and **DPS Wizard** for download, along with the **Interactive Control** service for the interactive solution of model control problems via the Internet.

In this chapter, for the control synthesis purpose, LDS models of temperature fields in the casting mould were created by means of evaluation of real-time experiments. Robust control synthesis based on internal model control (IMC) structure in the time domain has been done. Designed robust controllers were used for the robust control of preheating casting mould in the real-time experiment in accordance to casting technology requirements. Identification, uncertainty analysis of the models, robust control synthesis and experiments were performed with the software support of DPS Blockset and toolboxes of the MATLAB & Simulink, especially the System Identification Toolbox, Control Systems Toolbox, Robust

Control Toolbox, Optimization Toolbox, System Identification Toolbox, Real-Time Windows Target and Simulink Design Optimization.

2. LDS/HLDS representation of DPS

In general, DPS are systems whose state or output quantities, $X(x,y,z,t) / Y(x,y,z,t)$ are distributed quantities or fields of quantities, where (x,y,z) are spatial coordinates in 3D. These systems are often considered as systems whose dynamics is described by PDE. In the input-output relation, PDE define distributed-input/distributed-output systems (DDS) between distributed input, $U(x,y,z,t)$ and distributed output quantities, $Y(x,y,z,t)$, at initial and boundary conditions given. Distributed parameter systems are very frequently found in various technical and non-technical branches with limited number of manipulated input quantities, or actuators. These lumped input quantities by means of interaction of fields and quantities generate distributed output of real DPS. Representation of such DPS is either in the form of LDS, Fig. 1 a), or in the form of LDS with zero-order hold unit H (HLDS), when discrete-time lumped input quantities are used, Fig. 1. b) , (Hulkó et al., 1981, 1987, 1998).

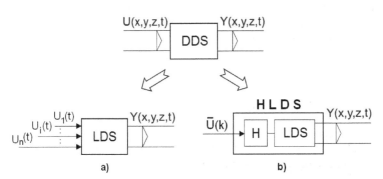

Figure 1. Representation of DPS: a) LDS - lumped-input/distributed-output system, b) HLDS –LDS with block of zero-order hold units H, $U(x,y,z,t)$ - distributed input quantity, $Y(x,y,z,t)$ - distributed output quantity, $\{U_i(t)\}_{i=1,n}$ - lumped input quantities, $\bar{U}(k)$ - vector of discrete-time lumped input quantities

2.1. Dynamics of LDS

Distributed output of the linear LDS from zero initial conditions either in continuous, or in discrete-time (DT) is in the form:

$$Y(\bar{x},t) = \sum_{i=1}^{n} Y_i(\bar{x},t) = \sum_{i=1}^{n} G_i(\bar{x},t) \otimes U_i(t) \tag{1}$$

$$Y(\bar{x},k) = \sum_{i=1}^{n} Y_i(\bar{x},k) = \sum_{i=1}^{n} GH_i(\bar{x},k) \oplus U_i(k) \tag{2}$$

where $\otimes$ denotes convolution product and $\oplus$ denotes convolution sum, $\overline{x} = (x,y,z)$ is position vector in 3D, $G_i(\overline{x},t)$ - distributed parameter impulse response of LDS to the i-th input, $GH_i(\overline{x},k)$ - DT distributed parameter impulse response of LDS with zero-order hold units H (HLDS) to the i-th input, $Y_i(\overline{x},t)$ - distributed parameter output quantity of LDS to the i-th input, $Y_i(\overline{x},k)$ - DT distributed parameter output quantity of HLDS to the i-th input, $U_i(t)$ - lumped input quantity, $U_i(k)$ - DT lumped input quantity, (Hulkó et al. 1998).

When $U_i(t)$ is a unit-step (Heaviside) function, $Y_i(\overline{x},t)$ is in the form of distributed step response function $\mathcal{H}_i(\overline{x},t)$. Similarly, for the unit-step function $U_i(k) : Y_i(\overline{x},k) \rightarrow \mathcal{H}H_i(\overline{x},k)$. For simplicity in this chapter distributed quantities are considered mostly as continuous scalar quantity fields with unit sampling interval in the time domain. Whereas DT distributed parameter step responses $\{\mathcal{H}H_i(\overline{x},k)\}_i$ of HLDS can be computed by common analytical or numerical methods, then DT distributed parameter impulse responses can be obtained as

$$\{GH_i(\overline{x},k) = \mathcal{H}H_i(\overline{x},k) - \mathcal{H}H_i(\overline{x},k-1)\}_i \tag{3}$$

For points $\{\overline{x}_i = (x_i,y_i,z_i)\}_i$ located in surroundings of lumped input quantities $\{U_i(t)\}_i$, where partial distributed transient responses $\{\mathcal{H}_i(\overline{x}_i,t)\}_i$ attains maximal amplitudes, partial distributed output quantities are obtained in time-domain and next either continuous $\{S_i(\overline{x}_i,s)\}_i$, or discrete transfer functions $\{SH_i(\overline{x}_i,z)\}_i$ with sampling period T are identified.

$$\{Y_i(\overline{x}_i,t) = G_i(\overline{x}_i,t) \otimes U_i(t)\}_i \quad \rightarrow \quad \{Y_i(\overline{x}_i,s) = S_i(\overline{x}_i,s)U_i(s)\}_i \tag{4}$$

$$\{Y_i(\overline{x}_i,k) = GH_i(\overline{x}_i,k) \oplus U_i(k)\}_i \quad \rightarrow \quad \{Y_i(\overline{x}_i,z) = SH_i(\overline{x}_i,z)U_i(z)\}_i \tag{5}$$

For the space dependency and in the steady-state we can define reduced transient step responses between i-th input quantity at point $\overline{x}_i = (x_i,y_i,z_i)$ and corresponding partial distributed output quantity in the steady-state:

$$\left\{\mathcal{H}HR_i(\overline{x},\infty) = \frac{\mathcal{H}H_i(\overline{x},\infty)}{\mathcal{H}H_i(\overline{x}_i,\infty)}\right\}_i \tag{6}$$

for $\{\mathcal{H}H_i(\overline{x}_i,\infty)\}_i \neq 0$.

Dynamics of LDS/HLDS is decomposed to the time and space components:

Time Components of Dynamics $\{S_i(\overline{x}_i,s)\}_i$, or $\{SH_i(\overline{x}_i,z)\}_i$ - for given i and chosen $\overline{x}_i$

Space Components of Dynamics $\{\mathcal{H}HR_i(\overline{x},\infty)\}_i$ - for given i in ∞

2.2. Feedback control loop based on HLDS dynamics

Decomposition of dynamics enables also to decompose the control synthesis (CS) to time synthesis (TS) and space synthesis (SS) tasks in the feedback control loop of the distributed parameter system, Fig. 2.

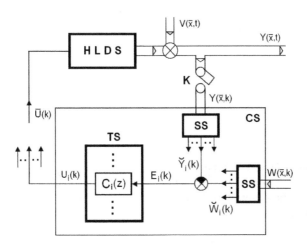

Figure 2. Distributed parameter feedback control loop: HLDS - LDS with zero-order holds $\{H_i\}_i$ on the input, CS - control synthesis, TS - control synthesis in time domain, SS - control synthesis in space domain, K - time/space sampling, $V(\bar{x},t)$ - disturbance quantity, $Y(\bar{x},t)$ - distributed controlled quantity, $Y(\bar{x},k)$ - sampled distributed controlled quantity, $\{\check{Y}_i(k)\}_i$ - approximation parameters of controlled quantity, $W(\bar{x},k)$ - reference quantity, $\{\check{W}_i(k)\}_i$ - approximation parameters of reference quantity, $\{E_i(k)\}_i$ - control errors, $\{C_i(z)\}_i$ - lumped parameter controllers, $\{U_i(k)\}_i$ - lumped control quantities

Let us consider a step change of distributed parameter control quantity $W(\bar{x},k)=W(\bar{x},\infty)$ and $V(\bar{x},t)=0$. The goal of the control synthesis is to generate a sequence of control inputs $\bar{U}(k)$ in such manner, that in the steady-state, for $k\to\infty$, the control error $E(\bar{x},k)$ will approach its minimal value $\|\check{E}(\bar{x},\infty)\|$ in the quadratic norm:

$$\min\|E(\bar{x},\infty)\|=\min\|W(\bar{x},\infty)-Y(\bar{x},\infty)\|=\|\check{E}(\bar{x},\infty)\| \tag{7}$$

First, in the SS blocks, the approximation both of sampled distributed controlled quantity $Y(\bar{x},k)$ and reference quantity $W(\bar{x},\infty)$, on the set of reduced steady-state distributed step responses $\{\mathcal{HHR}_i(\bar{x},\infty)\}_i$, are solved in following form:

$$\min_{\check{Y}_i}\left\|Y(\bar{x},k)-\sum_{i=1}^{n}Y_i(\bar{x}_i,k)\mathcal{HHR}_i(\bar{x},\infty)\right\|=\left\|Y(\bar{x},k)-\sum_{i=1}^{n}\check{Y}_i(k)\mathcal{HHR}_i(\bar{x},\infty)\right\| \tag{8}$$

$$\min_{\check{W}_i}\left\|W(\bar{x},\infty)-\sum_{i=1}^{n}W_i(\bar{x}_i,\infty)\mathcal{HHR}_i(\bar{x},\infty)\right\|=\left\|W(\bar{x},\infty)-\sum_{i=1}^{n}\check{W}_i\mathcal{HHR}_i(\bar{x},\infty)\right\| \tag{9}$$

Basis functions $\{\mathcal{HHR}_i(\bar{x},\infty)\}_i$ form a finite-dimensional subspace of approximation functions in the strictly convex normed linear space of distributed parameter quantities with quadratic norm, where the approximation problem is solved. From approximation theory involves, that solution of the approximation problems (8), (9) is guaranteed as a unique the best approximation in the form $\sum_{i=1}^{n} \breve{Y}_i(k) \mathcal{H}HR_i(\overline{x}, \infty)$ with the vector of optimal approximation parameters $\{\breve{Y}_i(k)\}_i$ in task (8) and the best approximation in the form $\sum_{i=1}^{n} \breve{W}_i \mathcal{H}HR_i(\overline{x}, \infty)$ with the vector of optimal approximation parameters $\{\breve{W}_i\}_i$ for approximation task (9).

Let us formulate a DPS control problem for the distributed reference quantity $W(\overline{x}, \infty)$. When $W(\overline{x}, k)$ is assumed, the space control synthesis is performed in each time step k, which gives $\{\breve{W}_i(k)\}_i$ parameters. Graphical interpretation of the approximation problem (9) for HLDS defined on 1D space $\overline{x}$ is on Fig. 3.

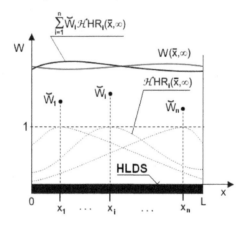

Figure 3. Solution of the approximation problem for the distributed reference quantity $W(\overline{x}, \infty)$

Next, based on the solution of approximation problem, the vector of control error is created:

$$\overline{E}(k) = \{E_i(k)\}_i = \{\breve{W}_i - \breve{Y}_i(k)\}_i \tag{10}$$

The control errors vector $\overline{E}(k) = \{E_i(k)\}_i$ enters into the block TS, where the vector of control quantities, $\overline{U}(k) = \{U_i(k)\}_i$ is generated by controllers $\{C_i(z)\}_i$ in single-parameter control loops. During the control process, for $k \to \infty$ the control task (7) is accomplished.

Finally, we may state as a summary, that in the feedback control of DPS with dynamics represented in the form of HLDS, the control synthesis is performed as:

Space Tasks of Control Synthesis – as approximation tasks.
Time Tasks of Control Synthesis – on the level of lumped parameter control loops.

3. Robust control system

In general, a mathematical model for the plant dynamics is the basis for analysis and design of control systems. Also for LDS representation of DPS lumped and distributed models are used. However, in practice, no mathematical model describes exactly a physical process. It is obvious, that although no model represents the process exactly, some of them will do so with greater accuracy than others.

The theory of the robust control represents one of the possible approaches to the control system design in the presence of uncertainty. The goal of the robust system design is to retain a good quality of system performance in spite of model inaccuracies and changes. For the design techniques, the following requirements are supposed to be fulfilled: formulation of nominal plant model, different plant uncertainty models and requirements for both, robust stability and performance.

3.1. Sources of uncertainties in the LDS structure

LDS representation of DPS means decomposition of dynamics to space and time components. Uncertainties may occur in both, time and space components.

In distributed parameter control system, according to Fig. 2, single-input, single-output control loops in the block TS are tuned as closed feedback control loops using usual methods. In these loops, as models of the controlled system, transfer functions $\left\{S_i\left(\overline{x}_i, s\right)\right\}_i$ and/or $\left\{SH_i\left(\overline{x}_i, z\right)\right\}_i$ in the z-domain are used. These transfer functions describe the dynamics between sequences $\left\{U_i\left(k\right)\right\}_i$ and $\left\{Y_i\left(\overline{x}_i, k\right)\right\}_i$.

In this case, the sources of uncertainties are given by:

- procedure of dynamics modelling and possible change of parameters in models (4), (5)
- solution of approximation problem (8), (9), where lumped quantities are obtained

In order to treat uncertainties, it will be further assumed that the dynamic behaviour of a plant is described not by a single linear time invariant model, but by a family of linear time invariant models, Ψ_i. This family in the frequency domain, e.g. for models $\left\{S_i\left(\overline{x}_i, s\right)\right\}_i$, takes the following form:

$$\Psi_i = \left\{S_i : \left|\ S_i\left(\overline{x}_i, j\omega\right) - \tilde{S}_i\left(\overline{x}_i, j\omega\right)\ \right| \le \overline{L}_{ai}\left(\omega\right)\right\} \tag{11}$$

where $\tilde{S}_i\left(\overline{x}_i, j\omega\right)$ is the nominal plant model. Any member of the family Ψ_i fulfils the conditions:

$$S_i\left(\overline{x}_i, j\omega\right) = \tilde{S}_i\left(\overline{x}_i, j\omega\right) + L_{ai}\left(j\omega\right) \tag{12}$$

$$\left|L_{ai}\left(j\omega\right)\right| \le \overline{L}_{ai}\left(\omega\right) \quad, \forall\ S_i \in \Psi_i \tag{13}$$

where $L_{ai}\left(j\omega\right)$ is an additive uncertainty and $\overline{L}_{ai}\left(\omega\right)$ is the bound of additive uncertainty. If we wish to work with multiplicative uncertainties, we define the relations:

$$L_{mi}(j\omega) = \frac{L_{ai}(j\omega)}{\tilde{S}_i(\overline{x}_i, j\omega)} \; ; \quad \overline{L}_{mi}(\omega) = \frac{\overline{L}_{ai}(\omega)}{\left|\tilde{S}_i(\overline{x}_i, j\omega)\right|} \tag{14}$$

where $L_{mi}(j\omega)$ is a multiplicative uncertainty and $\overline{L}_{mi}(\omega)$ is the bound of multiplicative uncertainty.

3.2. Design of IMC robust controllers

A robust control system for HLDS will be designed using the Internal Model Control (IMC) strategy (Morari & Zafiriou, 1989) with the general structure depicted in Fig. 4. a). It is possible to transform this structure to the classical feedback control loop, Fig. 4. b) and to incorporate it into the TS block of the DPS feedback control system. The relationship between the classical feedback controller C and the IMC controller Q for the nominal model $\tilde{P}$ of the controlled process P is as follows, and vice-versa:

$$Q = \frac{C}{1 + \tilde{P}C} \; ; \quad C = \frac{Q}{1 - \tilde{P}Q} \tag{15}$$

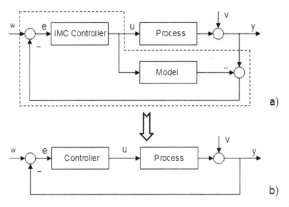

Figure 4. a) Internal Model Control structure, b) equivalent classical feedback control loop

It is well known that IMC strategy has the following properties:

1. *Dual stability*: Assume a perfect model, $(\tilde{P} = P)$ and if the controller and process are stable, then the IMC structure guarantees the closed-loop stability.
2. *Perfect control*: Assume a perfect model, $(\tilde{P} = P)$ and the closed-loop system is stable, while $Q = \tilde{P}^{-1}$, then there is no output steady-state error for set-point variance and disturbances.

The IMC structure thus provides the following benefits with respect to classical feedback: better dynamic response, system stability and robustness. One can search for Q instead of C without any loss of generality.

Structure of the distributed parameter feedback robust control system DPS with HLDS dynamics and IMC controllers is on Fig. 5.

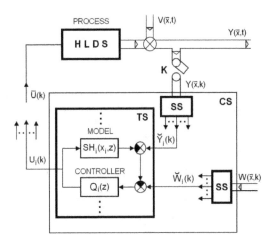

Figure 5. Distributed parameter feedback robust control system: HLDS - LDS with zero-order holds $\{H_i\}_i$ on the input, CS - control synthesis, TS - control synthesis in time domain, SS - control synthesis in space domain, K - time/space sampling, $V(\overline{x},t)$ - disturbance quantity, $Y(\overline{x},t)$ - distributed controlled quantity, $Y(\overline{x},k)$ - sampled distributed controlled quantity, $\{\breve{Y}_i(k)\}_i$ - approximation parameters of controlled quantity, $W(\overline{x},k)$ - reference quantity, $\{\breve{W}_i(k)\}_i$ - approximation parameters of reference quantity, $\{E_i(k)\}_i$ - control errors, $\{U_i(k)\}_i$ - lumped control quantities, $\{SH_i(x_i,z)\}_i$ - models of lumped controlled systems, $\{Q_i(z)\}_i$ - lumped parameter IMC controllers

H_2 optimal IMC controllers $\{Q_i(z)\}_i$ for inputs $\{\breve{W}_i(k)\}_i$ in the form unit-step function $\gamma(z) = \dfrac{z}{z-1}$ are obtained from solution of the following minimization problem:

$$\min_{Q_i(z)}\|e_i(z)\|_2 = \min_{Q_i(z)}\left\|\left(1 - SH_i(\overline{x}_i,z)Q_i(z)\right)\gamma_i(z)\right\|_2 \tag{16}$$

subject to the constraint $Q_i(z)$ to be stable and causal.

First, factorize the nominal stable transfer function $SH_i(x_i,z)$:

$$SH_i(\overline{x}_i,z) = SH_{Ni}(\overline{x}_i,z)\,SH_{Mi}(\overline{x}_i,z) \tag{17}$$

where $SH_{Ni}(\overline{x}_i,z)$ includes positive zeros or time-delays of the transfer function $SH_i(x_i,z)$. After this, optimal IMC controller $Q_i(z)$ is given by:

$$Q_i(z) = SH_{Mi}(\overline{x}_i,z)^{-1} \tag{18}$$

Finally, controller $Q_i(z)$ is augmented by low-pass filter $F_i(z)$ with parameter $0 < \alpha_i < 1$:

$$F_i(z) = \frac{1-\alpha_i}{z-\alpha_i} \tag{19}$$

Resulting IMC controller with filter $Q_{Fi}(z)$ is in following form:

$$Q_{Fi}(z) = Q_i(z) F_i(z) = Q_i(z) \frac{(1-\alpha_i)}{z-\alpha_i} \tag{20}$$

Parameter of the filter α_i is the only one tuning parameter to be selected by the user to achieve the appropriate compromise between performance and robustness and to keep the action of the manipulated variable within bounds. It must be chosen with respect to both, robust stability and robust performance condition:

$$\left| F_i\left(e^{j\omega T}\right) \right| < \left[\left| S_i\left(\bar{x}_i, j\omega\right) Q_i\left(e^{j\omega T}\right) \right| \bar{L}_{mi}(\omega) \right]^{-1}, \quad 0 \le \omega \le \frac{\pi}{T} \tag{21}$$

$$\left| Q_i(j\omega) \right| \bar{L}_{ai}(\omega) + \left| 1 - S_i\left(\bar{x}_i, j\omega\right) Q_i(j\omega) \right| G_{wi}(\omega) < 1, \quad 0 \le \omega \le \frac{\pi}{T} \tag{22}$$

where $G_{wi}(\omega)$ is weighting function

For $SH_i(x_i, z) = SH_{Mi}(\bar{x}_i, z)$ and low-pass filter (19), robust controller $C_i(z)$ in equivalent classical feedback control loop takes form:

$$C_i(z) = \frac{SH_{Mi}(\bar{x}_i, z)^{-1} F_i(z)}{1 - SH_i(\bar{x}_i, z) SH_{Mi}(\bar{x}_i, z)^{-1} F_i(z)} = \frac{1}{SH_{Mi}(\bar{x}_i, z)} \cdot \frac{F_i(z)}{1 - F_i(z)} \tag{23}$$

4. Benchmark casting plant

The casting mould is one of the key components of a casting. It is well known, that the quality of the castings is affected strongly by the surface quality and the distribution of temperature in the mould, which has both time and space dependence. For study of the physical phenomena occurring during the casting solidification, from a DPS control point of view, control system development as well as mathematical model validation, a benchmark of the casting processes was designed (Belavý et al., 2009). At the study of casting processes and design of experimental plant, simulation studies in virtual software environments ProCAST and COMSOL Multiphysics were used.

4.1. Construction of the benchmark casting plant

Scheme of the benchmark casting plant is depicted in Fig. 6. The core item is the two-part steel mould of a complex-shape mounted in the frame of the ejector mechanism, Fig. 7. This mechanism is hinge-mounted to the main frame, to enable tilting of the mould for optimal filling and metal flow. Further, a hydraulic cooling circuit, which consists of an array of induction motor driven roller vane pumps, a bunch of hoses, a flow divider, a collector with built-in check valves, a plate heat exchanger and an expansion tank. The main cooling circuit is divided into five independent circuits thus enabling the control of heat extraction from the casting via the chills. The coolant flow is controlled by means of frequency converters, since volumetric pumps are used. The main heating circuit is also divided into five independent circuits.

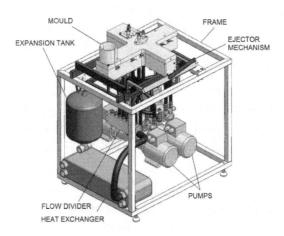

Figure 6. Scheme of the benchmark casting plant

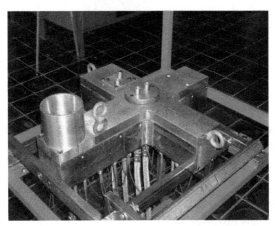

Figure 7. Two-part steel mould in detail

Inside of the casting mould are built-in 26 electric heating elements, each with maximal heating power 400 W. Heating elements are grouped to 5 zones and their heating power is actuated by the input voltage range of $(0 - 10)$ V. In the body of the mould is also placed 7 water-cooled copper chills and 11 thermocouples, Fig. 8., Fig 9. Coordinates of measuring points of thermocouples in x-y plane are given in Tab. 1 and z - coordinate is -0.05 m. Location of built-in elements has been carefully designed based on simulation studies in software environments ProCAST and COMSOL Multiphysics, in order to have the possibility of preheating the mould in 5 zones achieving desired temperature profile as well as directional solidification of the casting by means of active heat removal. The temperature field in the mould-casting system is possible to estimate through interpolation of data, measured by thermocouples.

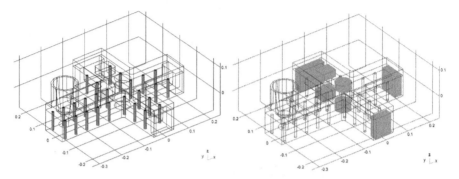

Figure 8. Location of heating elements (red) and copper chills (blue) in the mould

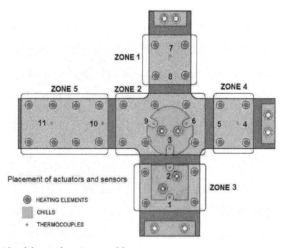

Figure 9. Bottom side of the steel casting mould

Position	1	2	3	4	5	6	7	8	9	10	11
x (m)	0	0	0	0.145	0.090	0.035	0	0	-0.035	-0.145	-0.255
y (m)	0.1585	0.0985	0.050	0	0	0	-0.135	-0.075	0	0	0

Table 1. Coordinates of thermocouples in x-y plane

4.2. Measurement and control scheme in MATLAB & Simulink

The measurement and control task of temperature field in the permanent casting mould was performed in the MATLAB & Simulink environment, where a *mould_exp_robust.mdl* scheme was setup, Fig. 10.

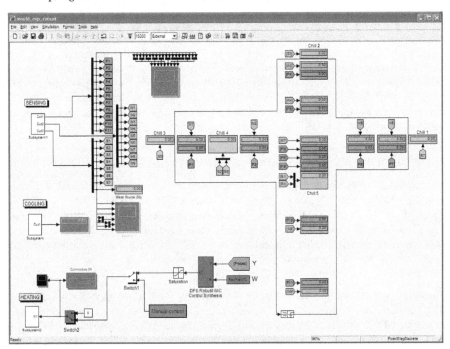

Figure 10. Measurement and control scheme in the MATLAB & Simulink

The scheme is composed of three main subsystems, namely: SENSING, HEATING and COOLING. Utilizing these subsystems and communication interface between process and computer, it is possible to measure dynamical characteristics of temperature field at zone heating. It is also possible to execute the experiment of controlled preheating of permanent mould before casting operation and controlled cooling during casting solidification. The above mentioned communication interface consists of data acquisition cards Advantech PCI-1710 [Ah], PCI-1710 [Ch] as analog input and Humusoft AD622 [Eh] as digital input.

Communication interface is performed by means of Simulink Real-Time Windows Target Toolbox and the communication is triggered by *Connect to Target* icon.

The SENSING subsystem enables the temperature measurement by thermocouples No. 1 to 11, which are permanently located in the bottom part of the steel mould, Fig. 9. These are marked on the scheme as P1 to P11. The subsystem also enables temperature measurements during casting solidification by temporal thermocouples W1 to W9, located in the casting domain. Thermocouple sensing junctions are located in the middle of the arm cross section, right above permanent thermocouples "P", except the node of the casting, where one temporal thermocouple points to the center of the node. Sensors S1 to S7 measure the temperature of cooling water in embedded chills. *Display* blocks of the sensors "P" and "W" in the scheme correspond to the real positions of sensors. Measured temperatures are saved to the data file and continuously displayed on the *Scope* block.

The HEATING subsystem has two basic operational regimes, which are activated by *Switch2* block. In the manual control regime, it is possible to set heating performance in range $(0 \div 10)$ Volt and measure the temperature transient characteristics with P1 to P11 thermocouples in given locations of the mould. The second regime activated by *Switch2* block enables to perform controlled preheating of the casting mould to desired temperature profile W defined in 11 points, where thermocouples P1 to P11 are located. The control task is performed by *DPS Robust IMC Control Synthesis* block.

5. Distributed Parameter Systems Blockset for MATLAB & Simulink

For the MATLAB & Simulink based software support of modelling, control and design of Distributed Parameter Systems given on complex 3D domains of definition, the programming environment **Distributed Parameter Systems Blockset for MATLAB & Simulink (DPS Blockset)** as Third-Party MathWorks Product has been developed by the Institute of Automation, Measurement and Applied Informatics, Faculty of Mechanical Engineering, Slovak University of Technology in Bratislava, within the program CONNECTIONS of The MathWorks Corporation, Fig. 11. , (Hulkó et al., 2003-2010).

The library of DPS Blockset shows Fig. 12. Blocks **HLDS** and **RHLDS** serve for modelling of distributed parameter systems as lumped-input/distributed-output systems with zero-order hold units. The block **DPS Control Synthesis** provides feedback to distributed parameter controlled systems in control loops with blocks for discrete-time **PID**, **Algebraic**, **State-Space** and **Robust Control**. The block **DPS Input** generates distributed quantities which can be used as distributed control quantities or distributed disturbances, etc. **DPS Display** presents distributed quantities with many options including export to AVI files. The block **DPS Space Synthesis** performs space synthesis as an approximation problem.

The block **DPS Wizard** in step-by-step operation, by means of several model examples with default parameters on 1D-3D definition domains, gives an automatized guide for arrangement and setting distributed parameter control loops. The block **Demos** contains examples oriented to methodology of modelling and control synthesis. The block **Show** contains motivation examples such as: *Control of temperature field of 3D metal body* (the controlled system was modelled in the virtual software environment COMSOL Multiphysics); *Control of 3D beam of „smart" structure* (the controlled system was modelled in the virtual software environment ANSYS); *Adaptive control of glass furnace* (the controlled system was modelled by Partial Differential Equations Toolbox of the MATLAB), and *Groundwater remediation control* (the controlled system was modelled in the virtual software environment MODFLOW). The block **Tutorial** presents methodological framework both for formulation and solution of control tasks for distributed parameter systems.

Robust Control of Distributed Parameter Systems with Demonstration in Casting Technology
and MATLAB/Simulink/DPS Blockset Software Support

83

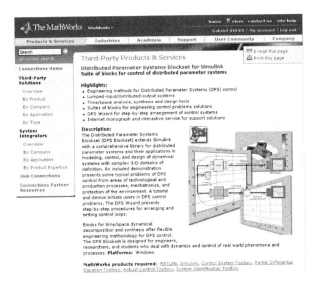

Figure 11. DPS Blockset on the web portal of The MathWorks Corporation

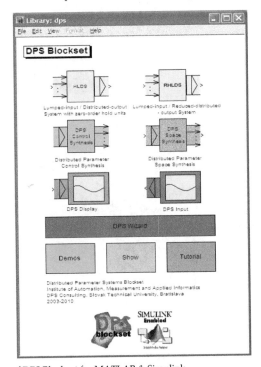

Figure 12. The library of DPS Blockset for MATLAB & Simulink

6. Dynamics of the temperature field in the casting mould

For control synthesis purpose, LDS/HLDS models of temperature fields in the casting mould have been created by means of evaluation of real-time experiments. The measurement of temperatures fields in the casting mould was performed by MATLAB & Simulink scheme *mould_exp_robust.mdl*, Fig. 10.

6.1. Experimental identification of transfer functions

In the casting mould lumped inputs $\{U_i\}_{i=1,5}$ are heating elements which act on sub-domains $\{\Omega_i\}_{i=1,5}$, (Zone 1 - 5). Distributed output is the temperature field of the casting mould.

Temperatures in the casting mould were measured by 11 thermocouples as a time-response to the step change of heating power, which was activated by the input voltage step from 0 to 2,5 V, for heating elements separately in each zone. Results of measurements for Zone #1, #3 and #5 are depicted in Fig. 13, where are time and x-y space dependences of temperatures and Fig. 14 presents temperature profiles in steady-states.

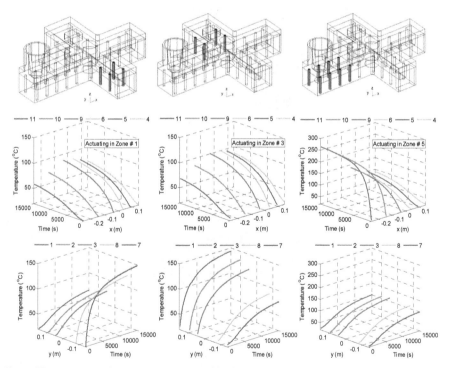

Figure 13. Time course of temperatures measured by thermocouples No. 1 - 11 after step change of the heating power separately in Zone #1, #3 and #5

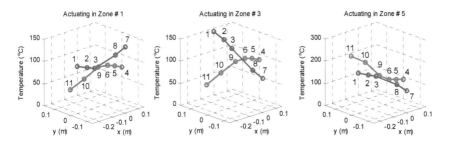

Figure 14. Temperature profiles in the steady-state measured by thermocouples No. 1 - 11 after step change of the heating power separately in Zone #1, #3 and #5

For identification of i-th transfer functions $\left\{S_i\left(\overline{x}_i, s\right)\right\}_{i=1,5}$, were determined points $\left\{\overline{x}_i = \left(x_i, y_i\right)\right\}_{i=1,5}$, located in each zone closely of lumped input quantities $\left\{U_i\right\}_{i=1,5}$, where temperatures attain maximal amplitudes by actuating the heating power in each zone separately. These points for actuating of the heating power in each zone are represented by positions of thermocouples given in Table 2.

Zone No.	1	2	3	4	5
Thermocouple No.	7	9	1	4	11

Table 2. Position of thermocouples for identification of measured temperatures

Identification of measured dynamical characteristics of temperatures was performed in the MATLAB software environment, where graphical user interface (GUI) *ident* from System Identification Toolbox was activated. There after importing the time domain input/output data, from the pop-up menu *Process models* transfer function in the form (24) for identification has been chosen, see Fig. 15., where are also results of identification from actuating in zone #1. Comparison of measured and identified model output in zone #1 is presented in Fig. 16. Identified parameters of transfer functions $\left\{S_i\left(\overline{x}_i, s\right)\right\}_{i=1,5}$ are in Table 3. Continuous transfer functions with structure (24) are converted by means of function *zpk* to zero-pole-gain format (ZPK). Then, for control synthesis purposes, they are transformed to discrete transfer functions $\left\{SH_i\left(\overline{x}_i, z\right)\right\}_{i=1,5}$ with sample time T= 10 s.

$$\frac{K\left(Tz\, s + 1\right)}{\left(Tp_1\, s + 1\right)\left(Tp_2\, s + 1\right)} \tag{24}$$

Zone No.	1	2	3	4	5
K	53.40	58.16	49.36	62.56	97.87
Tp_1	5881.68	4945.00	5489.58	5340.97	4578.71
Tp_2	939.66	1958.20	1398.20	973.90	1214.73
Tz	3616.81	3301.80	3201.10	3195.90	3410.50

Table 3. Identified parameters of transfer functions $\left\{S_i\left(\overline{x}_i, s\right)\right\}_{i=1,5}$ for actuating in each zone

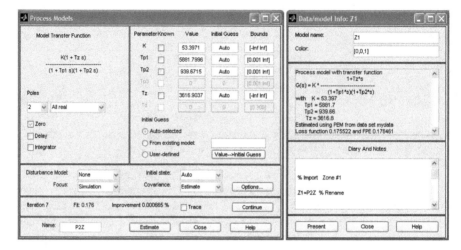

Figure 15. GUI Process Models menu and results of identification $S_i\left(\overline{x}_i,s\right)$ in Zone #1

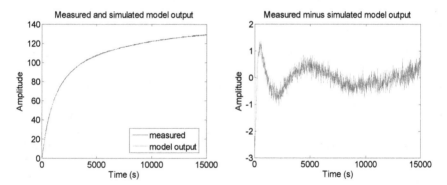

Figure 16. Comparison of measured and identified model output in Zone #1

6.2. Uncertainty analysis in the space and time domain

The proposed structure of the DPS control systems, Fig. 2, Fig. 5., are significant by decomposition of the control synthesis into the space and time subtasks. In the SS blocks, the approximation both of distributed controlled quantity $Y\left(\overline{x},k\right)$ and reference quantity $W\left(\overline{x},\infty\right)$, formulated as (8), (9) is solved. As the best approximation of controlled quantity $Y\left(\overline{x},k\right)$ vector of optimal approximation parameters $\left\{\breve{Y}_i\left(k\right)\right\}_i$ is obtained. Dynamics of these lumped quantities is different in compare with lumped quantities, $\left\{Y_i\left(\overline{x}_i,k\right)\right\}_i$, given by transfer functions $\left\{SH_i\left(\overline{x}_i,z\right)\right\}_i$ thus is created an uncertainty region in the time domain.

For uncertainty analysis, which takes place during the approximation problem solution, scheme from both, DPS Blockset blocks and Simulink blocks was arranged, see Fig. 17. There were obtained both, step responses $\{Y_i(\overline{x}_i,k)\}_i$ from each lumped input, $\{U_i\}_{i=1,5}$, to the corresponding output and approximated quantities corresponding to lumped output $\{\tilde{Y}_i(k)\}_i$ from the block SS. Characteristics with uncertainty regions for actuating in each zone are depicted in Fig. 18.

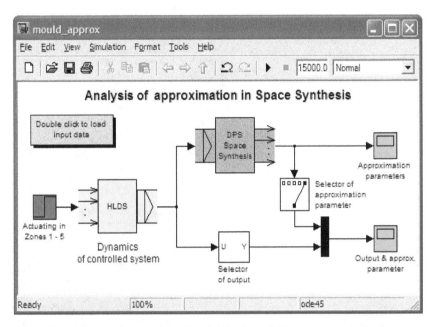

Figure 17. Block scheme in the MATLAB & Simulink for the analysis of approximation in the space synthesis and step responses in Zones 1 – 5

Identified transfer function $\{S_i(\overline{x}_i,s)\}_{i=1,5}$ in the structure (24) were also analysed in terms of uncertainties of their parameters. Analysis was performed in MATLAB environment, where functions from Robust Control Toolbox were used. Using functions *ureal* and *gridureal* were generated families of step responses with defined percentage variability of parameters in the nominal transfer functions $\{S_i(\overline{x}_i,s)\}_{i=1,5}$. Results for zone 1 are depicted in Fig. 19.

The gain variability K strongly affects to the value of the transient response in steady-state. The variability of the time constants Tp1 and Tp2 influences dynamics of transient response. Uncertainty region is caused by solution of the approximation task in the space synthesis. It would be appropriate to cover it by variability of nominal transfer function parameters. Cover of the uncertainty region in the time domain by variability of nominal parameters of the transfer function $S_i(\overline{x}_i,s)$ in Zone #1, #3 and #5 is presented in Fig. 20.

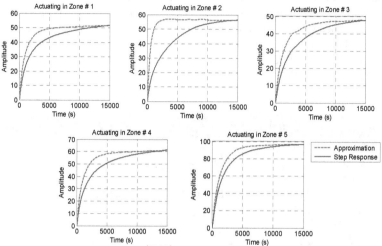

Figure 18. Approximation parameters $\left\{ \tilde{Y}_i(k) \right\}_i$ as a result of DPS space synthesis and step responses $\left\{ \mathcal{H}H_i\left(\overline{x}_i, k \right) \right\}_i$ for actuating in Zones 1 – 5

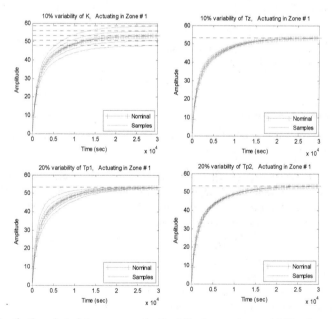

Figure 19. Family (Samples) of step responses for the defined percentage variability of parameters in the nominal transfer function $S_1\left(\overline{x}_i, s \right)$

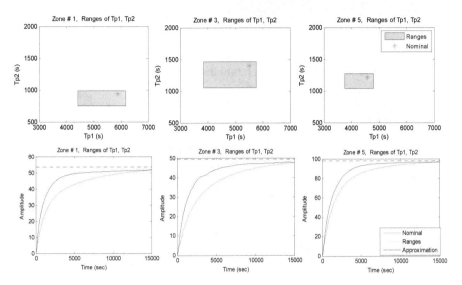

Figure 20. Cover of the uncertainty region in the time domain by variability of the nominal parameters Tp1 and Tp2 of the transfer function $S_i\left(\overline{x}_i, s\right)$ in Zone #1, #3 and #5

7. Robust control process

Robust control of temperature fields of the casting mould as distributed parameter system was performed with MATLAB & Simulink and DPS Blockset software support. Robust controllers designed by the IMC control strategy were first optimised through their tuning parameters $\left\{\alpha_i\right\}_i$ and then implemented to the control scheme for the real-time control of temperature fields of the casting mould in the benchmark casting plant.

7.1. Optimization of tuning parameters

In the MATLAB & Simulink environment, by means of the DPS Blockset, distributed parameter system of robust control, *mould_robust_DZPK.mdl* was arranged, see Fig. 21. It is DPS feedback control loop, where the *DPS Robust Control Synthesis* block includes both, time and spatial part of the control synthesis, see Fig. 22 a). In this case, the control system consists of five single parameter control loops, each for one zone of the mould, where discrete robust controllers based on IMC structure are used.

DPS Robust Control Synthesis contains two blocks named *DPS Space Synthesis*, where approximation of distributed controlled quantity $Y(\overline{x}, k)$ and reference quantity, $W(\overline{x}, \infty)$ is executed. The time control synthesis is performed by *Robust controllers based on IMC* block with five discrete controllers given by ZPK transfer function and filters with parameters $\left\{\alpha_i\right\}_{i=1,5}$, see Fig. 22 b).

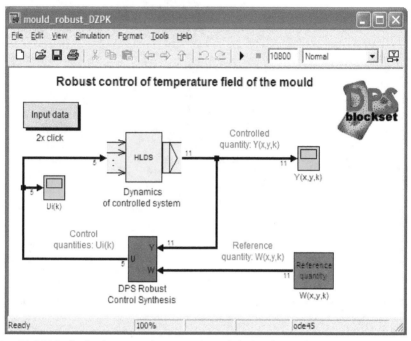

Figure 21. DPS feedback robust control system in the DPS Blockset for simulation of robust control of the temperature fields in the casting mould

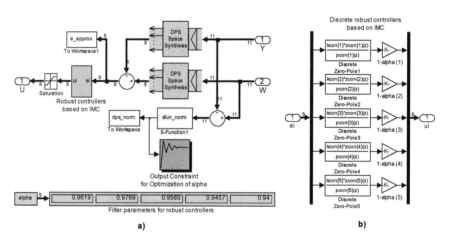

Figure 22. Structure of blocks in the scheme mould_robust_DZPK.mdl: a) DPS Robust Control Synthesis, b) Robust controllers based on IMC

The block *DPS Robust Control Synthesis* also contains block *Output Constraint for optimization of alpha*, where optimization of parameters $\{\alpha_i\}_{i=1,5}$ according to criterion function (25) is performed.

$$J = \min_{\alpha_i} \sum_{k=0}^{N} \left\| W(\overline{x},k) - Y(\overline{x},k) \right\| \tag{25}$$

Parameters of filters were optimized in the presence of constraints of the criterion function in order to assure nearly aperiodic course of the quadratic norm of the distributed control error with respect to the robust stability and robust performance conditions, see Fig. 23 and optimization progress presents Fig. 24. Control process was simulated for the reference quantities - temperatures on given 11 positions, where thermocouples are embedded. Robust stability was tested for ranges around the nominal parameters Tp1 and Tp2, of the transfer function $S_i(\overline{x}_i,s)$, see Fig. 20, with MATLAB function *robuststab*, from the Robust Control Toolbox, e.g. in the following is the printout of the robust stability testing for the control loop in zone 1.

Robust stability testing in Zone #1
StabilityMargin = UpperBound: 1.3333
                  LowerBound: 1.3296
DestabilizingFrequency: 8.0745e-004
DestbUnc =   Tp1: 1.7210
                Tp2: 438.5898
STABreport =   Uncertain System is robustly stable to modeled uncertainty.
-       It can tolerate up to 133% of the modeled uncertainty.

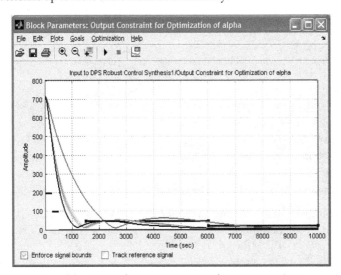

Figure 23. Minimization of the criterion function in presence of output constraints

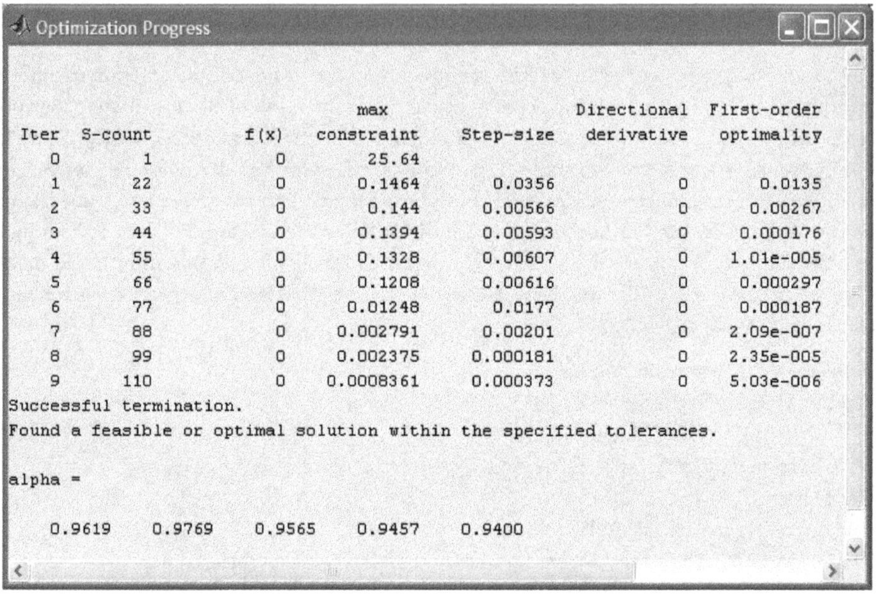

```
Optimization Progress                                                    _ □ X

                          max                    Directional  First-order
Iter   S-count    f(x)    constraint  Step-size   derivative   optimality
  0       1         0       25.64
  1      22         0       0.1464     0.0356         0           0.0135
  2      33         0       0.144      0.00566        0           0.00267
  3      44         0       0.1394     0.00593        0           0.000176
  4      55         0       0.1328     0.00607        0           1.01e-005
  5      66         0       0.1208     0.00616        0           0.000297
  6      77         0       0.01248    0.0177         0           0.000187
  7      88         0       0.002791   0.00201        0           2.09e-007
  8      99         0       0.002375   0.000181       0           2.35e-005
  9     110         0       0.0008361  0.000373       0           5.03e-006
Successful termination.
Found a feasible or optimal solution within the specified tolerances.

alpha =

    0.9619    0.9769    0.9565    0.9457    0.9400
```

Figure 24. Optimization progress for tuning parameters $\{\alpha_i\}_{i=1,5}$ of robust controllers

- A destabilizing combination of 133% of the modeled uncertainty exists, causing an instability at 0.000807 rad/s.
- Sensitivity with respect to uncertain element ...
  'Tp1' is 100%. Increasing 'Tp1' by 25% leads to a 25% decrease in the margin.
  'Tp2' is 54%. Increasing 'Tp2' by 25% leads to a 14% decrease in the margin.

7.2. Real-time robust control of preheating in the casting mould

Real-time robust control of the temperature fields of the casting mould in the benchmark casting plant was performed by means of Simulink designed block scheme *mould_exp_robust.mdl*. The structure of the block *DPS Robust IMC Control Synthesis* is depicted in Fig. 25, where are blocks *Space Synthesis Y* and *Space Synthesis W*, and block *Robust controllers based on IMC* with the same structure as in Fig. 22 b).

DPS Time and Space Control Synthesis

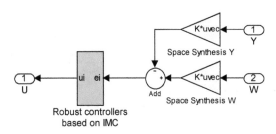

Figure 25. Structure of the block DPS Robust IMC Control Synthesis in the scheme mould_exp_robust.mdl for real-time control

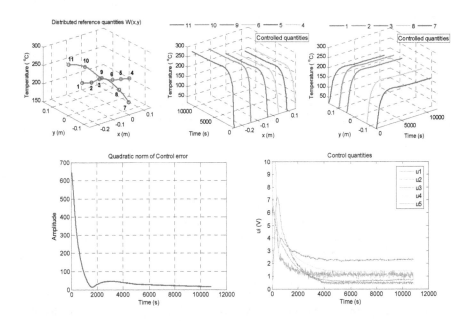

Figure 26. Robust control of the temperature field of the casting mould: distributed reference quantities, controlled quantities at given position of the mould, quadratic norm of distributed control error $\left\| E\left(\overline{x},k\right)\right\|$ and control quantities $\left\{U_i\left(k\right)\right\}_{i=1,5}$ in Zones 1-5

Control process was performed for the reference variable - temperature profile given in 11 positions, where thermocouples are embedded. Results of the real-time robust control process are on Fig. 26. The quality of control both in the time and space domain is given by the quadratic norm of the distributed control error.

8. Conclusion

The aim of this chapter was to present the engineering approach for the robust control of DPS, which opens a wide space for novel applications of the toolboxes and blocksets of the MATLAB & Simulink software environment. This approach is based on the general decomposition of controlled DPS dynamics, represented by transient and impulse characteristics, into time and space components. Starting out from this dynamics decomposition a methodical framework was presented for the decomposition of control synthesis into the space and time subtasks. In the space domain an approximation problems were solved, while in the time domain the control synthesis was performed by lumped parameter SISO control loops, where various well-known methods for design of controller is possible to utilize. The advantage of this approach is the relatively simple LDS model of DPS, which is directly suitable for control purposes and can be easily identified from input-output data by means of classical techniques.

Currently, it is interesting to formulate and solve tasks of control in various engineering branches, including the casting technology, by means of methods and tools of distributed parameter systems. Methodical approach presented in this chapter demonstrates simple possibilities, how to exploit the distributed dynamical characteristics on complex definition domains, obtained by evaluation of measured data for robust IMC control synthesis of DPS with respect to uncertainty of models and the real-time control according to technological requirements.

Author details

Cyril Belavý, Gabriel Hulkó and Karol Ondrejkovič
Institute of Automation, Measurement and Applied Informatics,
Faculty of Mechanical Engineering, Center for Control of Distributed Parameter Systems,
Slovak University of Technology in Bratislava, Slovak Republic

Acknowledgement

This work was supported by the Slovak Scientific Grant Agency VEGA under the contract No. 1/0138/11 and the Slovak Research and Development Agency under contracts No. APVV-0131-10 and No. APVV-0090-10 and also by the European Union with the co-financing of the European Social Fund, grant TAMOP-4.2.1.B-11/2/KMR-2011-0001.

9. References

Belavý, C. et al. (2009). Uncertainty Analysis and Robust Control of Temperature Fields of Casting Mould as Distributed Parameter Systems, *INCOM '09: Preprints of the 13th IFAC symposium on Information control problems in manufacturing*, Moscow, June 3-5, 2009

Butkovskij, A. G. (1965). *Optimal Control of Distributed Parameter Systems*, Nauka, Moscow

Curtain, R. & Morris K. (2009). Transfer Functions of Distributed Parameter Systems: A tutorial. *Automatica*, Vol. 45, (2009), pp. 1101-1116

Hulkó, G. et al. (1981). On Adaptive Control of Distributed Parameter Systems, *Proceedings of 8-th World Congress of IFAC*, Kyoto, 1981

Hulkó, G. et al. (1987). Control of Distributed Parameter Systems by means of Multi-Input and Multi-Distributed-Output Systems, *Proceedings of 10-th World Congress of IFAC*, Munich, 1987

Hulkó, G. et al. (1998). *Modeling, Control and Design of Distributed Parameter Systems with Demonstrations in MATLAB*, Publishing House STU, ISBN 80-227-1083-0, Bratislava

Hulkó, G. et al (2003-2007). Distributed Parameter Systems. Web portal [Online]. Available: www.dpscontrol.sk

Hulkó, G. et al. (2009a). Engineering Methods and Software Support for Modelling and Design of Discrete-time Control of Distributed Parameter Systems. *European Journal of Control*, Vol. 15, No. Iss. 3-4, *Fundamental Issues in Control*, (May-August 2009), pp. 407-417, ISSN 0947-3580

Hulkó, G. et al. (2009b). Engineering Methods and Software Support for Control of Distributed Parameter Systems, *ASC 2009: Proceedings of the 7th Asian Control Conference*, Honk Kong, China, August 27-29, 2009

Hulkó, G. et al. (2003-2010). *Distributed Parameter Systems Blockset for MATLAB & Simulink*, www.mathworks.com/products/connections/ - Third-Party Product of The MathWorks, Bratislava-Natick, Available from: www.dpscontrol.sk

Morari, M. & Zafirou, E. (1989). *Robust Process Control*, Prentice Hall, Englewood Cliffs

Lasiecka, I. & Triggiani, R. (2000). *Control Theory for Partial Differential Equations: Continuous and Approximation Theories I. Abstract Parabolic Systems*, Cambridge University Press, ISBN 0-521-43408-4, Cambridge, UK

Li, H. X. & Qi, Ch. (2010). Modeling of Distributed Parameter Systems for Application – A Synthesized Review from Time-Space Separation. *Journal of Process Control*, No 20, (2010), pp. 891-901

Lions, J. L. (1971). *Optimal Control of Systems Governed by Partial Differential Equations*, Springer - Verlag, Berlin - Heidelberg - New York

Wang, P. K. C. (1964). *Control of Distributed Parameter Systems* (Advances in Control Systems: Theory and Applications, 1.), Academic Press, New York

Chapter 4

Optimal Solution to Matrix Riccati Equation – For Kalman Filter Implementation

Bhar K. Aliyu, Charles A. Osheku, Lanre M.A. Adetoro and Aliyu A. Funmilayo

Additional information is available at the end of the chapter

1. Introduction

Matrix Riccati Equations arise frequently in applied mathematics, science, and engineering problems. These nonlinear matrix equations are particularly significant in optimal control, filtering, and estimation problems. Essentially, solving a Riccati equation is a central issue in optimal control theory. The needs for such equations are common in the analysis and synthesis of Linear Quadratic Gaussian (LQC) control problems. In one form or the other, Riccati Equations play significant roles in optimal control of multivariable and large-scale systems, scattering theory, estimation, and detection processes. In addition, closed forms solution of Riccti Equations are intractable for two reasons namely; one, they are nonlinear and two, are in matrix forms. In the past, a number of unconventional numerical methods were employed for the solutions of time-invariant Riccati Differential Equations (RDEs). Despite their peculiar structure, no unconventional methods suitable for time-varying RDEs have been constructed, except for carefully re-designed conventional linear multistep and Runge-Kutta(RK) methods.

Implicit conventional methods that are preferred to explicit ones for stiff systems are premised on the solutions of nonlinear systems of equations with higher dimensions than the original problems via Runge-Kutta methods. Such procedural techniques do not only pose implementation difficulties but are also very expensive because they require solving robust non-linear matrix equations.

In this Chapter, we shall focus our attention on the numerical solution of Riccati Differential Equations (RDEs) for computer-aided control systems design using the numerical algorithm with an adaptive step of *Dormand-Prince*. It is a key step in many computational methods for model reduction, filtering, and controller design for linear systems. In the meantime, we shall limit our investigation to the optimality in the numeric solution to Riccati equation as it affects the design of Kalman-Bucy filter state estimator, for an LQG control of an

Expendable Launch Vehicle (ELV) in pitch plane during atmospheric ascent. Furthermore, the approach in the paper by Aliyu Kisabo Bhar et al will be fully employed from a comparative standpoint of the solution to a differential Riccati equation and an Algebraic Riccati for Kalman-Bucy filter implementation.

2. Kalman filter

Theoretically the Kalman Filter is an estimator for the linear-quadratic problem, it is an interesting technique for estimating the instantaneous 'state' of a linear dynamic system perturbed by white -noise measurements that is linearly related to the corrupted white noise state. The resulting estimator is statistically optimal with respect to any quadratic function of the estimation error.

In estimation theory, Kalman introduced stochastic notions that applied to non-stationary time-varying systems, via a recursive solution. C.F. Gauss (1777-1855) first used the Kalman filter, for the least-squares approach in planetary orbit problems. The Kalman filter is the natural extension of the Wiener filter to non-stationary stochastic systems. In contrast, the theory of Kalman has provided optimal solutions for control systems with guaranteed performance. These control analyses were computed by solving formal matrix design equations that generally had unique solutions. By a way of reference, the U.S. space program blossomed with a Kalman filter providing navigational data for the first lunar landing.

Practically, it is one of the celebrated discoveries in the history of statistical estimation theory in the twentieth century. It has enable humankind to do many things, one obvious advantage, is its indispensability as silicon integration in the makeup of electronic systems. It's most dependable application is in the control of complex dynamic systems such as continuous manufacturing processes, aircraft, ships, or spacecraft. To control a dynamic system, you must first know what it is doing. For these applications, it is not always possible or desirable to measure every variable that you want to control, and Kalman filter provides a means of inferring the missing information from indirect (and noisy) measurements. Kalman Filter is also very useful for predicting the likely future course of dynamic systems that people are not likely to control, such as the flow of rivers during flood, the trajectory of celestial bodies, or the prices of traded commodities. Kalman Filter is 'ideally noted for digital computer implementation', arising from a finite representation of the estimated problem-by a finite number of variables. Usually, these variables are assumed to be real numbers-with infinite precision. Some of the problems encountered in its uses, arose from its distinction between 'finite' and 'manageable' problem sizes. These are significant issues on the practical side of Kalman filtering that must be considered in conjunction with the theory. It is also a complete statistical characterization of an estimated problem than an estimator, because it propagates the entire probability distribution of the variables in its task to be estimated. This is a complete characterization of the current state of knowledge of the dynamic system, including influence of all past measurements. These probability distributions are also useful for statistical analysis and predictive design of sensor systems.

The applications of Kalman filtering encompass many fields, but its use as a tool, is almost exclusively for two purposes: estimation and performance analysis of estimators. Figure 1 depicts the essential subject for the foundation for Kalman filtering theory.

Despite the indication of Kalman filtering process in the apex of the pyramid, it is an integral part in the foundation of another discipline *modern control theory*, and a proper subset of statistical decision theory.

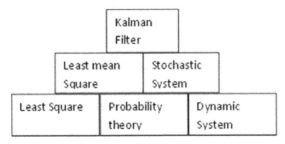

Figure 1. Foundation concept in Kalman filtering.

Kalman filter analyses a dynamic systems' behavior with external and measurement noise. In general, the output y is affected by noise measurement. In addition, the process dynamics are also affected by disturbances, such as atmospheric turbulence. Following this, we shall now present the model for the LQG control for the ELV via equation (1). The essential assumptions are viz; the dynamic system is linear, the performance cost function is quadratic, and the random processes are Gaussian.

By defining, a continuous –time process and measurement model is as follows;

$$\dot{x} = Ax + Bu + Gw,$$
$$y = Cx + v. \tag{1}$$

Where, w and v are zero-mean Gaussian noise processes (uncorrelated from each other). The following process and measurement covariance matrices hold namely:

$$\left. \begin{array}{l} Ev(t)v^T(s) = R_N\delta(t-s) \\ Ev(t)w^T(s) = 0 \\ Ew(t)w^T(s) = Q_N\delta(t-s) \end{array} \right\} \; t,s \in \Re \tag{2}$$

From the foregoing, a Kalman filter equation admits the form;

$$\dot{\hat{x}} = A\hat{x} + Bu + L(y - \hat{y}), \tag{3}$$

where L is the Kalman gain represented as

$$L = PC^T R_N^{-1}. \tag{4}$$

The covariance matrix P, in equation (4) is the solution to a Riccati Differential Equation (RDE) or an Algebraic Riccati Equation (ARE).

3. Riccati equation

In mathematics, a Riccati equation is any ordinary differential equation that is quadratic in the unknown function. In other words, it is an equation of the form

$$y'(x) = q_0(x) + q_1(x)y(x) + q_2(x)y^2(x),$$
(5)

where, $q_0(x) \neq 0$ and $q_2(x) \neq 0$ ($q_0(x)=0$ is Bernoulli equation and $q_2(x)=0$ is first order linear ordinary equation). It is named after Count Jacopo Francesco Riccati (1676-1754).

More generally, "Riccati equations" refer to matrix equations with analogous quadratic terms both in continuous-time and in discrete-time Linear-Quadratic-Gaussian Control. The steady-state (non-dynamic) versions of these equations are classified as algebraic Riccati equations.

3.1. Riccati differential equation (RDE)

The Riccati differential equation was first studied in the eighteen century as a nonlinear scalar differential equation, and a method was derived for transforming it to a linear matrix form. This same method works when the dependent variable of the original Riccati differential equation is a matrix.

The statistical performance of the Kalman filter estimator can be predicted a priori by solving the Riccati equations for computing the optimal feedback gain of the estimator. Also, the behaviors of their solutions can be shown analytically for the most trivial cases. These equations also provide a means for verifying the proper performance of the actual estimator when it is running.

For the LQG problem, the associated Riccati Differential Equation which provides the covariance $P(t)$ needed for the solution of Kalman gain is of the form,

$$\dot{P}(t) = A_\phi(t)P(t) + P(t)A_\phi^T(t) + G(t)Q_N(t)G(t) - P(t)C^T(t)R_N^{-1}(t)C(t)P(t)$$
(6)

where A_τ is the state transitional matrix defined as

$$\frac{d}{dt}x(t) = A(t)x(t) + G(t)w(t).$$
(7)

The Riccati Differential Equation in (6) can be solved by using a technique, called the Matrix Fraction Decomposition. A matrix product of the sort AB^{-1} is called a *matrix fraction*, and a representation of a matrix M in the form

$$M = AB^{-1}$$
(8)

A fractional decomposition of the covariance matrix results in a linear differential equation for the numerator and the denominator matrices. The numerator and denominator matrices as functions of time, such that the product $A(t)B^{-1}(t)$ satisfies the matrix Riccati equation and its boundary conditions. By taking the derivative of the matrix fraction $A(t)B^{-1}(t)$ with respect to t and using the fact that

$$\frac{d}{dt}B^{-1}(t) = -B^{-1}(t)\dot{B}(t)B^{-1}(t),$$ (9)

Now let us represent the covariance matrix $P(t)$ by

$$P(t) = A(t)B^{-1}(t),$$ (10)

and on applying equations (9-10) yields

$$\frac{dP(t)}{dt} = \dot{A}(t)B^{-1}(t) - A(t)B^{-1}(t)\dot{B}(t)B^{-1}(t)$$ (11)

From the Riccati equation in (6) substitution for $P(t)$ with $A(t)B^{-1}(t)$ in the right hand side of the equation, leads to the following namely

$$\frac{dP(t)}{dt} = A_\phi(t)A(t)B^{-1}(t) + A(t)B^{-1}(t)A_\phi^T(t) + G(t)Q_N(t)G^T(t)$$

$$-A(t)B^{-1}(t)C^T(t)R_N^{-1}(t)C(t)A(t)B^{-1}(t).$$ (12)

Equating (11) and (12) and multiplying through with $B(t)$ yields

$$\dot{A}(t) - A(t)B^{-1}(t)\dot{B}(t) = \left\{ A_\phi(t)A(t) + G(t)Q_N(t)G^T(t)B(t) \right\}$$

$$-A(t)B^{-1}(t)\left\{ C^T(t)R_N^{-1}(t)C(t)A(t) - A_\phi^T(t)B(t) \right\}$$ (13)

Therefore, if we find $A(t)$ and $B(t)$ that satisfy:

$$\dot{A}(t) = A_\phi(t) + G(t)Q_N(t)G^T(t)B(t),$$ (14)

$$\dot{B}(t) = C^T(t)R_N^{-1}(t)C(t)A(t) - A_\phi^T(t)B(t),$$ (15)

then $P(t)=A(t)B^{-1}(t)$ satisfies the Riccati differential equation. Note that equations (14) and (15) are the linear differential equations with respect to matrices $A(t)$ and $B(t)$. The foregoing can be arranged as follows viz;

$$\begin{pmatrix} \dot{A}(t) \\ \dot{B}(t) \end{pmatrix} = \begin{bmatrix} A_\phi(t) & G(t)Q_N(t)G^T(t) \\ C^T(t)R_N^{-1}(t)C(t) & -A_\phi(t) \end{bmatrix} \begin{pmatrix} A(t) \\ B(t) \end{pmatrix}$$ (16)

Such a representation is a Hamiltonian Matrix known as matrix Riccati differential equation.

$$\Psi(t) = \begin{bmatrix} A_\phi(t) & G(t)Q_N(t)G^T(t) \\ C^T(t)R_N^{-1}(t)C(t) & -A_\phi(t) \end{bmatrix} \tag{17}$$

The initial values of $A(t)$ and $B(t)$ must be constrained by the initial value of $P(t)$. This is easily satisfied by taking $P_0=I$, an identity matrix.

In the time-invariant case, the Hamiltonian matrix Ψ is also time-invariant. As a consequence, the solution for the numerator $A(t)$ and denominator $B(t)$ of the matrix fraction can be represented in matrix form as the product

$$\begin{bmatrix} A(t) \\ B(t) \end{bmatrix} = e^{\Psi t} \begin{bmatrix} P(0) \\ I \end{bmatrix}, \tag{18}$$

where $e^{\Psi t}$ is a $2n \times 2n$ matrix.

Convergence Properties of a Scalar Time-Invariant Case. In this case, the numerator $A(t)$ and the denominator $B(t)$ of the 'matrix fraction' $A(t)B^{-1}(t)$ will be scalars, but Ψ will be a $2n \times 2n$ matrix. Considering a case: $A(t) \rightarrow a(t)$, and $B(t) \rightarrow b(t)$ and the process and measurement equations becomes

$$\begin{aligned} A_\phi(t) &= A_\phi, \\ G(t) &= G, \\ Q(t) &= Q, \\ R(t) &= R, \\ C(t) &= C. \end{aligned} \tag{19}$$

The scalar time-invariant Riccati differential matrix equation and its linearized equivalent is

$$\dot{P}(t) = A_\phi P(t) + P(t)A_\phi - P(t)CR_N^{-1}CP(t) + GQG^T. \tag{20}$$

Hence, equation (16) reduces to

$$\begin{pmatrix} \dot{a} \\ \dot{b} \end{pmatrix} = \begin{bmatrix} A_\phi & GQG^T \\ CR^{-1}C & -A_\phi \end{bmatrix} \begin{pmatrix} a \\ b \end{pmatrix} \tag{21}$$

with the following initial conditions namely; $a(0)=P_0$ and $b(0)=1$. In the meantime, the eigenvalues of the Hamilton Matrix are;

$$\lambda_1, \lambda_2 = \pm \sqrt{A_\phi^2 + \frac{Q}{R}G^2C^2}. \tag{22}$$

Using λ_1 and λ_2, where, $q=G^2Q$, we can write the following:

$$a(t) = \frac{1}{2\lambda} \{ [P_0(\lambda - A_\phi) + q]e^{\lambda t} + [P_0(\lambda - A_\phi) + q]e^{-\lambda t} \} \tag{23}$$

$$b(t) = \frac{1}{2\lambda q} \{ (\lambda - A_\phi)[P_0(\lambda + A_\phi) + q]e^{\lambda t} - (\lambda + A_\phi)[P_0(\lambda - A_\phi) - q]e^{-\lambda t} \}. \tag{24}$$

Consequently, the covariance follows as;

$$P(t) = \frac{a(t)}{b(t)} = q \frac{[P_0(\lambda + A_\phi) + q] + [P_0(\lambda - A_\phi) - q]e^{-2\lambda t}}{(\lambda - A_\phi)[P_0(\lambda + A_\phi) + q] - (\lambda + A_\phi)[P_0(\lambda - A_\phi) - q]e^{-2\lambda t}}. \tag{25}$$

If the system is *observable*, i.e. (A,C): Observable Pair, then the RDE has a positive-definite, symmetric solution for an arbitrary positive-definite initial value of matrix $P_0 > 0$;

$$P(t) > 0 \quad p.d., \quad P(t) = P^T(t) \in R^{n \times n}, \quad \forall t > 0. \tag{26}$$

The need to solve Riccati equation is perhaps the greatest single cause of anxiety and agony on the part of people faced with implementing Kalman filter. Because there is no general formula for solving higher order polynomials equations (i.e., beyond quartic), finding closed-form solutions to algebraic Riccati equations by purely algebraic means is very rigorous. Thus, it is necessary to employ numerical solution methods. Numbers do not always provide us as much insight into the characteristics of the solution as formulas do, but readily amenable for most problems of practical significance.

3.2. Numerical example – An expendable launch vehicle (ELV) autopilot

This problem is taken from Aliyu et al, and it is significant for modeling and simulating an ELV autopilot problem in Matlab/Simulink®. It solves the symmetrical RDE:

$$\dot{P}(t) - AP(t) + P(t)A - P(t)CR_N^{-1}CP(t) + GQ_NG^T, \quad P_0 = I. \tag{27}$$

Where,

$$A = \begin{bmatrix} 0 & 1 & 0 \\ 14.7805 & 0 & 0.01958 \\ -100.858 & 0 & -0.1256 \end{bmatrix}, \quad Q_N = \begin{bmatrix} 1.1 \times 10^{-3} & 0 & 0 \\ 0 & 1.1 \times 10^{-3} & 0 \\ 0 & 0 & 1.1 \times 10^{-3} \end{bmatrix},$$

$$R_N = \begin{bmatrix} 4.0 \times 10^{-6} & 0 & 0 \\ 0 & 4.0 \times 10^{-6} & 0 \\ 0 & 0 & 4.0 \times 10^{-6} \end{bmatrix}, \quad C = \begin{bmatrix} 1 & 0 & 0 \\ 0 & 1 & 0 \\ 0 & 0 & 0 \end{bmatrix},$$

and

$$G = \begin{bmatrix} 0 & 14.7805 & -94.8557 \end{bmatrix}^T.$$

3.3. Numerical Methods and Problem Solving Environment (PSE), for Ordinary Differential Equations

In the last decade, two distinct directions have emerged in the way Ordinary Differential Equation (ODE) solvers software is utilized. These include Large Scale Scientific Computation and PSE. Most practicing engineers and scientists, as well as engineering and science students use numerical software for problem solving, while only a few very specific research applications require large scale computing.

MATLAB® provides several powerful approaches to integrate sets of initial value, Ordinary Differential Equations. We have carried out an extensive study of the requirements. For the simulation of the autopilot problem, we have used the mathematical development environment Matlab/Simulink®. Matlab/Simulink® was chosen, as it is widely used in the field of numerical mathematics and supports solving initial value ordinary differential equations like the type we have in (27) with easy.

From the humble beginnings of Euler's method, numerical solvers started relatively simple and have evolved into the more complex higher order Taylor methods and into the efficient Runge-Kutta methods. And the search for more efficient and accurate methods has led to the more complicated variable step solvers.

3.3.1. One step solver

For solving an initial value problem

$$y' = f(x,y), \quad y(x_0) = y_0, \tag{28}$$

a numerical method is needed. One step solvers are defined by a function $\Phi(x,y,h;f)$ which gives approximate values $y_i := y(x_i)$ for the exact solution $y(x)$:

$$y_{i+1} := y_i + h\Phi(x_i, y_i, h; f), \tag{29}$$

$$x_{i+1} := x_i + h, \tag{30}$$

where, h denotes the step size. In the following let x and y be arbitrary but fixed, and $z(t)$ is the exact solution of the initial value problem

$$z'(t) = f(t,z(t)), \quad z(x) = y \tag{31}$$

with the initial values x and y. Then the function

$$\Delta(x,y,h,f) := \begin{cases} \dfrac{z(x+h)-y}{h} & h \neq 0 \\ f(x,y) & h = 0 \end{cases} \tag{32}$$

describes the differential quotient of the exact solution $z(t)$ with step size h, whereas $\Phi(x,y,h;f)$ is the differential quotient of the approximated solution with step size h. The difference $\tau = \Delta - \Phi$ is the measure of quality of the approximation method and is denoted as local discretization error.

In the following, $F_N(a,b)$ is defined as the set of all functions f, for which exist all partial derivations of order N on the area

$$S = \left\{ x,y \mid a \leq x \leq b, y \in \Re^n \right\} \quad a,b \text{ finite,} \tag{33}$$

where they are continuous and limited.

One step solvers must fulfill

$$\lim_{h \to 0} \tau(x,y,h;f) = 0. \tag{34}$$

This is equivalent to

$$\lim_{h \to 0} \Phi(x,y,h;f) = f(x,y). \tag{35}$$

If this condition holds for all $x \in [a,b]$, $y \in F_1(a,b)$ then Φ and the corresponding one step method are called *consistent*. Thus, the one step method is of *order p*, if

$$\tau(x,y,h;f) = 0(h^p), \tag{36}$$

holds for all x ∈ [a,b], y ∈ R, f ∈ F_P(a,b). The global discretization error

$$e_n(X) := y(X) - y_n \quad X = x_n \text{ fix, } n \text{ variable} \tag{37}$$

is the difference between exact solution and the approximated solution. The one step method is denoted as *convergent*, if:

$$\lim_{n \to \infty} \left\| e_n(X) \right\| = 0. \tag{38}$$

Theorem: Methods of order $p > 0$ are convergent and it holds

$$e_n(X) = 0(h^p). \tag{39}$$

This means that the order of the global discretization error is equal to the order of the local discretization error. The crucial problem concerning one-step methods is the choice of the step size h. If the step size is too small, the computational effort of the method is unnecessary high, but if the step size is too large, the global discretization error increases. For initial values x_0, y_0 a step size as large as possible would be chosen, so that the global discretization error is below a boundary ε after each step. Therefore, a step size control is necessary.

3.3.2. Explicit Euler

The most elementary method of solving initial value problems is the explicit Euler. The value of y_{i+1} can be calculated the following way:

$$y_{i+1} = y_i + h \cdot f(x_i, y_i) \tag{40}$$

The explicit Euler calculates the new value y_{i+1} by following the tangent at the old value for a distance of h. The slope of the tangent is given by the value of $f(x_i, y_i)$. The explicit Euler uses no step size control; the step size h is fixed. Therefore, it is only useful in special cases, where the function to integrate is pretty flat. Nevertheless, it is very easy to implement and calculates very fast, so it can be a good choice.

3.3.3. Runge-Kutta method

The Runge-Kutta methods are a special kind of one-step solvers, which evaluate the right side in each step several times. The intermediate results are combined linearly. The general discretization schema for one-step of a Runge-Kutta method is

$$y_1 = y_0 + h(b_1 K_1 + b_2 K_2 + \cdots + b_a K_a), \tag{41}$$

with corrections

$$K_i = f(x_0 + c_i h, y_0 + h \sum_{j=1}^{i-1} a_{ij} K_j), \quad i = 1, \cdots s. \tag{42}$$

The coefficients are summarized in a tableau, the so-called Butcher-tableau, see figure 2.

$$
\begin{array}{c|ccccc}
c_1 & 0 \\
c_2 & a_{21} & \ddots & 0 \\
\vdots & \vdots & \ddots & \ddots \\
c_s & a_{s1} & \cdots & a_{ss-1} & 0 \\
\hline
 & b_1 & b_2 & \cdots & b_s
\end{array}
$$

Figure 2. Butcher-tableau.

3.4. Step size control

The Runge-Kutta methods use an equidistant grid, but this is for most applications inefficient. A better solution is to use an adaptive step size control. The grid has to be chosen so that

- a given accuracy of the numerical solution is reached
- the needed computational effort is minimized.

As the characteristics of the solution are a priori unknown, a good grid structure cannot be chosen before the numerical integration. Instead, the grid points have to be adapted during the computation of the solution. Trying to apply this to Runge-Kutta methods lead to the following technique:

To create a method of order p (for y_{i+1}), it is combined with a method of order $P+1$(for $\hat{y}_{k+1}$).

This method for y_{i+1} is called the embedded method. The idea of embedding was developed by Fehlberg and methods using this technique therefore are called *Runge-Kutta-Fehlberg* methods. This leads to a modified Butcher-tableau (see figure 3). The new step size is calculated with

$$h_{new} = h \sqrt[p+1]{\frac{\varepsilon}{\|y - \hat{y}\|}}, \tag{43}$$

where ε denotes the tolerance.

$$\begin{array}{c|c}
c & A \\
\hline
 & b^T \\
\hline
 & \hat{b}^T
\end{array}
\qquad
\begin{array}{l}
\\
\longrightarrow \quad y_1 = y_0 + h \sum_{i=1}^{s} b_i K_i \\
\longrightarrow \quad \hat{y}_1 = y_0 + h \sum_{i=1}^{\hat{s}} \hat{b}_i K_i
\end{array}$$

Figure 3. Modified Butcher-tableau for embedded Runge-Kutta-methods.

3.4.1. Error control and variable step size

The main concern with numerical solvers is the error made when they approximate a solution. The second concern is the number of computations that must be performed. Both of these can be addressed by creating solvers that use a variable step size in order to keep the error within a specified tolerance. By using the largest step size allowable while keeping the error within a tolerance, the error made is reduced.

The way to keep the error under control is to determine the error made at each step. A common way to do this is to use two solvers of orders p and $p+1$, as earlier explained. Any approximations made of order p will have an error no larger than the value of the $p + 1$ term. This leads us to take the difference of the two solvers to find the value of the error term.

Since the downside of using two distinct methods is a dramatic increase in computations, another method is typically used. An example of this method is the Rung-Kutta-Fehlberg Algorithm. The Rung-Kutta-Fehlberg combines Rung-Kutta methods of order four and order five into one algorithm. Doing this reduces the number of computations made while returning the same result.

3.4.2. Dormand-Prince method

The *Dormand-Prince* method is a member of the *Runge-Kutta-Fehlberg* class with order 4(5).It means that the method has order 5 and the embedded method has order 4. This is described by the following equations:

$$y(x_0 + h) = y_0 + h \sum_{k=0}^{4} b_k f_k(x_0, y_0; h)$$

$$\hat{y}(x_0 + h) = y_0 + h \sum_{k=0}^{5} \hat{b}_k f_k(x_0, y_0; h) \tag{44}$$

$$f_k = f(x_0 + c_k h, y_0 + h \sum_{t=0}^{k-1} a_{ki} f_i)$$

The coefficients from Dormand and Prince can be seen in figure 4.

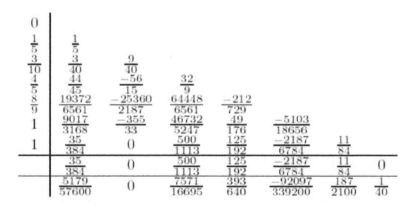

Figure 4. Butcher-tableau for Dormand-Prince-method.

For solving an initial value problem like the one we have in (27) Matlab was chosen, as it is widely used in the field of numerical mathematics and supports solving ordinary differential equations. Moreover, it is possible to visualize the simulation results of the autopilot. In our program we used the *ode45*, a standard solver included in Matlab/Simulink. The solver *ode45* implements the method of *Dormand-Prince*, which is a member of the class of *Runge-Kutta-Fehlberg* methods. More specifically, the *Dormand–Prince* method uses six function evaluations to calculate fourth- and fifth-order accurate solutions. The difference between these solutions is then taken to be the error of the (fourth-order) solution. This error estimate is very convenient for adaptive step size integration algorithms. This adaptive step-size control algorithm monitors the estimate of the integration error, and reduces or increases the step size of the integration in order to keep the error below a specified threshold. The accuracy requested is that both the relative and absolute (maximal) errors be less than the truncation error tolerance. In MATLAB, both relative (*RelTol*) and absolute (*AbsTol*) tolerances can be specified. The default values (that were used in solving the problem) are *RelTol*= 0.001 and *AbsTol*= 10^{-6} .We intend to integrate the DRE from *t*=0 up to *t*=1. The Simulink model for the DRE is as shown in Figure 5.

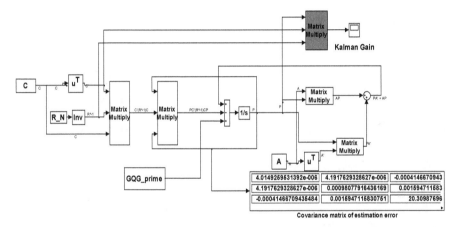

Figure 5. Simulink model for matrix Differential Riccati Equation.

After successfully simulating the above model, it was used to design an Linear Quadratic Gaussian (LQG) autopilot with the following Linear Quadratic Regulator (LQR) Characteristics;

$$Q = \begin{bmatrix} 2.5 & 0 & 0 \\ 0 & 4 & 0 \\ 0 & 0 & 173.6 \end{bmatrix}, \text{ and } R = 0.1. \tag{45}$$

For this autopilot, the Kalman-Bucy filter model was implemented as shown in Fig.6. It should be noted that if for any reason the initial condition P_0 in (27) is taking as a matrix with entries less than 1, then initial covariance matrix could be used as a tuning parameter to meet a specific *time response* characteristics as was presented in Aliyu, et al.

4. Filter performance

The dependent variable in the Riccati differential equation of the Kalman-Bucy filter is the covariance matrix of the *estimation error*, defined as the difference between the estimated state vector x-*hat* and the true state vector x. Matrix P is a matrix of covariance of an error estimate of the state vector x. The initial value of which is chosen as

$$P_0 = E\{[x(t) - \hat{x}(t)][x(t) - \hat{x}(t)]^T\} \quad \text{At } t \to \infty. \tag{46}$$

The state error covariance matrix is $n \times n$ and symmetric, and must remain positive definite to retain filter stability. Diagonal elements of this matrix are variances of errors of the estimations for corresponding components of the state vector. These also serve as a definition of accuracy for the estimation.

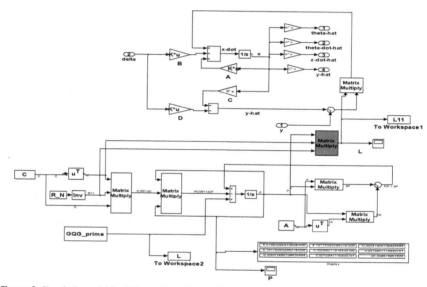

Figure 6. Simulink model for Kalman-Bucy filter with a RDE.

The solution of the matrix Riccati equation was found to provide a quantitative measure of how well the state variables can be estimated in terms of mean-squared estimation errors. Therefore, the matrix Riccati equation from the Kalman filter was soon recognized as a practical model for predicting the performance of sensor systems, and it became the standard model for designing aerospace sensor systems to meet specified performance requirements. More importantly, covariance analysis is crucial in exploring what-if scenarios with new measurement sources.

Note that in (27) we increase estimation uncertainty by adding in process noise and we decrease estimation uncertainty by the amount of information (R^{-1}) inherent in the measurement.

For an initial guess for the value of covariance, a very large value could be selected if one is using a very poor sensor for measurement. This makes the filter very conservative. Converse is the case if very good sensors are used for measurement.

The LQG autopilot simulation for tracking a pitch angle of 3 degrees (0.05rads) with the observer as designed in Fig.6 gave the result presented in Fig.7. It is interesting to note that the time response characteristics of the simulated autopilot in Fig. 7 meets all the design specifications of; *percentage overshoot* less than 10 percent; *settling time of less* than 4 seconds; *rise time* of less than 1 second and *steady state error* of less than 2 percent.

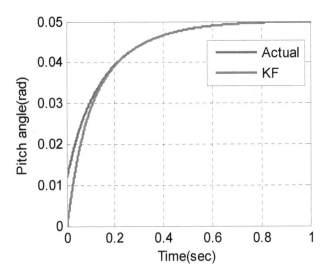

Figure 7. Set-point command tracking of LQG autopilot for a RDE solution to Kalman gain.

The numerical result at *t=1* for the covariance matrix with respect to Fig.5 is given in (47) and hence the associated Kalman gain is given in (48). The Kalman gain harnessed at this point urged us to re-design the Kalman filter model as shown in Fig. 8 for our LQG autopilot.

$$P = \begin{bmatrix} 5.228197174 \times 10^{-6} & 4.261615461 \times 10^{-6} & -0.000394471297 \\ 4.261615461 \times 10^{-6} & 0.0009807093782 & 0.0006722035747 \\ -0.0003944771297 & 0.0006722035747 & 8.750905161 \end{bmatrix}, \tag{47}$$

$$L = \begin{bmatrix} 1.30704929362596 & 1.06540386549228 & 0 \\ 1.06540386549228 & 245.177344558508 & 0 \\ -98.6192824463156 & 168.050893692856 & 0 \end{bmatrix}. \tag{48}$$

A further investigation was carried out-the single point value of Kalman filter gain given in (48) was used to implement the Kalman filter algorithm as popular represented in most textbooks-as a constant gain. For which, the Kalman-Bucy model in Fig. 8 was developed.

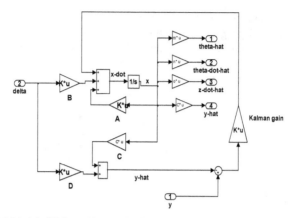

Figure 8. Simulink Model of Kalman filter model for a constant gain value of Kalman gain.

Hence, the same LQG autopilot was simulated with the Kalman filter based observer as shown in Fig.8. Simulation result for the system is as shown in Fig. 9. It is also interesting to note that all the time response characteristics as earlier mentioned were met. Though, the LQR controller could bring the ELV to a *settling time* at about 2 seconds.

The Matlab in-built command function $[K,P,E]=lqr(A,B,C,D,Q,R)$ was used to obtain the solution for the design of the LQR controller. Where, K is the controller gain, P is the associated solution to the Algebraic Riccati Equation of the controller design and E, the closed-loop eigenvalues of the plant dynamics. Note, that for LQR design the pair (A,B) must be *controllable* then, a state feedback control law can be constructed to arbitrarily locate the closed-loop eigenvalues.

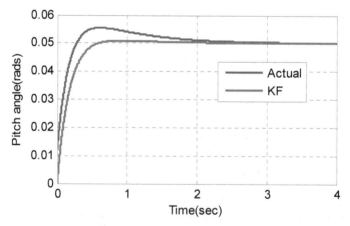

Figure 9. Set point command tracking of ELV autopilot for a Kalman gain obtained by evaluating covariance matrix to a Riccati Differential Equation at *t=1sec*.

5. Algebraic Riccati equation

Assume that the Riccati differential equation has an asymptotically stable solution for $P(t)$:

$$\lim_{t \to \infty} P(t) = P_\infty. \tag{49}$$

Then the time derivative vanishes

$$\lim_{t \to \infty} \frac{dP(t)}{dt} = 0. \tag{50}$$

Substituting this into the (6) yields

$$AP + PA^T + GQG^T - PC^T R^{-1}CP = 0. \tag{51}$$

This is called the Algebraic Riccati Equation. This is a nonlinear matrix equation, and need a numerical solver to obtain a solution for P_∞.

Consider a scalar case: $P_\infty \in R^{1 \times 1}$, A_τ ,C, Q, R ,$G \in R^{1 \times 1}$. The Algebraic Riccati Equation can be solved analytically

$$\frac{C^2}{R} P_\infty^2 - 2 A_\phi P_\infty - G^2 Q = 0,$$

$$P_\infty = \frac{R}{C^2} \left\{ A_\phi \pm \sqrt{A_\phi^2 + \frac{Q}{R} C^2 G^2} \right\}. \tag{52}$$

From (52) there exist two solutions; one positive and the other negative, corresponding to the two values for the signum ($\pm$). There is no cause for alarm. The solution that agrees with (52) is the non-negative one. The other solution is non-positive. We are only interested in the non-negative solution, because the variance P of uncertainty is, by definition, non-negative. Thus, taking the positive solution

$$\lim_{t \to \infty} P(t) = P_\infty = \frac{R}{C^2} \left\{ A_\phi + \sqrt{A_\phi^2 + \frac{Q}{R} C^2 G^2} \right\} \tag{53}$$

For the numerical example at hand, the Kalman gain for this problem is easily solved with the following Matlab command [L, P,E]=lqe(A,G,C,Q,R). This command solves a continuous time Algebraic Riccati Equation associated with the described model. Where, L, is the Kalman gain, P, the covariance matrix, and E, the closed-loop eigenvalues of the observer. The numeric values are as follows respectively:

$$L = \begin{bmatrix} 0.999999834557877 & 1.0005722536001 & 0 \\ 1.00057522536001 & 23530.07308334456 & 0 \\ -12.5039701153711 & -150868.724947992 & 0 \end{bmatrix}, \tag{54}$$

$$P = \begin{bmatrix} 3.99999938 \times 10^{-6} & 4.0023 \times 10^{-6} & -5.0016 \times 10^{-5} \\ 4.0023 \times 10^{-6} & 0.0941 \times 10^{-6} & -0.6035 \\ -5.0016 \times 10^{-6} & -0.6035 & 673.4535 \end{bmatrix},$$ (55)

and

$$E = \begin{bmatrix} -23530.19862489 \\ -1.00000017144017 \\ -5.81187094955956 \times 10^{-5} \end{bmatrix}.$$ (56)

Based, on the result in (54), the LQG autopilot was simulated with the Kalman-Bucy filter state observer as modeled in Fig. 8. The result obtained from this was used in designing an LQG controller for the case of an ELV during atmospheric ascent. This seeks to track and control a pitch angle of 3 degrees (0.05rads) and the result is as shown Figure 10. Though, in this case the controller could bring the ELV to a *Settling Time* at 3 seconds. A minute further, compared to that obtained in Fig. 9. In both cases a negligible difference in *Percentage Overshoot* was observed.

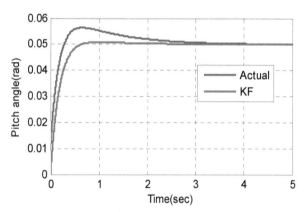

Figure 10. Set-point command tracking of LQG autopilot for an Algebraic Riccati Equation's solution to Kalman gain.

6. Comparative analysis

It can be clearly seen from figure 7 that the result of applying Kalman gain in the LQG problem of an ELV is most suitable by solving the associated Riccati Equation in its differential form (RDE). All time response characteristics were met within a second and with a zero *percent overshoot*! Though, issues might arise when hardware implementation is to be carried out. This basically will be due to the computational demand that will be placed on the selected micro-controller. In view of that, if we choose to design the

Kalman filter in the traditional manner but still not solving the associated Riccati equation as an algebraic one but as a differential one as done earlier and then harvesting the value of the Kalman gain at some specific point (in this research, we chose 1 second). Then, applying the Kalman gain, as a constant gain throughout the regime of simulation (RDE@1sec). It is obvious that for this example, this result still out performs that obtained from solving an Algebraic Riccati Equation (ARE). Actually, it could be clearly seen in Fig. 9 that the *settling time* is 2 second and in Fig. 10 is 3 seconds as the case applies. Figure 11 tries to give a holistic view of the three cases considered in this research for perusal.

Though one might be tempted to look at the difference in *settling time* of 1 second between the case of harvesting the Kalman gain value after solving a RDE at *t=1sec.*, With that of ARE as negligible or insignificant. On the contrary, considering an aerospace vehicle like the ELV, moving with a speed rage of *Mach* number *0.8-1.2* (transonic). One will be force to rethink. Let alone, compared to a *settling time* of 0.7sec obtained when Kalman gain is obtained from solving a RDE.

It is of paramount interest to add here that the plant and observer dynamics for all cases explored in this research gave a dynamic system with stable poles (*separation principle*). Contrary to that obtained in the paper Aliyu et al and in the book Aliyu Bhar Kisabo.

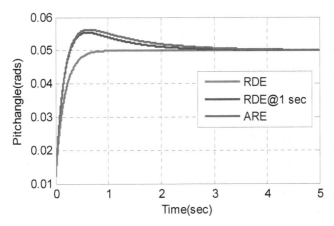

Figure 11. Compared results of the three approaches to the solution of Kalman gain as applied to an autopilot.

7. Conclusion

It can be clearly seen in Figure 6, that the synthesized LQG autopilot, with Kalman gain obtained by solving an Algebraic Riccati Equation (ARE) has 6 *percent overshoot* and a *settling time* of 3seconds. While, that in Fig. 3, is most preferred in all *time-domain* characteristics-zero *percentage overshoot* and *settling time* of 0.7second. This is the result of implementing

Kalman gain as a solution to a Riccati Differential Equation (RDE). Thus, the solution to *Riccati Differential Equation* for the implementation of Kalman filter in LQG controller design is the most optimal for pitch plane control of an ELV in the boast phase.

It is required that after designing Kalman filter, the accuracy of estimation is also assessed from the covariance matrix. It could be seen that both cases gave a very good estimation (very small covariance). Though, that of ARE gave a much smaller value. This has less significance to our research since we are majorly interested in the time response characteristic of the controlled plant. MATLAB 2010a was used for all the simulations in this paper.

Author details

Bhar K. Aliyu, Charles A. Osheku, Lanre M.A. Adetoro and Aliyu A. Funmilayo
Federal Ministry of Science and Technology (FMST), National Space Research & Development Agency (NASRDA), Center For Space Transport & Propulsion (CSTP) Epe, Lagos, Nigeria

Acknowledgement

The authors will like to specially appreciate the Honourable *Minister* of Science and Technology, Prof. Ita Okon Bassey Ewe, for his special intereste in the Research and Development activities at National Space Research and Development Agency (NASRDA). His support has been invaluable. Also, in appreciation is the *Director-General* of NASRDA, Dr. S. O Mohammed for making CSTP a priority agency among others Centres of NASRDA. We also thank Dr. Femi A. Agboola, *Director*, Engineering and Space Systems (ESS) at NASRDA, for his meaningful suggestions and discussions.

8. References

Aliyu Bhar Kisabo. (2011). *Expendable Launch Vehicle Flight Control; Design & Simulation With Matlab/Simulink*, ISBN 973-3-8443-2729-8, Germany.

L. F. Shampine, I. Gladwell, S. Thompson (2003). *Solving ODEs with MATLAB*, ISBN 978-0-511-07707-4, USA.

Robert H. Bishop. (2002). *The mechatronics Handbook*, Second Edition, ISBN 0-8493-0066-5, Boca Raton, London, New York, Washington D.C

Mohinder S Grewal.; & Angus P. Anderson. (2001). *Applications of kalman Filtering; Theory & practice Using Matlab*, Second Edition, ISBN 0-471-26638-8, New York, Chichester, Weinhem, Brisban,Sigapore,Toronto

Aliyu Bhar Kisabo et al (2011). Autopilot Design for a Generic Based Expendable Launch Vehicle, Using Linear Quadratic gaussian (LQG) Control. *European Journal of Scientific Research*, Vol.50, No.4, (February 2011), pp. 597-611, ISSN 1450-216X

Reza, Abazari. (2009). Solution of Riccati Type Differential Equations Using Matrix Differential Transform. *Journal of Applied Mathematics & Informatics*, Vol.27, No.5-6, (December 2009), pp. 1133-1143

Chapter 5

Numerical Simulation of the Frank-Kamenetskii PDE: GPU vs. CPU Computing

Charis Harley

Additional information is available at the end of the chapter

1. Introduction

The efficient solution of the Frank-Kamenetskii partial differential equation through the implementation of parallelized numerical algorithms or GPUs (Graphics Processing Units) in MATLAB is a natural progression of the work which has been conducted in an area of practical import. There is an on-going interest in the mathematics describing thermal explosions due to the significance of the applications of such models - one example is the chemical processes which occur in grain silos. Solutions which pertain to the different geometries of such a physical process have different physical interpretations, however in this chapter we will consider the Frank-Kamenetskii partial differential equation within the context of the mathematical theory of combustion which according to Frank-Kamenetskii [16] deals with the combined systems of equations of chemical kinetics and of heat transfer and diffusion. A physical explanation of such a system is often a gas confined within a vessel which then reacts chemically, heating up until it either attains a steady state or explodes.

The focus of this chapter is to investigate the performance of the parallelization power of the GPU vs. the computing power of the CPU within the context of the solution of the Frank-Kamenetskii partial differential equation. GPU computing is the use of a GPU as a co-processor to accelerate CPUs (Central Processing Units) for general purpose scientific and engineering computing. The GPU accelerates applications running on the CPU by offloading some of the compute-intensive and time consuming portions of the code. The rest of the application still runs on the CPU. The reason why the application is seen to run faster is because it is using the extreme parallel processing power of the GPU to boost performance. A CPU consists of 4 to 8 CPU cores while the GPU consists of 100s of smaller cores. Together they operate to crunch through the data in the application and as such it is this massive parallel architecture which gives the GPU its high compute performance.

The methods which will be investigated in this research are implicit methods, such as the Crank-Nicolson method (CN) and the Crank-Nicolson method incorporating the Newton method (CN_N) [26]. These algorithms pose a serious challenge to the implementation of parallelized architecture as we shall later discuss. We will also consider Rosenbrock methods which are iterative in nature and as was indicated in Harley [22] showed drastically increased running times as the time period over which the problem was considered increased. Further pitfalls which arise when trying to obtain a solution for the partial differential equation in question when using numerical techniques is firstly the singularity which exists at $x = 0$. This complexity may be dealt with through the use of a Maclaurin expansion which splits the problem into two cases: $x = 0$ and $x \neq 0$.

The second hurdle is the nonlinear source term which may be dealt with using different techniques. In this chapter we will implement the Newton method which acts as an updating mechanism for the nonlinear source term and in so doing maintains the implicit nature of the scheme in a consistent fashion. While the incorporation of the Newton method leads to an increase in the computation time for the Crank-Nicolson difference scheme (see [22]) there is also an increase in the accuracy and stability of the solution. As such we find that the algorithms we are attempting to employ in the solution of this partial differential equation would benefit from the processing power of a GPU.

In this chapter we will focus on the implementation of the Crank-Nicolson implicit method, employed with and without the Newton method, and two Rosenbrock methods, namely ROS2 and ROWDA3. We consider the effectiveness of running the algorithms on the GPU rather than the CPU and discuss whether these algorithms can in fact be parallelized effectively.

2. Model

The steady state formulation of the equation to be considered in this chapter was described by Frank-Kamenetskii [16] who later also considered the time development of such a reaction. The reaction rate depends on the temperature in a nonlinear fashion, generally given by Arrhenius' law. This nonlinearity is an important characteristic of the combustion phenomena since without it the critical condition for inflammation would disappear causing the idea of combustion to lose its meaning [16]. Thus, in the case of a thermal explosion, the Arrhenius law is maintained by the introduction of the exponential term which acts as a source for the heat generated by the chemical reaction. As such we are able to write an equation modelling the dimensionless temperature distribution in a vessel as

$$\frac{\partial u}{\partial t} = \nabla^2 u + \delta e^{u/(1+\epsilon u)} \tag{1}$$

where u is a function of the spatial variable x and time t and the Frank-Kamenetskii parameter δ is given by

$$\delta = \frac{Q}{\lambda}\frac{E}{RT_0^2}r^2\kappa\alpha e^{\left(-\frac{E}{RT_0}\right)}. \tag{2}$$

The value of the Frank-Kamanetskii parameter [16] δ is related to the critical temperature at which ignition of a thermal explosion takes place and is thus also referred to as the critical value. At values below its critical value δ_{cr} a steady state is reached for a given geometry and set of boundary conditions whereas an explosion ensues for values above it. The Laplacian operator takes the form

$$\nabla^2 = \frac{\partial^2}{\partial x^2} + \frac{k}{x}\frac{\partial}{\partial x}, \qquad 0 < x < 1 \tag{3}$$

where k is indicative of the shape of the vessel within which the chemical reaction takes place: $k = 0, 1$ and 2 represent an infinite slab, infinite circular cylinder and sphere, respectively. The dimensionless parameter $\epsilon = \frac{RT_0}{E}$ is introduced as the critical activation parameter. To be able to speak of combustion the condition $\epsilon \ll 1$ must be satisfied due to the fact that the ambient temperature can normally be seen as much smaller in magnitude than the ignition temperature [16]. Equation (1) for $\epsilon = 0$ was derived by Frank-Kamenetskii [16]. Further work was done by Steggerda [31] on Frank-Kamenetskii's original criterion for a thermal explosion showing that a more detailed consideration of the situation is possible. For small x a solution was derived for the cylindrical system by Rice [27], Bodington and Gray [6] and Chambré [10]. While the steady state case - often termed the Lane-Emden equation of the second kind - has been considered extensively, the time dependent case is also of import and has been studied in [2], [32] and [33].

In this chapter we consider numerical solutions for equation (1) modelling a thermal explosion within a cylindrical vessel, i.e. $k = 1$. A thermal explosion occurs when the heat generated by a chemical reaction is far greater than the heat lost to the walls of the vessel in which the reaction is taking place. As such this equation is subject to certain boundary conditions given at the walls of the vessel. The appropriate boundary conditions for this problem are

$$u(x,0) = 0, \tag{4}$$

$$\frac{\partial u}{\partial x}(0, t) = 0, \quad (a) \qquad u(R, t) = 0 \quad (b) \tag{5}$$

where $R = 1$ is the radius of the cylinder. The boundary conditions (4) and (5) imply that the temperature at the vessel walls is kept fixed and the solution is symmetric about the origin.

Frank-Kamenetskii [16] obtained a steady state solution to this problem with $\epsilon = 0$. Zeldovich et al. [34] considered similarity solutions admitted by (1) for $k = 1$ that exhibit blow-up in finite time. These kinds of solutions, while noteworthy, have limited significance due to the restricted form of the initial profiles compatible with the similarity solutions. These solutions correspond to very special initial conditions for the temperature evolution profile, limiting the degree to which results obtained in this manner are applicable. This disadvantage has been noted by Anderson et al. [3] while analytically investigating the time evolution of the one-dimensional temperature profile in a fusion reactor plasma. A solution which also models blow-up in finite time has been obtained by Harley and Momoniat [18] via nonlocal symmetries of the steady-state equation.

In Harley [21] a Crank-Nicolson- and hopscotch scheme were implemented for equation (1) subject to (4) and (5) where $\delta = 1$ and $\epsilon = 0$. The nonlinear source term was kept explicit when the Crank-Nicolson method was employed, as commented on by Britz et al. [9] in whose work the nonlinear term was incorporated in an implicit manner in a style more consistent with the Crank-Nicolson method. Britz et al. [9] implemented the Crank-Nicolson scheme with the Newton iteration and showed that it outperformed the explicit implementation of the nonlinearity as in [21] in terms of accuracy. However it does require more computer time as would be expected.

In recent work (see [22]) the Crank-Nicolson method was implemented with the Newton iteration as done by Britz et al. [9] by computing a correction set in each iteration to obtain approximate values of the dependent variable at the next time step. The efficiency of the Crank-Nicolson scheme, hopscotch scheme (both of these methods were implemented with an explicit and then an implicit discretisation of the source term) and two versions of the Rosenbrock method were compared [22]. Using the pdepe function in MATLAB and the steady state solution obtained by Frank-Kamenetskii [16] as a means of comparison, it was found that the incorporation of the Newton method for the Crank-Nicolson- and hopscotch scheme led to increased running times as T, where $0 \leq t \leq T$, increased.

Furthermore, it was shown that while the Crank-Nicolson- and hopscotch method (with or without the implementation of the Newton method) performed well in terms of accuracy for $T = 0.3$ and 0.5, they were in fact able to outperform pdepe at $T = 4$. The Rosenbrock methods employed (ROS2 and ROWDA3) performed similarly with regards to accuracy, however showed almost an exponential increase in their running times as T increased, indicating that using the Crank-Nicolson- or hopscotch scheme may be more efficient. Thus, given that the Rosenbrock methods performed even poorer with regards to running time, it seems reasonable to suggest that implementing the Crank-Nicolson- or hopscotch scheme with a Newton iteration is most ideal. The Crank-Nicolson method using the Newton method as a means of maintaining the implicit nature of the source term in the difference scheme has been used by Anderson and Zienkiewicz [2]. In Harley [21] and Abd El-Salam and Shehata [1] the discretisation of the exponential terms were kept explicit, thereby removing the nonlinearity.

As a consequence of these findings and due to the complexity created by the nonlinear source term which serves a critical function in the model, further work regarding faster algorithms for the solution of such an equation are of interest. This chapter will not consider the hopscotch scheme directly as an appropriate method for the solution of the Frank-Kamenetskii partial differential equation due to work done by Feldberg [15] which indicated that for large values of $\beta = \frac{\Delta t}{\Delta x^2}$ the algorithm produces the problem of propagational inadequacy which leads to inaccuracies - similar results were obtained in [22]. Given the improved accuracy of the Crank-Nicolson method incorporating the Newton method [22] - the order of the error for this method is $O(\Delta t^2)$ which is only approximately the case for the Crank-Nicolson method without the Newton iteration incorporated [9] - it seems more fitting to consider an improvement in the computing time of this method. Hence a consideration of such an improvement on the algorithm's current running time will be the focus of this chapter. The means by which we wish to accomplish this is through the use of the the Parallel Computing Toolbox in MATLAB. It is hoped that this is the next step towards creating fast and effective numerical algorithms for the solution of a partial differential equation such as the one originating from the work of Frank-Kamenetskii [16].

3. Executing MATLAB on a GPU

The advantage of using the Parallel Computing Toolbox in MATLAB is the fact that it allows one to solve computationally and data-intensive problems using multicore processors, GPUs, and computer clusters. In this manner one can parallelize numerical algorithms, and in so doing MATLAB applications, without CUDA or MPI programming. Parallelized algorithms such as parfor, used within the context of what is usually a for loop, allows you to offload work from one MATLAB session (the client) to other MATLAB sessions, called workers. You can use multiple workers to take advantage of parallel processing and in this way improve the performance of such loop execution by allowing several MATLAB workers to execute individual loop iterations simultaneously. In this context however we are not able to implement in-built MATLAB functions such as parfor due to the numerical algorithms which we have chosen to consider. The CN- and CN_N method, both implicit, loop through the index m until $t_0 + m \triangle t = T$. These iterative steps are not independent of each other, i.e to obtain data at the $m + 1^{th}$ step the data at the mth step is required. In a similar fashion the ROS2 and ROWDA3 methods also iterate through dependent loops to obtain a solution. As such we attempt to run the code directly on the GPU instead of the CPU in order to decrease the running time of the algorithms.

The Parallel Computing Toolbox in MATLAB allows one to create data on and transfer it to the GPU so that the resulting GPU array can then be used as an input to enhance built-in functions that support them. The first thing to consider when implementing computations on the GPU is *keeping* the data on the GPU so that we do not have to transfer it back and forth for each operation - this can be done through the use of the gpuArray command. In this manner computations with such input arguments run on the GPU because the input arguments are already in the GPU memory. One then retrieves the results from the GPU to the MATLAB workspace via the gather command. Having to recall the results from the GPU is costly in terms of computing time and can in certain instances make the implementation of an algorithm on the GPU less efficient than one would expect. Furthermore, the manner in which one codes algorithms for GPUs is of vital importance given certain limitations to the manner in which functions of the Toolbox may be implemented (see [25]). More importantly however, is whether the method employed can allow for the necessary adjustments in order to improve its performance. In this chapter we will see that there are some problems with implementing the kind of algorithms considered here on the GPU.

In this chapter we are employing MATLAB under Windows 7 (64 bits) on a PC equipped with an i7 2.2 GHz processor with 32 GB of RAM.

3.1. Crank-Nicolson implicit scheme

We will implement the Crank-Nicolson method while maintaing the explicit nature of the nonlinear source term and also apply the method by computing a correction set in each iteration to obtain approximate values of the dependent variable at the next time step through the use of the Newton method [26]. The methodology will be explained briefly here; the reader is referred to [7–9] for clarification.

When implementing the Crank-Nicolson method we employ the following central-difference approximations for the second-and first-order spatial derivatives respectively

$$\frac{\partial^2 u}{\partial x^2} \approx \frac{u_{n+1}^m - 2u_n^m + u_{n-1}^m}{\triangle x^2}, \tag{6}$$

$$\frac{\partial u}{\partial x} \approx \frac{u_{n+1}^m - u_{n-1}^m}{2\triangle x} \tag{7}$$

while a forward-difference approximation

$$\frac{\partial u}{\partial t} \approx \frac{u_n^{m+1} - u_n^m}{\triangle t} \tag{8}$$

is used for the time derivative. We implement a Crank-Nicolson scheme by approximating the second-derivative on the right-hand side of (1) by the implicit Crank-Nicolson [12] approximation

$$\frac{\partial^2 u}{\partial x^2} \approx \frac{u_{n+1}^{m+1} - 2u_n^{m+1} + u_{n-1}^{m+1}}{2\triangle x^2} + \frac{u_{n+1}^m - 2u_n^m + u_{n-1}^m}{2\triangle x^2}. \tag{9}$$

In a similar fashion the first-derivative on the right-hand side becomes

$$\frac{\partial u}{\partial x} \approx \frac{u_{n+1}^{m+1} - u_{n-1}^{m+1}}{4\triangle x} + \frac{u_{n+1}^m - u_{n-1}^m}{4\triangle x}. \tag{10}$$

To impose zero-shear boundary conditions at the edges we approximate the spatial first-derivative by the central-difference approximation (7) which leads to the following condition

$$u_{-1}^m = u_1^m. \tag{11}$$

As mentioned before the boundary condition (5a) at $x_0 = 0$ can pose a problem for the solution of equation (1). One could discretise it directly as a forward difference formula, such as the three-point approximation $-3u_0^m + 4u_1^m - u_2^m = 0$, and add this to the set of equations to solve when using the Crank-Nicolson scheme. Alternatively one could use the more accurate symmetric approximation, $u_{-1}^m = u_1^m$, which introduces a 'fictitious point' at $x = -\triangle x$. This however, would lead to another problem due to the singularity in the differential equation at $x_0 = 0$. Instead we choose to overcome this difficulty by using the Maclaurin expansion

$$\lim_{x \to 0} \frac{1}{x}\frac{\partial u}{\partial x} = \frac{\partial^2 u}{\partial x^2}\bigg|_{x=0} \tag{12}$$

which simplifies the equation for the case $x_0 = 0$. It has been noted by Britz et al. [9] that using (12) turns out to be more convenient and accurate. Due to the fact that the point $x_0 = 0$ would lead to a singularity in equation (1) we structure the code to account for two instances: $x = 0$ and $x \neq 0$. Using (12) for equation (1) we attain the following approximation

$$\frac{\partial u}{\partial t} = 2\frac{\partial^2 u}{\partial x^2} + e^u \tag{13}$$

to equation (1) at $x_0 = 0$. This approximation has been taken into account in the system given by (16) below. Such an approximation has been used in many numerical algorithms. In Crank and Furzeland [13], for instance, they presented a modified finite-difference method which eliminates inaccuracies that occur in the standard numerical solution near singularities. The approximation has also been used by Harley and Momoniat [19] to generate a consistency criteria for initial values at $x_0 = 0$ for a Lane-Emden equation of the second-kind. From the equation under consideration (1) an initial condition for $u(x,t)$ is obtained at $x_0 = 0$ giving the following

$$(1 + 2\beta)\, u_0^{m+1} - 2\beta u_1^{m+1} - \triangle t\delta e^{u_0^{m+1}} = (1 + 2\beta)\, u_0^m + 2\beta u_1^m + \triangle t\delta e^{u_0^m} \tag{14}$$

as the initial difference scheme with $\beta = \frac{\triangle t}{\triangle x^2}$. Implementing the difference approximations discussed above we obtain the general numerical scheme

$$-\frac{\lambda_n}{2} u_{n-1}^{m+1} + (1 + \beta)\, u_n^{m+1} - \frac{\gamma_n}{2} u_{n+1}^{m+1} - \triangle t\delta e^{u_n^{m+1}} = \frac{\lambda_n}{2} u_{n-1}^m + (1 - \beta)\, u_n^m + \frac{\gamma_n}{2} u_{n+1}^m + \triangle t\delta e^{u_n^m} \tag{15}$$

where $x_n = n\triangle x$ and $\beta = \frac{\triangle t}{\triangle x^2}$ such that $\gamma_n = \beta \left(1 - \frac{1}{2n}\right)$ and $\lambda_n = \beta \left(1 + \frac{1}{2n}\right)$. This difference scheme (15), including the initial difference condition (14), form a system of equations which are to be solved iteratively.

As indicated by the boundary conditions (5a) and (5b) we consider the problem for $x \in [0, 1]$ and $t \in [0, T]$. The domain $[0, 1]$ is sub-divided into N equidistant intervals termed $\triangle x$, i.e. $0 = x_0 < x_1 < x_2 < \cdots < x_{N-1} < x_N$ where $x_{n+1} = x_n + \triangle x$. In a similar fashion the domain $[0, T]$ is sub-divided into M intervals of equal length, $\triangle t$, through which the scheme iterates. The system will iterate until $t_m + \triangle t = T$, i.e. for $M = T/\triangle t$ steps. The system generated by (15) can be written in compact form as

$$A\mathbf{u}^{m+1} = B\mathbf{u}^m + \triangle t\delta e^{\mathbf{u}^m} + \triangle t\delta e^{\mathbf{u}^{m+1}} \tag{16}$$

and is solved as follows

$$\mathbf{u}^{m+1} = (A)^{-1} \left(B\mathbf{u}^m + \triangle t\delta e^{\mathbf{u}^m} + \triangle t\delta e^{\mathbf{u}^{m+1}}\right). \tag{17}$$

The inverse of A is calculated using the \ operator in MATLAB which is more efficient than the inv function. The nonlinear term on the $m + 1^{th}$ level is dealt with through an implementation of the Newton method [26] in an iterative fashion as done by Britz et al. [9] and discussed in [8]. The system $J\delta\mathbf{u} = -\mathbf{F}(\mathbf{u})$ is solved where $\mathbf{F}$ is the set of difference equations created as per (16) such that $\mathbf{F}(\mathbf{u}) = 0$. The starting vector at $t = 0$ is chosen as per the initial condition (4) such that $\mathbf{u} = 0$. The Newton iteration converges within 2-3 steps given that changes are usually relatively small.

3.2. Rosenbrock method

We now consider two particular Rosenbrock methods, ROS2 and ROWDA3, as a means of comparison for the effectiveness of the methods discussed in the previous section. The Rosenbrock methods belong to the class of linearly implicit Runge - Kutta methods [11, 17]. They were used successfully for the numerical solution of non-electrochemical stiff partial differential equations, including equations of interest to electrochemistry. For further information regarding the particulars of such methods interested readers are referred to the numerical literature of [17, 28–30].

The reason for the use of the Rosenbrock methods in this paper is the ease with which they are able to deal with the nonlinear source term and the fact that no Newton iterations are necessary. The advantages of these methods are great efficiency, stability and a smooth error response if ROS2 or ROWDA3 are used (see [4] for instance) and the ease with which they are able to handle time-dependent and/or nonlinear systems.

We consider equation (1) as the following system

$$\frac{du_n}{dt} == \begin{cases} \frac{(1+k)}{\Delta x^2}(2u_1 - 2u_0) + \delta e^{u_0} & \text{if } n = 0 \\ \frac{\gamma_n}{\Delta t}u_{n-1} - \frac{2}{\Delta x^2}u_n + \frac{\lambda_n}{\Delta t}u_{n+1} + \delta e^{u_n} & \text{if } n = 1, 2, ..., n-2 \\ -\frac{2}{\Delta x^2}u_{N-1} + \frac{\lambda_{N-1}}{\Delta t}u_{N-2} + \delta e^{u_{N-1}} & \text{if } n = N-1 \end{cases} \tag{18}$$

which along with $0 = u_N$ can be written in the compact form

$$\mathbf{S}\frac{d\mathbf{u}}{dt} = \mathbf{F}(t, \mathbf{u}) \tag{19}$$

where $\mathbf{S} = \text{diag}(1, 1, 1, ..., 1, 0)$ is the selection matrix containing zeros in those positions where the set of differential algebraic equations has an algebraic equation (i.e. zero on the left-hand side of (18)) and unity in those positions corresponding to the ordinary differential equations. The function $\mathbf{F}(t, \mathbf{u})$ can be written as: $\mathbf{F}(t, \mathbf{u}) = \mathbf{J}\mathbf{u} + \mathbf{s}$ where the matrix $\mathbf{J}$ is the Jacobian and the vector $\mathbf{s}$ arises from the constant terms of the set of differential algebraic equations. We can thus write $\mathbf{F}(t, \mathbf{u}) = \mathbf{J}\mathbf{u} + \mathbf{s}$ as

$$= \frac{1}{\Delta t} \begin{bmatrix} -2(1+k)\beta & 2(1+k)\beta & 0 & 0 & 0 & \cdots & 0 & 0 & 0 & 0 \\ 0 & \gamma_1 & -2\beta & \lambda_1 & 0 & \cdots & 0 & 0 & 0 & 0 \\ 0 & 0 & \gamma_2 & -2\beta & \lambda_2 & \cdots & 0 & 0 & 0 & 0 \\ \vdots & \vdots & \vdots & \vdots & \cdots & \cdots & \vdots & \vdots & \vdots & \vdots \\ 0 & 0 & 0 & \cdots & 0 & 0 & \gamma_{N-2} & -2\beta & \lambda_{N-2} & 0 \\ 0 & 0 & 0 & 0 & \cdots & 0 & 0 & \gamma_{N-1} & -2\beta & 0 \\ 0 & 0 & 0 & 0 & \cdots & 0 & 0 & 0 & 0 & 1 \end{bmatrix} \begin{bmatrix} u_0 \\ u_1 \\ u_2 \\ \vdots \\ u_{N-2} \\ u_{N-1} \\ u_N \end{bmatrix}$$

$$+ \begin{bmatrix} \delta e^{u_0} \\ \delta e^{u_1} \\ \delta e^{u_2} \\ \vdots \\ \delta e^{u_{N-2}} \\ \delta e^{u_{N-1}} \\ 0 \end{bmatrix} \tag{20}$$

such that

$$\mathbf{F}_u = \frac{1}{\Delta t} \begin{bmatrix} (1+k)\beta(2u_1 - 2u_0) + \delta e^{u_0} \\ \gamma_1 u_0 - 2\beta u_1 + \lambda_1 u_2 + \delta e^{u_1} \\ \gamma_2 u_1 - 2\beta u_2 + \lambda_2 u_3 + \delta e^{u_2} \\ \vdots \\ \gamma_{N-2} u_{N-3} - 2\beta u_{N-2} + \lambda_{N-2} u_{N-1} + \delta e^{u_{N-2}} \\ -2\beta u_{N-1} + \lambda_{N-1} u_N - 2 + \delta e^{u_{N-1}} \\ u_N \end{bmatrix}. \tag{21}$$

In order to implement the Rosenbrock methods a number s of $\mathbf{k}_i$ vectors are computed with s the order chosen. The general equation given by (22) is solved iteratively to obtain each vector $\mathbf{k}_i$ for all i specified which will then be used to update the vector $\mathbf{u}$ for the next time step. We use the notation employed in [7] for the general equation to be used to obtain the values for $\mathbf{k}_i$

$$-\frac{\mathbf{M}}{\beta}\mathbf{k}_i = -\frac{\triangle t}{\beta}\mathbf{F}\left(t + \varphi_i \triangle t, \mathbf{u} + \sum_{j=1}^{i-1} a_{ij}\mathbf{k}_j\right)$$

$$-\frac{\mathbf{S}}{\beta}\sum_{j=1}^{i-1} c_{ij}\mathbf{k}_j - \frac{\kappa_i}{\beta}\triangle t^2 \mathbf{F}_t(t, \mathbf{u}) \tag{22}$$

where we define $M = \frac{\mathbf{S}}{\kappa} - \triangle t\mathbf{F}_u$ were the function $\mathbf{F}$ is applied at partly augmented t and $\mathbf{u}$ values and the time derivative $\mathbf{F}_t$ is zero in this case since the system does not include functions of time. Having calculated the s $\mathbf{k}_i$ vectors the solution is obtained from

$$\mathbf{u}_{m+1} = \mathbf{u}_m + \sum_{i=1}^{s} m_i\mathbf{k}_i \tag{23}$$

where the m_i are weighting factors included in the tables of constants specified for each method (see [4] and [7]).

In this chapter we implement the ROS2 and ROWDA3 methods though there are other variants of the Rosenbrock methods. Lang [24] described a L-stable second-order formula called ROS2. A third-order variant thereof is called ROWDA3 and described by Roche [28] and later made more efficient by Lang [23]. The latter is a method favoured by Bieniasz who introduced Rosenbrock methods to electrochemical digital simulation [4, 5]. For a more detailed explanation and discussion regarding the method and its advantages refer to [7]. The focus of the work done here is with regards to whether the Rosenbrock algorithms lend themselves toward parallelized implementation. It has already been noted that functions such as the `parfor` command cannot be used in this instance. It now remains to consider the method's performance when run on a GPU via the MATLAB Parallel Computing Toolbox.

4. Discussion of numerical results

The results noticed, as per Table 1, indicate the extent to which implementing the code on the GPU slows down overall performance of the CN, CN_N, ROS2 and ROWDA3 methods. The question is why this would be the case. In Table 1 the results for the different methods run on a CPU were obtained by running the code on one CPU only instead of all of those available to MATLAB on the computer employed. This was done to get a better understanding of the one-on-one performance between the processing units, and yet implementing the code on the GPU still led to poor performance.

To gain a better understanding of these results we consider the baseline structure for our CN code:

```
A = gpuArray(A);
B = gpuArray(B);
```

```
u0 = gpuArray(u0);
for m = 1 : T
    b = delta. * dt. * exp((1 + eps. * u0).\(u0));
    u0 = mldivide(A, (B * u0 + b));
end
```

In doing so, we realise that the main components thereof are matrix and elementwise vector operations. In order to understand why we are achieving the results we do (see Table 1) we run a few simple 'test'-codes to consider the speed taken by the CPU vs. the GPU to perform such elementary operations as C\d and d. * f where C is a matrix and d and f are vectors. In Figure 1 we see the speed of the CPU over the GPU computed as $\frac{CPU\ running\ time}{GPU\ running\ time}$. You will notice that as the size of the matrix and corresponding vector increases so too does the speed at which the GPU is able to compute C\d allowing it to overtake the CPU. This is what one would expect given that the GPU will only 'kick in' once the CPU is overloaded with data structures too large for it to compute effectively. Thus the efficiency in terms of running time of the code provided above is heavily dependent upon the size of the matrices A and B. At this juncture it is important to remember that we are considering the range $x \in [0,1]$ with $\triangle x = 0.1$ which means that our A matrix is a 10×10 matrix and as such not large enough to give the GPU the chance to expose its ability to improve the performance of the algorithm. The reason for the choice in the size of the matrix for the problem considered is twofold: (1) it is due to the influence of the ratio $\beta = \triangle t / \triangle x^2$ which one usually tries to keep close to 1 for reasons of stability, and (2) the limitations of memory of the PC being used.

The next step in this evaluative process is to now consider the speed at which vector operations are performed. This was done in a similar fashion to the previous case by considering the speed taken by the CPU and GPU to perform the elementwise operation d. * f where d and f are vectors. The ratios of the speeds $\frac{CPU\ running\ time}{GPU\ running\ time}$ were also considered for the in-built function arrayfun which performs elementwise operations on all its inputs. It can clearly be seen in Figure 2 that the in-built function outperforms the normal .* operation. What is interesting in this case is that the size of the vector required for the GPU to outperform the CPU is very large - we considered vectors of sizes between 200 000 and 201 000 as indicated. For smaller vector lengths the GPU is completely outperformed by the speed at which calculations are done on the CPU. As such, to improve the speed at which these vector calculations are performed we would either (1) have to diminish $\triangle x$ to the degree needed to obtain vectors of the required length (2) or be required to move the vectors from the GPU memory to the CPU memory every time calculations need to be made. The first approach would require a memory capacity beyond that of the computer used here and the second would greatly increase the running time of the algorithm and as such is not worth implementing.

As a means of further investigation we consider the CN code as a test case for the use of the arrayfun function. Obviously implementing this in-built function as follows

```
A = gpuArray(A);
B = gpuArray(B);
u0 = gpuArray(u0);
u0 = arrayfun(@myCrank, u0, A, B)
```

$\beta = 0.01$ and $T = 0.3$			
	CN	CN_N	$ROS2$	$ROWDA3$
CPU	7.8449e-05	2.7737e-04	2.3002e-05	9.1288e-05
GPU	0.0014	0.0960	0.0033	0.0063
$\beta = 0.01$ and $T = 5$			
	CN	CN_N	$ROS2$	$ROWDA3$
CPU	1.4783e-05	2.0018e-04	1.5354e-05	6.3574e-05
GPU	8.0940e-04	0.0047	0.0028	0.0047
$\beta = 2$ and $T = 5$			
	CN	CN_N	$ROS2$	$ROWDA3$
CPU	2.4573e-05	0.0033	1.7146e-05	6.8119e-05
GPU	0.0048	0.4731	0.0042	0.0073

Table 1. Running times per iteration of $\triangle t$ for the relevant methods implemented for $\triangle t = 0.0001$, $\triangle x = 0.1, \delta = 1$ and $\epsilon = 0$.

$\epsilon = 0.01$			
CN	CN_N	$ROS2$	$ROWDA3$
0.0137	0.0025	0.0059	0.0138
$\epsilon = 0.05$			
CN	CN_N	$ROS2$	$ROWDA3$
0.0133	0.0024	0.0067	0.0149
$\epsilon = 0.1$			
CN	CN_N	$ROS2$	$ROWDA3$
0.0146	0.0025	0.0057	0.0128
$\epsilon = 0.25$			
CN	CN_N	$ROS2$	$ROWDA3$
0.0145	0.0024	0.0059	0.0133

Table 2. The ratio $\frac{CPU\ running\ time}{GPU\ running\ time}$ for the relevant methods implemented for $\triangle t = 0.0001$, $\triangle x = 0.1$, $\delta = 1$ and $T = 0.3$.

$\delta = 0.5$			
CN	CN_N	$ROS2$	$ROWDA3$
0.0146	0.0012	0.0064	0.0150
$\delta = 1$			
CN	CN_N	$ROS2$	$ROWDA3$
0.0275	0.0026	0.0061	0.0160
$\delta = 2$			
CN	CN_N	$ROS2$	$ROWDA3$
0.0151	0.0030	0.0062	0.0151
$\delta = 3$			
CN	CN_N	$ROS2$	$ROWDA3$
0.0160	0.0042	0.0063	0.0140

Table 3. The ratio $\frac{CPU\ running\ time}{GPU\ running\ time}$ for the relevant methods implemented for $\triangle t = 0.0001$, $\triangle x = 0.1$, $\epsilon = 0$ and $T = 0.3$.

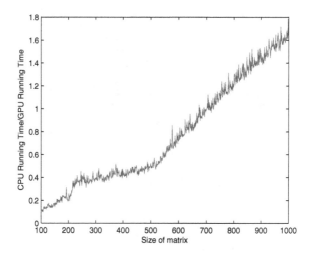

Figure 1. Plot showing the CPU Running Time/GPU Running Time for matrices and corresponding vectors of sizes 100 to 1000.

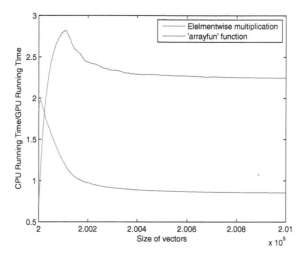

Figure 2. Plot showing the CPU Running Time/GPU Running Time for vectors of sizes 200 000 to 201 000.

where the @myCrank function performs the loop through m, instead of the code presented previously produces incorrect results. The results obtained do however support our findings that the arrayfun function is able to increase the speed with which elementwise operations are performed. In this instance arrayfun is computing on the GPU since the inputs are all GPU array objects. We found for $T = 10$ with $\triangle t = 0.0001$ as we decreased $\triangle x$ that computing on the GPU was faster than doing so on the CPU: for $\triangle x = 0.1$ and 0.01 the ratios were $\frac{CPU\ running\ time}{GPU\ running\ time} = 1.5709$ and $\frac{CPU\ running\ time}{GPU\ running\ time} = 6.5906$ respectively. This makes sense given that smaller values of $\triangle x$ would increase the sizes of the matrices A and B and the vectors b and $u0$. As such, it seems likely that using a PC with a greater memory capacity would lead to the GPU outperforming the CPU by a large margin as $\triangle x$ decreases.

4.1. Influence of changing parameter values on the running time of the algorithms

Just a few brief comments upon the results obtained for CN, CN_N, ROS2 and ROWDA3 for varying values of ϵ and δ will be made in this section. Firstly we considered the schemes for $\delta = 1$ and $\epsilon = 0.01, 0.05, 0.1$ and 0.25 and then we also considered the case for $\epsilon = 0$ with $\delta = 0.1, 1, 2$ and 3. The reader will notice considering Tables 2 and 3 that there does not seem to be any noticeable trend to the results obtained. As such the values of ϵ and δ do not seem to have a meaningful impact on the speed at which the algorithms compute.

5. Concluding remarks

The implementation of numerical algorithms such as those considered in this chapter are widely used for the solution of many differential equations which model physical processes and applications. As such it is of vital importance that we be able to perform such calculations at high speed given the requirement of fine grids to improve accuracy. It is in this context that the use of GPUs becomes of prime importance. However it is not simply a matter of running the algorithm on the GPU - the method employed needs to lend itself to being adjusted in the required manner so that the parallel processing power of the GPU may be taken advantage of. Though we found that the numerical methods considered here were not entirely suited to being implemented on the GPU as we would have hoped we were able to explain why this was the case.

This work has investigated the effectiveness of matrix and elementwise operations when run on a GPU vs. a CPU and found that the speed taken to do such operations heavily relies on the choice of $\triangle x$. It was discovered that the introduction of the nonlinear source term is problematic due to the length of time taken to do elementwise calculations on the GPU. While matrix operations were also shown to be slow it was more specifically this aspect of the code which increased the running time.

We also discovered the power of the in-built function `arrayfun` which was able to improve upon the performance of the GPU with regards to computing time to the degree that it outperformed the CPU even for a grid with 'large' $\triangle x$, i.e. small matrices and vectors within the computations. As the grid became finer the performance of the GPU over the CPU improved, indicating the impact of the size of the matrices upon which computations are being performed and the degree to which `arrayfun` is able to improve computations occurring on the GPU. Thus, the manner in which `arrayfun` computes elementwise is extremely efficient and if such a structure could be developed for matrix operations then that would truly allow the performance of the GPU to overtake that of CPU computing.

What the work in this chapter has shown is that the structures of the GPU and the Parallel Computing Toolbox in MATLAB are such that while certain algorithms have the ability to be adjusted for improved performance not all methods do. In particular it seems clear that implicit methods with matrix and vector operations will in fact run much slower on the GPU than the CPU. Thus whether GPU computing is able to improve the performance of a numerical scheme is very much dependent upon the type of computations which need to be done. In our case we discovered that the implicit and nonlinear nature of our numerical schemes do not lend themselves towards improved performance via the implementation of the parallel processing power of a GPU.

Acknowledgements

I would like to thank Mr. Dario Fanucchi for invaluable discussions.

Author details

Charis Harley
Faculty of Science, University of the Witwatersrand, School of Computational and Applied Mathematics, Centre for Differential Equations, Continuum Mechanics and Applications, South Africa

6. References

[1] Abd El-Salam, M. R. & Shehata, M. H. (2005). The numerical solution for reaction diffusion combustion with fuel consumption, *Appl. Math. Comp.*, 160:423Û-435.

[2] Anderson, C. A.; Zienkiewicz, O. C. (1974). Spontaneous ignition: finite element solutions for steady and transient conditions, *J. Heat Transfer*, 96(3):398–404

[3] Anderson, D.; Hamnén, H.; Lisak, M.; Elevant T. & Persson, H (1991). Transition to thermonuclear burn in fusion plasmas, *Plasma Physics and Controlled Fusion*, 33(10):1145–1159

[4] Bieniasz, L. K. (1999). Finite-difference electrochemical kinetic simulations using the Rosenbrock time integration scheme, *Journal of Electroanalytical Chemistry*, 469:97–115

[5] Bieniasz, L. K. & Britz, D. (2001). Chronopotentiometry at a Microband Electrode: Simulation Study Using a Rosenbrock Time Integration Scheme for Differential-Algebraic Equations, and a Direct Sparse Solver, *Journal of Electroanalytical Chemistry*, 503:141–152

[6] Boddington, T. & Gray, P. (1970). Temperature profiles in endothermic and exothermic reactions and interpretation of experimental rate data, *Proc. Roy. Soc. Lond Ser A - Mat. Phys. Sci.*, 320(1540):71–100

[7] Britz, D. (2005). Digital Simulation in Electrochemistry, 3rd Edition, Lecture Notes in Physics, Springer, 3 − 540 − 23979 − 0, Berlin Heidelberg

[8] Britz, D.; Baronas, R.; Gaidamauskaitė, E. & Ivanauskas, F. (2009). Further Comparisons of Finite Difference Schemes for Computational Modelling of Biosensors, *Nonlinear Analysis: Modelling and Control*, 14(4):419–433

[9] Britz, D.; Strutwolf J. & Østerby, O. (2011). Digital simulation of thermal reactions, *Appl. Math. and Comp.*, 218(4), 15:1280–1290

[10] Chambré, P. L. (1952). On the solution of the Poisson-Boltzmann equation with application to the theory of thermal explosions, *J*. Chem. Phys., 20:1795–1797

[11] Chan, Y. N. I.; Birnbaum, I. & Lapidus, L. (1978). Solution of Stiff Differential Equations and the Use of Imbedding Techniques, *Ind*. Eng. Chem. Fundam., 17(3):133–148

[12] Crank J. & Nicolson, E. (1947). A practical method for numerical evaluation of solutions of partial differential equations of the heat-conduction type, *Proc*. Camb. Phil. Soc., 43:50–67

[13] Crank J. & Furzeland, R. M. (1977). The treatment of boundary singularities in axially symmetric problems containing discs, *J*. Inst. Math. Appl., 20(3):355–370

[14] Evans. D. J. & Danaee, A. (1982). A new group Hopscotch method for the numerical solution of partial differential equations, *SIAM J*. Numer. Anal., 19(3):588–598

[15] Feldberg, S. W. (1987). Propagational inadequacy of the hopscotch finite difference algorithm: the enhancement of performance when used with an exponentially expanding grid for simulation of electrochemical diffusion problems, *J*. Electroanal. Chem., 222:101–106

[16] Frank-Kamenetskii, D. A. (1969). *Diffusion and Heat Transfer in Chemical Kinetics*, Plenum Press, New York

[17] Hairer E. & Wanner, G. (1991). Solving Ordinary Differential Equations II, Stiff and Differential-Algebraic Problems, Springer-Verlag, $3 - 540 - 60452 - 9$, Berlin

[18] Harley, C. & Momoniat, E. (2007). Steady state solutions for a thermal explosion in a cylindrical vessel, *Modern Physics Letters B (MPLB)*, 21(14):831–841.

[19] Harley, C. & Momoniat, E. (2008). Instability of invariant boundary conditions of a generalized Lane-Emden equation of the second-kind, *Applied Mathematics and Computation*, 198:621–633

[20] Harley, C. & Momoniat, E. (2008). Alternate derivation of the critical value of the Frank-Kamenetskii parameter in the cylindrical geometry, *Journal of Nonlinear Mathematical Physics*, 15(1):69–76

[21] Harley, C. (2010). Explicit-implicit Hopscotch method: The numerical solution of the Frank-Kamenetskii partial differential equation, *Journal of Applied Mathematics and Computation*, 217(8):4065–4075

[22] Harley, C. (2011). Crank-Nicolson and Hopscotch method: An emphasis on maintaining the implicit discretisation of the source term as a means of investigating critical parameters. Special Issue on 'Nonlinear Problems: Analytical and Computational Approach with Applications', *Abstract and Applied Analysis*, Submitted.

[23] Lang, J. (1996). High-resolution self-adaptive computations on chemical reaction-diffusion problems with internal boundaries, *Chemical Engineering Science*, 51(7):1055–1070

[24] Lang, J. (2001). Adaptive Multilevel Solution of Nonlinear Parabolic PDE Systems, Springer, 9783540679004, Berlin

[25] The MathWorks, Inc. ©1994-2012. Parallel Computing Toolbox Perform parallel computations on multicore computers, GPUs, and computer clusters, *http* : *//www.mathworks.com/products/parallel − computing/*.

[26] Press, W. H.; Teukolsky, S. A.; Vetterling, W. T. & Flannery, B. P. (1986). Numerical Recipes in Fortran, 2nd Edition, Cambridge University Press, $0 - 521 - 43064 - X$, Cambridge

[27] Rice, O. K. (1940). The role of heat conduction in thermal gaseous explosions, *J. Chem. Phys.*, 8(9):727–733

[28] Roche, M. (1988). Rosenbrock methods for differential algebraic equations, *Numerische Mathematik*, 52:45–63

[29] Rosenbrock, H. H. (1963). Some general implicit processes for the numerical solution of differential equations, *The Computer Journal*, 5(4):329–330

[30] Sandu, A.; Verwer, J. G.; Blom, J.G.; Spee, E. J. & Carmichael, G. R. (1997). Benchmarking Stiff ODE Solvers for Atmospheric Chemistry Problems II: Rosenbrock Solvers, *Atmospheric Environment*, 31:3459–3472

[31] Steggerda, J. J. (1965). Thermal stability: an extension of Frank-Kamenetskii's theory, *J. Chem. Phys.*, 43:4446–4448

[32] Zhang, G.; Merkin J. H. & Scott, S. K. (1991). Reaction-diffusion model for combustion with fuel consumption: Ii. Robin boundary conditions, *IMA J. Appl. Math.*, 51:69–93

[33] Zhang, G.; Merkin J. H. & Scott, S. K. (1991). Reaction-diffusion model for combustion with fuel consumption: I. Dirichlet boundary conditions, *IMA J. Appl. Math.*, 47:33–60

[34] Zeldovich, Y. B.; Barenblatt, G. I.; Librovich, V. B. & Makhviladze, G. M. (1985). The Mathematical Theory of Combustion and Explosions, Consultants Bureau, New York

Chapter 6

Fuzzy Analytical Network Process Implementation with Matlab

Xiaoguang Zhou

Additional information is available at the end of the chapter

1. Introduction

In many complex decision-making problems, the decision information provided by the decision makers is often imprecise or uncertain due to time limit, lack of data, or the decision makers' limited attention and information processing capabilities. Decision-making in a fuzzy environment means a decision process in which the goals and/or the constraints, but not necessarily the system under control, are fuzzy in nature. This means that the goals and/or the constraints constitute classes of alternatives whose boundaries are not sharply defined. Fuzzy set, whose basic component is a membership function (Zadeh, 1965), was introduced in the following several decades. Fuzzy set theory has been applied successfully in the decision-making field.

Matlab is a suitable tool for solving fuzzy decision-making problems. This chapter is focusing on how to solve a specific class of fuzzy decision-making problem, that is, Fuzzy Analytical Network Process (FANP) by Matlab. Project selection is chosen as an example to illustrate the proposed method. The reason is that project selection is a complex decision-making process. It involves a search from the environment of opportunities, the generation of project options, and the evaluation of multiple attributes, both qualitative and quantitative, by different stakeholders.

There are various mathematic techniques for selecting an optimal project. Mathematical programming models can be used to accomplish this decision. For example, the R&D project selection can be presented based on linear, non-linear, dynamic, goal, and stochastic mathematical programming (Wang & Hwang, 2007). Based on the idea of moments approximation method via linear programming, Fang et al. (2008) proposed a scenario generation approach for the mixed single-stage Research and Development (R&D) projects and multi-stage securities portfolio selection problem, etc.

Also, project selection has been presented in regard with multiple objectives. For instance, Gabriel et al. (2006) developed a multiobjective, integer-constrained optimization model with competing objectives for project selection, and the subjective rank is determined via the Analytic Hierarchy Process (AHP). Ghorbani & Rabbani (2009) proposed a multi-objective algorithm for project selection. Two objective functions have been considered to maximize total expected benefit of selected projects and minimize the summation of the absolute variation of allotted resource between each successive time periods. Gutjahr et al. (2010) presented a multi-objective optimization model for project portfolio selection taking employee competencies and their evolution into account, and so on.

Fuzzy sets theory is utilized to cover the vagueness inherent in the nature of project selection problem as well. For example, Huang et al. (2008) presented a fuzzy analytic hierarchy process method and utilize crisp judgment matrix to evaluate subjective expert judgments. Bhattacharyya et al. (2011) developed a fuzzy multi-objective programming approach to facilitate decision making in the selection of R&D projects. Ebrahimnejad et al. (2011) considered a two-phase decision making approach, combining a modified version of the Analytic Network Process (ANP) method and an improved compromise ranking method under uncertainty. Chang & Lee (2012) proposed a Data Envelopment Analysis (DEA), knapsack formulation and fuzzy set theory integrated model to deal with the project selection , etc.

Some researchers tried the project selection problem in other ways. Dey (2006) proposed a decision support system, which analyses projects with respect to market, technicalities, and social and environmental impact in an integrated framework using analytic hierarchy process. Liesiö et al. (2007) developed the Robust Portfolio Modeling methodology which extends Preference Programming methods into portfolio problems, where a subset of project proposals are funded in view of multiple evaluation criteria. Smith-Perera et al. (2010) proposed an approach to prioritize project portfolio in an efficient and reliable way based on analytic network process method and the information obtained from the experts during the decision-making process. Shakhsi-Niaei et al. (2011) presented a procedure which used the PROMETHEE method linked to a Monte Carlo simulation in order to consider and possibly make lower all kinds of uncertainties of project selection problem in an acceptable complexity level, and so on.

As mentioned above, AHP or ANP was widely used during the process of selecting or evaluating an optimal project (Gabriel et al., 2006; Dey, 2006; Smith-Perera et al., 2010; Ebrahimnejad et al., 2011), and these literatures (Cheng & Li, 2005; Amiri, 2010; Aragonés-Beltrán et al., 2010; Jung & Seo, 2010; etc) are also about project selection based on AHP/ANP. In addition, AHP/ANP was proverbially used in other decision-making fields as well (Kahraman et al., 2006; Lee et al., 2009; Arunraj & Maiti, 2010; Huang et al., 2011; etc.). The main reason is that AHP/ANP can deal with qualitative and quantitative information at the same time, and ANP can take into account the interaction and feedback relationships between criteria and/or indices. However, due to the vagueness and uncertainty on the judgments of decision-makers, the crisp pairwise comparison in the conventional AHP/ANP seems insufficient and imprecise to capture the right judgments of decision-makers.

In this study, a fuzzy logic is introduced for the pairwise comparison of ANP to make up the deficiency of the conventional AHP/ANP, referred to as FANP. The objective of this chapter is to present a FANP-based approach for the construction project selection problem using triangular fuzzy numbers. According to the fuzzy preference programming (FPP) method, local weights of fuzzy pairwise comparison matrices can be achieved. Then an unweighted and weighted supermatrix based on its network structure can be formed. For FANP, the key steps are to calculate the local weights and the limit supermatrix. Both of them can be solved by Matlab. A case will be given by the proposed method, and Matlab codes will be provided as well.

2. What's FANP?

The ANP, introduced by Saaty, is a generalization of the AHP (Saaty, 1996). ANP is the first mathematical theory that makes it possible to deal with all kinds of dependences and feedbacks by replacing hierarchies with networks (Saaty, 1996). ANP allows for complex inter-relationships among decision dimensions and attributes. The ANP feedback approach replaces hierarchies with networks in which the relationships between dimensions are not easily represented as higher or lower, dominant or subordinate, direct or indirect. For instance, not only does the importance of the criteria determine the importance of the attributes, as in a hierarchy, but also the importance of the attributes may have impact on the importance of the criteria. A hierarchical structure with a linear top-to-bottom form is not suitable for a complex system.

As we know, AHP/ANP has been proposed as a suitable multi-criteria decision analysis tool for project selection and evaluation. However, the conventional AHP/ANP-based decision model seems to be ineffective in dealing with the inherent fuzziness or uncertainty in judgment during the pairwise comparison process. Although the use of the discrete scale of 1-9 to represent the verbal judgment in pairwise comparisons has the advantage of simplicity, it does not take into account the uncertainty associated with the mapping of one's perception or judgment to a number. In real-life decision-making situations, the decision makers or stakeholders could be uncertain about their own level of preference, due to incomplete information or knowledge, complexity and uncertainty within the decision environment. Such situations will occur when selecting and evaluating an optimal project. Therefore, it's better to make project selection and assessment under fuzzy conditions. This chapter will focus on FANP in fuzzy decision-making based on triangular fuzzy numbers. Actually, some researchers have focused on decision-making based on FANP (Promentilla et al., 2008 ; Ayağ & Özdemir, 2009 ; Boran & Goztepe, 2010; Dağdeviren & Yüksel, 2010; Pires et al., 2011 ; Ju et al., 2012 ; etc.).

2.1. Triangular fuzzy number

A fuzzy set is a class of objects with a continuum of grades of membership. Such a set is characterized by a membership function, which assigns to each object a grade of membership ranging between zero and one.

A triangular fuzzy number (TFN) M is shown in Fig. 1. A TFN is denoted simply as (l, m, u). The parameters l, m and u, respectively, denote the smallest possible value, the most promising value, and the largest possible value that describe a fuzzy event. Each TFN has linear representations on its left and right side such that its membership function can be defined as

$$u_M(x) = \begin{cases} (x-l)/(m-l) & l \leq x \leq m \\ (u-x)/(u-m) & m \leq x \leq u \\ 0 & otherwise \end{cases} \tag{1}$$

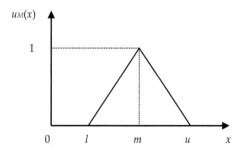

Figure 1. A triangular fuzzy number M

2.2. Fuzzy preference programming method

A number of methods have been developed to handle fuzzy comparison matrices. For instance, Van Laarhoven & Pedrycz (1983) suggested a fuzzy logarithmic least squares method to obtain the fuzzy weights from a triangular fuzzy comparison matrix. Buckley (1985) utilized the geometric mean method to calculate fuzzy weights. Chang (1996) proposed an extent analysis method, which derives crisp weights for fuzzy comparison matrices. Xu (2000) brought forward a fuzzy least squares priority method (LSM). Csutora & Buckley (2001) came up with a Lambda-Max method, which is the direct fuzzification of the well-known $k$max method. Mikhailov (2003, 2004) developed a fuzzy preference programming method, which also derives crisp weights from fuzzy comparison matrices. Srdjevic (2005) proposed a multicriteria approach for combining prioritization methods within the AHP, including additive normalization, eigenvector, weighted least-squares, logarithmic least-squares, logarithmic goal programming and fuzzy preference programming. Wang et al. (2006) presented a modified fuzzy logarithmic least square method. Yu & Cheng (2007) developed a multiple objective programming approach for the ANP to obtain all local priorities for crisp or interval judgments at one time, even in an inconsistent situation. Huo et al. (2011) proposed new parametric prioritization methods (PPMs) to determine a family of priority vectors in AHP.

FPP method, as a reasonable and effective means, is adopted in this study. This method can acquire the consistency ratios of fuzzy pairwise comparison matrices without additional study, and the local weights can be easily solved by Matlab software. The stages of Mikhailov's fuzzy prioritization approach are given as follows (Mikhailov, 2003).

Consider a prioritization problem with n elements, where the pairwise comparison judgements are represented by normal fuzzy sets or fuzzy numbers. Supposing that the decision-maker can provide a set $F=\{\tilde{a}_{ij}\}$ of $m \leq n(n-1)/2$ fuzzy comparison judgements, $i=1, 2,$ ..., $n-1; j=2, 3, ..., n; j>i$, represented as triangular fuzzy numbers $\tilde{a}_{ij}=(l_{ij}, m_{ij}, u_{ij})$. The problem is to derive a crisp priority vector $w=(w_1, w_2, ..., w_n)^T$, such that the priority ratios w_i/w_j are approximately within the scopes of the initial fuzzy judgments, or

$$l_{ij} \,\tilde{\leq}\, \frac{w_i}{w_j} \,\tilde{\leq}\, u_{ij} \qquad (2)$$

where the symbol $\tilde{\leq}$ denotes the statement "fuzzy less or equal to".

Each crisp priority vector w satisfies the double-side inequality (2) with some degree, which can be measured by a membership function, linear with respect to the unknown ratio w_i/w_j

$$u_{ij}\left(\frac{w_i}{w_j}\right) = \begin{cases} \dfrac{(w_i/w_j) - l_{ij}}{m_{ij} - l_{ij}}, & \dfrac{w_i}{w_j} \leq m_{ij}, \\[3mm] \dfrac{u_{ij} - (w_i/w_j)}{u_{ij} - m_{ij}}, & \dfrac{w_i}{w_j} \geq m_{ij}. \end{cases} \qquad (3)$$

The membership function (3) is linearly increasing over the interval $(-\infty, m_{ij})$ and linearly decreasing over the interval (m_{ij}, ∞). The function takes negative values when $w_i/w_j<l_{ij}$ or $w_i/w_j>u_{ij}$, and has a maximum value $u_{ij}=1$ at $w_i/w_j=m_{ij}$. Over the range (l_{ij}, u_{ij}), the membership function (3) coincides with the fuzzy triangular judgment (l_{ij}, m_{ij}, u_{ij}).

The solution to the prioritization problem by the FPP method is based on two main assumptions. The first one requires the existence of non-empty fuzzy feasible area P on the $(n-1)$ dimensional simplex Q^{n-1}

$$Q^{n-1} = \{(w_1, w_2, ... w_n) \,\Big|\, w_i > 0, \sum_{i=1}^{n} w_i = 1\}, \qquad (4)$$

defined as an intersection of the membership functions, similar to (3) and the simplex hyperplane (4). The membership function of the fuzzy feasible area is given by

$$u_P(w) = \min_{ij}\{u_{ij}(w) \,|\, i = 1,2,...,n-1; j = 2,3,...,n; j > i\}. \qquad (5)$$

If the fuzzy judgements are very inconsistent, then $u_P(w)$ could take negative values for all normalized priority vectors $w \in Q^{n-1}$.

The second assumption of the FPP method specifies a selection rule, which determines a priority vector, having the highest degree of membership in the aggregated membership function (5). It can easily be proved that $u_P(w)$ is a convex set, so there is always a priority vector $w^* \in Q^{n-1}$ that has a maximum degree of membership

$$\lambda^* = u_P(w^*) = \max_{w \in Q^{n-1}} \min_{ij} \left\{ u_{ij}(w) \right\}. \tag{6}$$

The maximum prioritization problem (6) can be represented in the following way:

$$\text{Max}\,\lambda$$
$$\lambda \le u_{ij}(w), i = 1,2,\ldots,n-1; j = 2,3,\ldots,n; j > i,$$
$$\sum_{k=1}^{n} w_k = 1, w_k > 0, k = 1,2,\ldots,n. \tag{7}$$

Taking the specific form of the membership functions (3) into consideration, the problem (7) can be further transformed into a bilinear program of the type

$$\text{Max}\,\lambda$$
$$(m_{ij} - l_{ij})\lambda w_j - w_i + l_{ij}w_j \le 0,$$
$$(u_{ij} - m_{ij})\lambda w_j + w_i - u_{ij}w_j \le 0,$$
$$\sum_{k=1}^{n} w_k = 1, w_k > 0, k = 1,2,\ldots,n. \tag{8}$$
$$i = 1,2,\ldots,n-1; j = 2,3,\ldots,n; j > i.$$

The optimal solution to the non-linear problem above (w^*, λ^*) might be obtained by employing some appropriate numerical method for non-linear optimization. The optimal value λ^*, if it is positive (the maximum value is one), indicates that all solution ratios satisfy the fuzzy judgment completely, which means that the initial set of fuzzy judgments is rather consistent. A negative value of λ^* shows that the solutions ratios approximately satisfy all double-side inequalities (2). Therefore, the optimal value λ^* can be used for measuring the consistency of the initial set of fuzzy judgments.

3. Proposed project selection and evaluation framework

This study proposes an analytic approach based on the fuzzy ANP to assist in project selection and evaluation. We first identify the selection and evaluation criteria. Then we present the evaluation model in the following subsections.

3.1. Criteria of project selection

Some researchers investigated which factors have an effect on project selection. For example, Mohanty (1992) pointed out that a potential project should have four important features: minimum investment, low complex of technology, short period and high returns. Lin & Chen (2004) suggested that the contractors should consider the essence of bidding, competition, the value of tendering opportunities, resources, and corporate reputation.

Kumar (2006) pointed out that project selection belongs to the strategic level for any organizations, and today it is seriously influenced by environmental and social factors. Wang et al. (2009) suggested that during project selection, the evaluation index system can be divided into two parts: the bid/non-bid and which project to bid, then make a comprehensive evaluation, etc.

With the interaction and feedback relationships between dimensions and/or attribute-enablers being considered, a four-level evaluation index system is presented, as shown in Fig. 2. The first level is the objective, which is to find out an optimal project; the second level is the dimensions including project profitability, project risk, project owners and project bidding competition; the third level is attribute-enablers, 15 indicators included; and the lowest level is the alternatives.

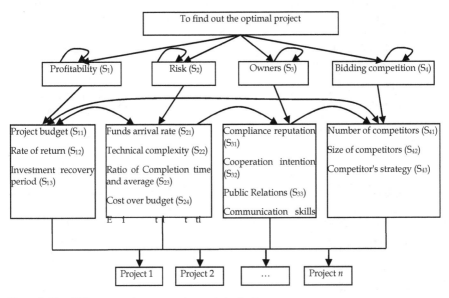

Figure 2. The ANP structure for construction project selection

Generally, if project profitability (S_1) has an effect on project bidding competition (S_4), then a line with arrow from S_4 to S_1 is added. If the sub-criteria of project risk (S_2) has interaction with itself, then S_2 is inner dependent, and an arc with arrow is added to S_2.

3.2. FANP-based approach

The fuzzy ANP-based approach is presented step-by-step as follows:

Step 1. Model construction and problem structuring. With the relationships among dimensions and attribute-enablers being considered, a four levels selection and evaluation index system is proposed, as shown in Fig. 2.

During the process of project selection and evaluation, experts tend to specify their preferences in the form of natural language expressions. The fuzzy linguistic variable, whose value represents the range from natural to artificial language, is a variable that reflects different aspects of human language. When the values or meanings of a linguistic factor are being reflected, the resulting variable must also reflect appropriate modes of change for that linguistic factor. Moreover, variables describing a human word or sentence can be divided into numerous linguistic criteria, such as equally important, moderately important, important, very important or absolutely important. For the purposes of the present study, a 9-point scale is presented for the relative importance of pairwise comparison, as shown in Table 1.

Step 2. Establishing pairwise comparison matrices by decision committee using the linguistic scales for relative importance given in Table 1. For example, complication of technique (S_{11}) and maturity of technique (S_{12}) are compared using the question "How important is the complication of technique when it is compared with the maturity of technique at the dimension of technique risk?" and the answer is "moderately important (MI)", so this linguistic scale is placed in the relevant cell against the triangular fuzzy numbers (2, 3, 4). All the fuzzy evaluation matrices are produced in the same manner.

Linguistic scale for importance	Triangular fuzzy scale	Triangular fuzzy reciprocal scale
Equally important(EI)	(1, 1, 1)	(1, 1, 1)
Intermediate1(IM₁)	(1, 2, 3)	(1/3, 1/2, 1)
Moderately important(MI)	(2, 3, 4)	(1/4, 1/3, 1/2)
Intermediate2(IM₂)	(3, 4, 5)	(1/5, 1/4, 1/3)
Important(I)	(4, 5, 6)	(1/6, 1/5, 1/4)
Intermediate3(IM₃)	(5, 6, 7)	(1/7, 1/6, 1/5)
Very important(VI)	(6, 7, 8)	(1/8, 1/7, 1/6)
Intermediate4(IM₄)	(7, 8, 9)	(1/9, 1/8, 1/7)
Absolutely important(AI)	(9, 9, 9)	(1/9, 1/9, 1/9)

Table 1. Linguistic scales for relative importance

Step 3. Calculating the local weights of the factors and sub-factors taking part in the second and third levels of the ANP model by FPP method according to formulation (8).

Step 4. Constructing an unweighted supermatrix based on the interdependencies in the network. The supermatrix is a partitioned matrix, in which each submatrix is composed of a set of relationships between dimensions and attribute-enablers in the graphical model.

Step 5. Acquiring the weighted supermatrix. Because in each column it consists of several eigenvectors which of them sums to one (in a column of a stochastic), and hence the entire column of the matrix may sum to an integer greater than one, the unweighted supermatrix needs to be stochastic to derive the weighted supermatrix.

Step 6. Obtaining the limit supermatrix. The weighted supermatrix will not be in a steady state until the row values of which converge to the same value for each column of the matrix, then the limit supermatrix is achieved.

$$\overline{W} = \lim_{t \to \infty} W^t. \tag{9}$$

Step 7. Calculating the comprehensive weights. A comprehensive weight of each index can be obtained by multiplying the weight of the criterion level indicator, the weight of independent sub-criterion and the weight of interdependent sub-index.

$$w_{ij} = P_i \times A_{ij}^D \times A_{ij}^I, \tag{10}$$

where w_{ij} is the comprehensive weight of each factor, P_i is relative importance weight of dimension i on final goal; A_{ij}^D, relative importance weight for attribute-enabler j of dimension i, and for the dependency (D) relationships within attribute-enabler's component level; A_{ij}^I, stabilized relative importance weight for attribute-enabler j of dimension i, and for the independency (I) relationships within attribute-enabler's component level; $i=1, 2, ..., m$; $j=1, 2, ..., n$.

Step 8. Selecting an optimal construction project. The equation of desirability index, D_k for alternative k is calculated using the following equation:

$$D_k = \sum_{i=1}^{m} \sum_{j=1}^{n} w_{ij} S_{kij} \tag{11}$$

where w_{ij} is the comprehensive weight; S_{ikj}, relative impact of construction project alternative k on attribute-enabler j of dimension i of selection network.

4. How to use Matlab during the process of decision-making with FANP?

Two key steps in the process of FANP will be solved by Matlab. One is acquiring local weights of fuzzy pairwise comparison matrices (step 3); the other is obtaining the limit supermatrix (step 6). Both of them are associated with matrix calculation. Matlab is selected for its excellent performance on matrix operation and data processing.

4.1. Acquiring local weights of fuzzy pairwise comparison matrices

$$\text{Max}\, \lambda$$
$$(m_{ij} - l_{ij})\lambda w_j - w_i + l_{ij} w_j \le 0,$$
$$(u_{ij} - m_{ij})\lambda w_j + w_i - u_{ij} w_j \le 0,$$
$$\sum_{k=1}^{n} w_k = 1, w_k > 0, k = 1, 2, ..., n.$$
$$i = 1, 2, ..., n-1; j = 2, 3, ..., n; j > i.$$

As mentioned before, the local weights of fuzzy pairwise comparison matrices are acheived by FPP method. That is, the local weights will be obtained by solving the non-linear problem above.

As criteria and sub-criteria have different numbers, there are different orders of fuzzy pairwise comparison matrices, such as matices of order (2×2), (3×3), ..., (n×n). Therefore, the local weights and consistency index may be derived from matrix of different orders. Function definition and non-linear program calculation will be first concerned in this section, then some examples will be given to illustrate the proposed method.

4.1.1. Function definition

To acquire the local weights of fuzzy comparison matrices, some functions need to be defined. A procedure can be saved as the format - ".m" file in Matlab. The name of which can be used directly when you need to call it.

To obtain the local weights, a main program file is developed, named as "networkmain.m". The local weights can be easily acquired by inputting "networkmain" in the command window. As there are different forms of comparison matrices, we need to change slightly the main program file for matrices of different orders.

Matlab contains a lot of functions to solve linear and non-linear problems. For instance, non-linear problems can be solved by function "fmincon", which is also the key function of the file "networkmain.m". The full expression of the function is "fmincon (fun, $x0$, A, b, Aeq, beq, VLB, VUB, nonlcon)". During the process of decision-making with FANP, in accordance with the FPP method, the fuzzy pairwise comparison matrices first need to be transformed into non-linear programming formats. Then it can be solved by the function "fmincon". The detail description of the function is as follows:

"Fun" is the objective function of a non-linear problem. A variable in the objective function is marked as $x(i)$. If the total number of variables is n, then they are correspondingly named as $x(1)$, $x(2)$, ..., $x(n)$. There are $(n+1)$ variables for a $(n \times n)$ comparison matrix, including n local weights and a consistency index λ. The objective function in FPP method is to acquire the maximum value, but the default standard objective function of "fmincon" in Matlab is to find the minimum value, so it is necessary to convert $x(n+1)$ into $-x(n+1)$ in the function "fmincon". Of course, it might be solved by changing the constraints instead of changing the objective function as well.

"$x0$" is the initial value of the non-linear problem, and it has the same scale as the number of variables. Every local weight $x(i)$ takes values in the range $[0, 1]$, and their sum satisfies $x(1)+x(2)+...+x(n)=1$. Consistency index $x(n+1)$ takes values in the range $(-\infty, 1]$.

"A and b" are the coefficients of linear inequality constraint $Ax<=b$. As there are no linear inequality constraints in FANP, a and b can be ignored or replaced with two empty arrays.

"Aeq and beq" are both the coefficients of linear equality constraint Aeq*x=beq. According to FANP, the sum of local weights should be one, then

$$x(1) + x(2) + \ldots + x(n) + 0x(n+1) = 1,$$

where $x(1)$, $x(2)$, ..., $x(n)$ are the first, second, ..., nth local weight respectively, and $x(n+1)$ is the consistency index. Then we have Aeq=[1 1 ... 1 0] and beq=[1].

"VLB and VUB" are the upper and lower bounds of the variables. According to the FPP method and FANP, all the local weights have a lower bound of zero, and the lower bound of consistency index is negative infinity. Since all the upper bounds are subject to the constraints, they can be replaced with empty arrays. In matlab, the postive and negative infinity symbols are named as inf and –inf respectively.

"nonlcon" is the non-linear constraints, including non-linear inequality constraint c and non-linear equality constraint ceq. As there is no non-linear equality constaint for FPP method, we can let ceq=[ ].

To solve the non-linear problem (8), the following main program file "networkmain.m" is developed.

```
Aeq=[1 1 ... 1 0];
beq=[1];
VLB = [0; 0;...; 0; -inf];
VUB = [ ];
x0 = [0.1; 0.2; ...; 1];
OPT = optimset('LargeScale', 'off');
[x, fval] = fmincon('networkf', x0, [ ], [ ],Aeq, beq, VLB, VUB, 'networknonlcon', OPT)
```

The LargeScale option specifies a preference for which algorithm to use. It is only a preference because certain conditions must be met to use the large-scale algorithm. For this function "fmincon", we choose the medium-scale algorithm. LargeScale use the medium-scale algorithm when set to 'off'. Two files, "networkf.m" and "networknonlcon.m", are called in the procedure above. They are defined for objective function and non-linear constraints independently.

The program of "networkf.m" is developed as follows:

```
function f =networkf(x);
f = -x(n+1);
```

where the value of function f is related to n. For example, for a matrix of order 3, $n=3$, $f=-x(4)$; for a matrix of order 4, $n=4$, $f=-x(5)$. Therefore, objective function f has different formats as a result of different sizes of matrices.

According to the FPP method, every triangular fuzzy number (l_{ij}, m_{ij}, u_{ij}) needs to be transformed into the following inequality constraints.

$$(m_{ij}-l_{ij})^*x(n+1)^*x(j) -x(i)+(l_{ij})^*x(j)\leq0;$$
$$(u_{ij}-m_{ij})^*x(n+1)^*x(j)+x(i)-(u_{ij})^*x(j) \leq0.$$

As we know, a triangular fuzzy comparison matrix is symmetric. Therefore, for the following matrix, we only need to consider the constraints above the diagonal.

$$
\begin{pmatrix}
(l_{11}, m_{11}, u_{11}) & (l_{12}, m_{12}, u_{12}) & \cdots & (l_{1n}, m_{1n}, u_{1n}) \\
(l_{21}, m_{21}, u_{21}) & (l_{22}, m_{22}, u_{22}) & \cdots & (l_{2n}, m_{2n}, u_{2n}) \\
\vdots & \vdots & \vdots & \vdots \\
(l_{n1}, m_{n1}, u_{n1}) & (l_{n2}, m_{n2}, u_{n2}) & \cdots & (l_{nn}, m_{nn}, u_{nn})
\end{pmatrix}
$$

For instance, for a 3-by-3 fuzzy comparison matrix, only three elments need to be taken into account, which is, (l_{12}, m_{12}, u_{12}), (l_{13}, m_{13}, u_{13}) and (l_{23}, m_{23}, u_{23}). Then, the corresponding "networknonlcon.m" file is given by

function [c, ceq] = networknonlcon3(x);

c = [
    $(m_{12}-l_{12})^{*}x(4)^{*}x(2)-x(1)+(l_{12})^{*}x(2)$;
    $(u_{12}-m_{12})^{*}x(4)^{*}x(2)+x(1)-(u_{12})^{*}x(2)$;
    $(m_{13}-l_{13})^{*}x(4)^{*}x(3)-x(1)+(l_{13})^{*}x(3)$;
    $(u_{13}-m_{13})^{*}x(4)^{*}x(3)+x(1)-(u_{13})^{*}x(3)$;
    $(m_{23}-l_{23})^{*}x(4)^{*}x(3)-x(2)+(l_{23})^{*}x(3)$;
    $(u_{23}-m_{23})^{*}x(4)^{*}x(3)+x(2)-(u_{23})^{*}x(3)$;
    ];
ceq = [ ];

The programs for (4×4), (5×5), ..., ($n \times n$) matrices can be developed in the same manner. Several examples for acquiring the local weights are given as follows.

4.1.2. Local weights of a fuzzy pairwise comparison matrix of order 3

Example 1. How to solve the local weights of the following fuzzy pairwise comparison matrix of order 3?

$$
\begin{pmatrix}
(1,1,1) & (1/6, 1/5, 1/4) & (1/4, 1/3, 1/2) \\
(4,5,6) & (1,1,1) & (2,3,4) \\
(2,3,4) & (1/4, 1/3, 1/2) & (1,1,1)
\end{pmatrix}
$$

First, the initial parameter of the main function "networkmain" needs to be set for this (3×3) matrix, which has three local weights, named as $x(1)$, $x(2)$ and $x(3)$, and a consistency index, referred to as $x(4)$. That means there are four variables in linear equality constraint. The corresponding "networkmain.m" file is as follows:

Aeq=[1 1 1 0];
beq=[1];
VLB = [0; 0; 0; -inf];
VUB = [ ];
x0 = [0.2; 0.5; 0.3; 1];
OPT = optimset('LargeScale', 'off');
[x, fval] = fmincon('networkf', x0, [ ], [ ],Aeq, beq, VLB, VUB, 'networknonlcon3', OPT)

As it mentioned before, the opposite number of consistency index in the function "network" is taken. The corresponding objective function file "networkf.m" is as follows:

function f = networkf(x);
f = -x(4);

Since the triangular fuzzy comparison matrix is symmetric, only three constraints above the diagonal need to be considered, that is (1/6, 1/5, 1/4), (1/4, 1/3, 1/2) and (2, 3, 4). The "networknonlcon3.m" file for this matrix is as follows:

function [c,ceq] = networknonlcon3(x);

c = [
    (1/5-1/6)*x(4)*x(2)-x(1)+(1/6)*x(2);
    (1/4-1/5)*x(4)*x(2)+x(1)-(1/4)*x(2);
    (1/3-1/4)*x(4)*x(3)-x(1)+(1/4)*x(3);
    (1/2-1/3)*x(4)*x(3)+x(1)-(1/2)*x(3);
    (3-2)*x(4)*x(3)-x(2)+(2)*x(3);
    (4-3)*x(4)*x(3)+x(2)-(4)*x(3);
    ];
ceq = [ ];

```
>> networkmain
Optimization terminated: first-order optimality measure less
  than options.TolFun and maximum constraint violation is less
  than options.TolCon.
Active inequalities (to within options.TolCon = 1e-006):
  lower      upper      ineqlin     ineqnonlin
                                        1
                                        4
                                        5


  x =

        0.1128
        0.6265
        0.2607
        0.4031


  fval =

        -0.4031
```

Figure 3. The local weights and consistency index of Example 1

In Fig. 3, x is the optimal solution and fval is the optimal value. The first three values of x are the local weights of the matrix, and the last one is the consistency index.

The final step, is to run "networkmain" in the command window to acquire the local weights. The local weights $x(1)$, $x(2)$, $x(3)$ are 0.1128, 0.6265, 0.2607 respectively, as shown in Figure 3. The consistency index $x(4)$ is 0.4031>0, which means the fuzzy comparison matrix has a good consistency, and the results are acceptable.

4.1.3. Local weights of a fuzzy pairwise comparison matrix of order 4

Example 2. How to solve the local weights of the following fuzzy pairwise comparison matrix of order 4?

$$\begin{pmatrix} (1,1,1) & (3/2,2,5/2) & (1,3/2,2) & (5/2,3,7/2) \\ (2/5,1/2,2/3) & (1,1,1) & (2/3,1,2) & (3/2,2,5/2) \\ (1/2,2/3,1) & (1/2,1,3/2) & (1,1,1) & (2,5/2,3) \\ (2/7,1/3,2/5) & (2/5,1/2,2/3) & (1/3,2/5,1/2) & (1,1,1) \end{pmatrix}$$

The calculation process for a matrix of order 4 is similar to that of a matrix of order 3. A matrix of order 4 has four local weights, named as $x(1)$, $x(2)$, $x(3)$ and $x(4)$, and a consistency index, referred as $x(5)$. The following program is the corresponding "networkmain.m" file for this matrix.

```
Aeq=[1 1 1 1 0];
beq=[1];
VLB = [0; 0; 0; 0; -inf];
VUB = [ ];
x0 = [0.1; 0.4; 0.2; 0.3; -1];
OPT = optimset('LargeScale', 'off');
[x, fval] = fmincon('networkf', x0, [ ], [ ],Aeq, beq, VLB, VUB, 'networknonlcon4', OPT)
```

The corresponding objective function file for this matrix is as follows:

```
function f = networkf(x);
f = -x(5);
```

Six constraints for this fuzzy pairwise comparison matrix need to be calculated, that is, (3/2, 2, 5/2), (1, 3/2, 2), (5/2, 3, 7/2), (2/3, 1, 2), (3/2, 2, 5/2) and (2, 5/2, 3). The "networknonlcon4.m" file for this matrix of order 4 is as follows:

```
function [c, ceq] = networknonlcon4(x);
c = [
    (2-3/2)*x(5)*x(2) - x(1) + (3/2)*x(2);
    (5/2 - 2)*x(5)*x(2) + x(1) - (5/2)*x(2);
    (3/2-1)*x(5)*x(3) - x(1) + (1)*x(3);
```

```
(2 - 3/2)*x(5)*x(3) + x(1) - (2)*x(3);
(3-5/2)*x(5)*x(4) - x(1) + (5/2)*x(4);
(7/2-3)*x(5)*x(4) + x(1) - (7/2)*x(4);
(1-2/3)*x(5)*x(3) - x(2) + (2/3)*x(3);
(2-1)*x(5)*x(3) + x(2) - (2)*x(3);
(2-3/2)*x(5)*x(4) - x(2) + (3/2)*x(4);
(5/2-2)*x(5)*x(4) + x(2) - (5/2)*x(4);
(5/2 - 2)*x(5)*x(4) - x(3) + (2)*x(4);
(3 - 5/2 )*x(5)*x(4) + x(3) - (3)*x(4);
];
ceq = [ ];
```

Finally, "networkmain" is run in the command panel to obtain the local weights. The optimal solutions are $x(1)=0.3891$, $x(2)=0.2229$, $x(3)=0.2685$, $x(4)=0.1196$, $x(5)=0.4910$, as shown in Figure 4. The consistency index $x(5)$ is $0.4910>0$, which means the fuzzy comparison matrix has a good consistency, and the results are acceptable.

```
>> networkmain
Optimization terminated: first-order optimality measure less than options.TolFun
 and maximum constraint violation is less than options.TolCon.
Active inequalities (to within options.TolCon = 1e-006):
   lower      upper      ineqlin    ineqnonlin
                                       1
                                       6
                                       7
                                      11

x =

    0.3891
    0.2229
    0.2685
    0.1196
    0.4910

fval =

   -0.4910
```

Figure 4. The local weights and consistency index of Example 2

where x is the optimal solution and fval is the optimal value. The first four values of x are the local weights of the matrix, and the last one is the consistency index.

4.1.4. Local weights of a fuzzy pairwise comparison matrix of order n

Example 3. How to solve the local weights of the following fuzzy pairwise comparison matrix of order n?

$$\begin{pmatrix} (l_{11},m_{11},u_{11}) & (l_{12},m_{12},u_{12}) & \cdots & (l_{1n},m_{1n},u_{1n}) \\ (l_{21},m_{21},u_{21}) & (l_{22},m_{22},u_{22}) & \cdots & (l_{2n},m_{2n},u_{2n}) \\ & & \vdots & \\ (l_{n1},m_{n1},u_{n1}) & (l_{n2},m_{n2},u_{n2}) & \cdots & (l_{nn},m_{nn},u_{nn}) \end{pmatrix}$$

A ($n\times n$) matrix has ($n+1$) variables, including n local weights and one consistency index, named as $x(1)$, $x(2)$, ..., $x(n+1)$. Linear equality constraint is as follows:

$$x(1) + x(2) + \ldots + x(n) + 0^*x(n+1) = 1$$

Then, Aeq = [1 1 ... 1 0], beq = [1].

The lower bounds of the local weights are zero, and the lower bound of consistency index is negative infinity. There is no specific upper bound. Then we have

$$VLB = [0; 0;\ldots; 0; -inf]; VUB = [\ ].$$

The initial values of the variables can be arbitrary in the range of feasible region. If different initial values lead to different results, it means the nonlinear problem has multiple optimal solutions. Then, we have

$x0 = [1; 1; \ldots; 1]$,
[x, fval] = fmincon('networkf', x0, [ ], [ ],Aeq, beq, VLB, VUB, 'networknonlcon').

The corresponding objective function file networkf.m is as follows:

```
function f = networkf(x);
f = -x(n+1);
```

For the non-linear constraints, only those elements above the diagonal need to be considered. That is, these triangular fuzzy numbers (l_{ij}, m_{ij}, u_{ij}) need to be taken into account, $i<j$; i=1, 2, ..., n; j= 2, 3,..., n.

The "networknonlcon$n$.m" file in this case is as follows:

```
function [c,ceq] = networknonlconn(x);
c = [
    (m12-l12)*x(n+1)*x(2)-x(1)+(l12)*x(2);
    (u12-m12)*x(n+1)*x(2)+x(1)-(u12)*x(2);
    (m13-l13)*x(n+1)*x(3)-x(1)+(l13)*x(3);
    (u13-m13)*x(n+1)*x(3)+x(1)-(u13)*x(3);
        ...
    (m1n-l1n)*x(n+1)*x(n)-x(1)+(l1n)*x(n);
```

$(u_{1n}-m_{1n})^*x(n+1)^*x(n)+x(1)-(u_{1n})^*x(n);$
$(m_{23}-l_{23})^*x(n+1)^*x(3)-x(2)+(l_{23})^*x(3);$
$(u_{23}-m_{23})^*x(n+1)^*x(3)+x(2)-(u_{23})^*x(3);$
...
$(m_{(n-1)n}-l_{(n-1)n})^*x(n+1)^*x(n)-x(n-1)+(l_{(n-1)n})^*x(n);$
$(u_{(n-1)n}-m_{(n-1)n})^*x(n+1)^*x(n)+x(n-1)-(u_{(n-1)n})^*x(n);$
];
ceq = [ ];

Finally, we run "networkmain" in the command panel to obtain the local weights. If the consistency index is positive, the fuzzy comparison matrix has a good consistency and the results are acceptable. Otherwise, we need to modify the fuzzy pairwise comparison matrix until it is satisfied with consistency requirement.

4.2. Obtaining limit supermatrix

A limit supermatrix is a weighted supermatrix in a stable state. The weighted supermatrix may be convergent or not. If it is convergent, the limit supermatrix can be achieved. Unfortunately, it is usually not convergent, and then a periodic result is obtained. Under this condition, the limit supermatrix will be achieved only after the periodicity of the supermatrix is determined.

4.2.1. The program for acquiring stable limit supermatrix

To obtain a limit supermatrix, four functions named as "fanp_limitedsupermatrix.m", "fanp_multiMatrix.m", "fanp_circulantCheck.m" and "fanp_equal.m" are developed. The first file is the main program by which limit supermatrix can be solved; supermatrix multiplication is implemented by the second file; the third file is used to determine whether a supermatrix is stable or periodic; and the last one is used to test whether a supermatrix after iterations is the same as it was before or not. The second and third files will be called in the main procedure, and the last one will be used in the third program. File "fanp_limitedsupermatrix.m" is given as follows:

```
function B = fanp_limitedsupermatrix( );
weightedsupermatrix = [0.00000,0.00000,0.00000,0.63400,0.25000,0.40000;
         0.00000,0.00000,0.00000,0.19200,0.25000,0.20000;
         0.00000,0.00000,0.00000,0.17400,0.50000,0.40000;
         0.63700,0.58200,0.13600,0.00000,0.00000,0.00000;
         0.10500,0.10900,0.65400,0.00000,0.00000,0.00000;
         0.25800,0.30900,0.21000,0.00000,0.00000,0.00000];
newMatrix = fanp_multiMatrix(weightedsupermatrix,weightedsupermatrix);
matrixRecord = weightedsupermatrix;
times = 1;
matrixRecord(:, :, 2) = newMatrix;
circulantCheckResult = fanp_circulantCheck(matrixRecord, newMatrix)
while circulantCheckResult(1) == 0
```

```
times = times + 1;
   disp(times)
   newMatrix = fanp_multiMatrix(newMatrix,weightedsupermatrix);
   matrixRecord(:, :, times+1) = newMatrix;
   circulantCheckResult = fanp_circulantCheck(matrixRecord, newMatrix);
end
disp('total multied :')
disp(times)
disp('times')
```

where the "weighted supermatrix" can be arbitrary, which is derived from an unweighted supermatrix. It needs to use a semicolon to separate each row of the supermatrix. "newMatrix" is the new matrix after an iteration. The variable "time" is to keep count of iterations. Variable "matrixRecord" is a three-dimensional variable used to record the output of each iteration.

After each iteration, "matrixRecord" is called to check whether the "newMatrix" is stable or periodic. Whenever the "newMatrix" reaches a stable or periodic state, the program terminates. Otherwise, the program will keep on iterating. Finally, the total number of iterations will be displayed.

The program for a matrix or supermatrix multiplication is as follows:

```
function array3 = fanp_multiMatrix(array1, array2)
   n = size(array1);
   for i = 1: n
     for j = 1: n
       sum = 0;
       for m = 1: n
         sum = sum + array1(i, m)*array2(m, j);
       end
       array3(i, j) = sum;
     end
   end
```

where the parameters "array1" and "array2" are the results of current iteration, and the return value "array3" records the result of a new iteration.

The following function "fanp_circulantCheck" is for determining whether the new supermatrix is stable or periodic. Function "fanp_equal" will be called in this procedure.

```
function [circulantFlag,rLength,limitedMatrix,cycles] = fanp_circulantCheck(matrixRecord,
newMatrix);
circulantFlag = 0;
limitedMatrix = [ ];
   cycles = 1;
a = size(matrixRecord);
```

```
rLength = a(3);
for i = rLength-1 : -1 : 1
  if fanp_equal(matrixRecord(:, :, i),newMatrix) == 1
    disp('cycle started...')
    circulantFlag = 1;
    limitedMatrix = matrixRecord(:,:,i);
    for j = i + 1 : rLength - 1
      limitedMatrix = limitedMatrix + matrixRecord(:, :, j);
      cycles = cycles + 1;
    end
    limitedMatrix = limitedMatrix / cycles;
    disp('stable matrix  : ')
    limitedMatrix
    disp('cycle : ')
    cycles
    disp('cycle start times : ')
    i
    return
  end
end
```

In the program above, "matrixRecord" and "newMatrix" are the input parameters, and "circulantFlag" is the output and the sign of a cycle. If the supermatrix has a cycle, "1" is returned. The limit supermatrix, cycles and iterative times of the cycle starting will be displayed.

Comparisons will be made between the iterative output and the existing results one by one. If any two of them are equal, then the cycle of the supermatrix occurs. In this case, the final limit supermatrix is acquired by dividing the summation of all the supermatrices in the cycle by the value of period. For a supermatrix without a cycle, we can assume that its period is one. Therefore, whatever the results of the comparison, we can use the procedure above to obtain the ultimate limit supermatrix.

The following function "fanp_equal" is used to test whether the new supermatrix is the same as the former one or not.

```
function equalFlag = fanp_equal(array1,array2)
  n = size(array1);
  for i=1: n
    for j=1: n
      if array1(i, j) ~= array2(i, j)
        disp('the two matrix are not equal')
        equalFlag = 0;
        return
      end
    end
```

end
disp('the two matrix are equal')
equalFlag = 1;
return

where elements of "array1" and "array2" will be compared one by one. If they are equal, return 1; otherwise, return 0.

4.2.2. Acquiring the limit supermatrix from a supermatrix without a cycle

Example 4. Acquiring the limit supermatrix from the following weighted supermatrix.

$$
\begin{pmatrix}
0.0000 & 0.2000 & 0.0000 & 0.0000 \\
0.2000 & 0.0000 & 0.5000 & 0.0000 \\
0.4000 & 0.4000 & 0.0000 & 1.0000 \\
0.4000 & 0.4000 & 0.0000 & 0.0000
\end{pmatrix}
$$

As mentioned before, the weighted supermatrix can be specified in the function "fanp_limitedsupermatrix". The result obtained by running it in the command window, as shown in Fig. 5.

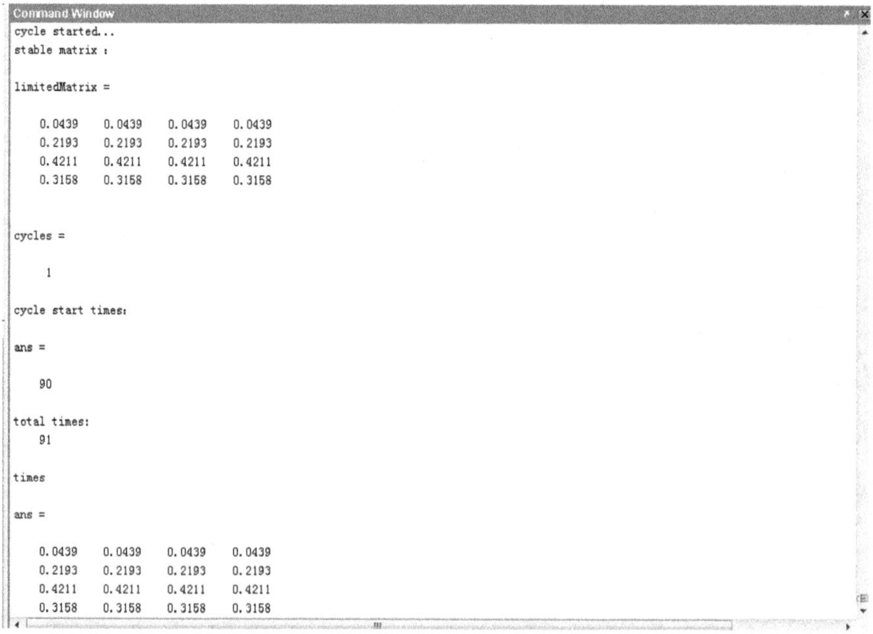

Figure 5. The operation result of Example 4

According to the result, the limit supermatrix is

$$\begin{pmatrix} 0.0439 & 0.0439 & 0.0439 & 0.0439 \\ 0.2193 & 0.2193 & 0.2193 & 0.2193 \\ 0.4211 & 0.4211 & 0.4211 & 0.4211 \\ 0.3158 & 0.3158 & 0.3158 & 0.3158 \end{pmatrix}.$$

where "cycles" is 1 means the limit supermatrix is not periodic, and "cycle start times" is 90 means the cycle appears at the ninetieth iteration. The total number of iterations is 91. The limit supermatrix is obtained at the end of ninetieth iteration though the program was implemented one more time. The local weights are (0.0439, 0.2193, 0.4211, 0.3158) for this supermatrix.

4.2.3. Acquiring the limit supermatrix from a supermatrix with a cycle

Example 5. Acquiring the limit supermatrix from the following supermatrix

0.000	0.250	0.266	0.086	0.269	0.100	0.250	0.269	0.000	0.000	0.000	0.000	0.133	0.133	0.083
0.083	0.000	0.067	0.268	0.085	0.200	0.125	0.085	0.000	0.000	0.000	0.000	0.133	0.133	0.167
0.250	0.083	0.000	0.146	0.146	0.200	0.125	0.146	0.000	0.000	0.000	0.000	0.067	0.067	0.083
0.123	0.106	0.104	0.000	0.263	0.132	0.230	0.206	0.290	0.315	0.298	0.250	0.000	0.000	0.000
0.052	0.039	0.033	0.233	0.000	0.084	0.128	0.115	0.032	0.035	0.033	0.028	0.000	0.000	0.000
0.052	0.058	0.104	0.087	0.093	0.000	0.071	0.115	0.065	0.057	0.081	0.120	0.000	0.000	0.000
0.075	0.106	0.059	0.127	0.093	0.230	0.000	0.064	0.081	0.057	0.055	0.074	0.000	0.000	0.000
0.032	0.024	0.033	0.053	0.051	0.054	0.071	0.000	0.032	0.035	0.033	0.028	0.000	0.000	0.000
0.000	0.000	0.000	0.000	0.000	0.000	0.000	0.000	0.000	0.288	0.116	0.086	0.043	0.088	0.058
0.000	0.000	0.000	0.000	0.000	0.000	0.000	0.000	0.286	0.000	0.321	0.268	0.150	0.154	0.156
0.000	0.000	0.000	0.000	0.000	0.000	0.000	0.000	0.143	0.157	0.000	0.146	0.097	0.056	0.084
0.000	0.000	0.000	0.000	0.000	0.000	0.000	0.000	0.071	0.056	0.063	0.000	0.043	0.036	0.036
0.177	0.102	0.102	0.000	0.000	0.000	0.000	0.000	0.000	0.000	0.000	0.000	0.000	0.083	0.111
0.100	0.056	0.176	0.000	0.000	0.000	0.000	0.000	0.000	0.000	0.000	0.000	0.111	0.000	0.222
0.056	0.176	0.056	0.000	0.000	0.000	0.000	0.000	0.000	0.000	0.000	0.000	0.223	0.250	0.000

```
Command Window                                                                    ⫶ ×

cycle started...
stable matrix :

limitedMatrix =

   0.1372   0.1372   0.1372   0.1372   0.1372   0.1372   0.1372   0.1372   0.1372   0.1372   0.1372   0.1372   0.1372   0.1372   0.1372
   0.1064   0.1064   0.1064   0.1064   0.1064   0.1064   0.1064   0.1064   0.1064   0.1064   0.1064   0.1064   0.1064   0.1064   0.1064
   0.1091   0.1091   0.1091   0.1091   0.1091   0.1091   0.1091   0.1091   0.1091   0.1091   0.1091   0.1091   0.1091   0.1091   0.1091
   0.1231   0.1231   0.1231   0.1231   0.1231   0.1231   0.1231   0.1231   0.1231   0.1231   0.1231   0.1231   0.1231   0.1231   0.1231
   0.0655   0.0655   0.0655   0.0655   0.0655   0.0655   0.0655   0.0655   0.0655   0.0655   0.0655   0.0655   0.0655   0.0655   0.0655
   0.0588   0.0588   0.0588   0.0588   0.0588   0.0588   0.0588   0.0588   0.0588   0.0588   0.0588   0.0588   0.0588   0.0588   0.0588
   0.0729   0.0729   0.0729   0.0729   0.0729   0.0729   0.0729   0.0729   0.0729   0.0729   0.0729   0.0729   0.0729   0.0729   0.0729
   0.0327   0.0327   0.0327   0.0327   0.0327   0.0327   0.0327   0.0327   0.0327   0.0327   0.0327   0.0327   0.0327   0.0327   0.0327
   0.0478   0.0478   0.0478   0.0478   0.0478   0.0478   0.0478   0.0478   0.0478   0.0478   0.0478   0.0478   0.0478   0.0478   0.0478
   0.0276   0.0276   0.0276   0.0276   0.0276   0.0276   0.0276   0.0276   0.0276   0.0276   0.0276   0.0276   0.0276   0.0276   0.0276
   0.0132   0.0132   0.0132   0.0132   0.0132   0.0132   0.0132   0.0132   0.0132   0.0132   0.0132   0.0132   0.0132   0.0132   0.0132
   0.0578   0.0578   0.0578   0.0578   0.0578   0.0578   0.0578   0.0578   0.0578   0.0578   0.0578   0.0578   0.0578   0.0578   0.0578
   0.0586   0.0586   0.0586   0.0586   0.0586   0.0586   0.0586   0.0586   0.0586   0.0586   0.0586   0.0586   0.0586   0.0586   0.0586
   0.0601   0.0601   0.0601   0.0601   0.0601   0.0601   0.0601   0.0601   0.0601   0.0601   0.0601   0.0601   0.0601   0.0601   0.0601

cycles =

   2

cycle start times:

ans =

   72
```

Figure 6. The operation result of Example 5

Specify the weighted supermatrix in the function "fanp_limitedsupermatrix" and run the program in the command window, the result is shown in Fig. 6. Where "cycles" is 2 means the limit supermatrix is periodic, and the period is 2. "cycle start times" is 72 means the cycle appears since the 72nd iteration, and the limit supermatrix is obtained at the end of the 73rd iteration. According to the FPP method, the local weights are (0.1372, 0.1064, 0.1091, 0.1231, 0.0655, 0.0588, 0.0729, 0.0327, 0.0292, 0.0478, 0.0276, 0.0132, 0.0578, 0.0586, 0.0601). This example is actually the weighted supermatrix of the following case in section 5, and the result is the limit supermatrix of the case.

5. Case study

Supposing that a company has the opportunity to select an optimal project from a number of alternatives. Through pre-test, three projects, named as D_1, D_2 and D_3, need further evaluation. A cross-functional project team consists of various departments working to select the best project. Firstly the selection criteria are identified. Then according to the FANP method, the optimal alternative is derived. The decision-making process of choosing an optimal project based on FANP is as follows:

Step 1. Model construction and problem structuring. Taking the interaction among dimensions and attribute-enablers into account, a four-level evaluation index system is proposed, as shown in Fig. 2.

Step 2. Pairwise comparison matrices among dimensions/attributes are formed by the decision committee using the scales given in Table 1, and the scores of the three projects are determined as well. For instance, Table 2. is the pairwise comparison matrix for the profitability (S_1), risk (S_2), owners (S_3) and Bidding competition (S_4) at the dimension of choosing an optimal project. All the fuzzy comparison matrices are produced in the same way.

optimal project	S_1	S_2	S_3	S_4
S_1	EI	$1/IM_2$	$1/MI$	$1/IM_1$
S_2	IM_2	EI	IM_1	IM_1
S_3	MI	$1/IM_1$	EI	$1/IM_1$
S_4	IM_1	$1/ IM_1$	IM_1	EI

Table 2. The comparison matrix using linguisitc scales at the dimension of optimal project

Expert opinions will be converted into the corresponding triangular fuzzy numbers, as shown in Table 3.

optimal project	S_1	S_2	S_3	S_4	Local weights
S_1	(1, 1, 1)	(1/5, 1/4, 1/3)	(1/4, 1/3, 1/2)	(1/3, 1/2, 1)	0.0989
S_2	(3, 4, 5)	(1, 1, 1)	(1, 2, 3)	(1, 2, 3)	0.4240
S_3	(2, 3, 4)	(1/3, 1/2, 1)	(1, 1, 1)	(1/3, 1/2, 1)	0.2544
S_4	(1, 2, 3)	(1/3, 1/2, 1)	(1, 2, 3)	(1, 1, 1)	0.2226
λ=0.6667					

Table 3. The comparison matrix using TFNs at the dimension of optimal project

Step 3. Local weights of the factors and sub-factors which take part in the second and third levels of the ANP model, provided in Fig. 2, are calculated by FPP method. For example, according to equation (8), the local weights of Table 3 can be achieved by solving the following non-linear programming.

$$\text{Max}\,\lambda$$

$$(1/20)\lambda w_2 - w_1 + (1/5)w_2 \le 0;$$
$$(1/12)\lambda w_2 + w_1 - (1/3)w_2 \le 0;$$
$$(1/12)\lambda w_3 - w_1 + (1/4)w_3 \le 0;$$
$$(1/6)\lambda w_3 + w_1 - (1/2)w_3 \le 0;$$
$$(1/6)\lambda w_4 - w_1 + (1/3)w_4 \le 0;$$
$$(1/2)\lambda w_4 + w_1 - w_4 \le 0;$$
$$\lambda w_3 - w_2 + w_3 \le 0;$$
$$\lambda w_3 + w_2 - 3w_3 \le 0;$$
$$\lambda w_4 - w_2 + w_4 \le 0;$$
$$\lambda w_4 + w_2 - 3w_4 \le 0;$$
$$(1/6)\lambda w_4 - w_3 + (1/3)w_4 \le 0;$$
$$(1/2)\lambda w_4 + w_3 - w_4 \le 0;$$
$$w_1 + w_2 + w_3 + w_4 = 1;$$
$$w_1, w_2, w_3, w_4{}^3 \ge 0.$$

	S_{11}	S_{12}	S_{13}	S_{21}	S_{22}	S_{23}	S_{24}	S_{25}	S_{31}	S_{32}	S_{33}	S_{34}	S_{41}	S_{42}	S_{43}
S_{11}	0.000	0.750	0.800	0.171	0.538	0.200	0.500	0.538	0.000	0.000	0.000	0.000	0.400	0.400	0.250
S_{12}	0.250	0.000	0.200	0.536	0.170	0.400	0.250	0.170	0.000	0.000	0.000	0.000	0.400	0.400	0.500
S_{13}	0.750	0.250	0.000	0.293	0.293	0.400	0.250	0.293	0.000	0.000	0.000	0.000	0.200	0.200	0.250
S_{21}	0.368	0.318	0.313	0.000	0.526	0.263	0.458	0.412	0.581	0.631	0.595	0.500	0.000	0.000	0.000
S_{22}	0.155	0.118	0.099	0.467	0.000	0.169	0.256	0.230	0.065	0.070	0.066	0.056	0.000	0.000	0.000
S_{23}	0.155	0.173	0.313	0.174	0.186	0.000	0.143	0.230	0.129	0.115	0.162	0.241	0.000	0.000	0.000
S_{24}	0.226	0.318	0.176	0.253	0.186	0.460	0.000	0.128	0.161	0.115	0.110	0.148	0.000	0.000	0.000
S_{25}	0.095	0.073	0.099	0.107	0.102	0.108	0.143	0.000	0.065	0.070	0.066	0.056	0.000	0.000	0.000
S_{31}	0.000	0.000	0.000	0.000	0.000	0.000	0.000	0.000	0.000	0.575	0.231	0.171	0.130	0.263	0.174
S_{32}	0.000	0.000	0.000	0.000	0.000	0.000	0.000	0.000	0.571	0.000	0.644	0.536	0.450	0.460	0.467
S_{33}	0.000	0.000	0.000	0.000	0.000	0.000	0.000	0.000	0.286	0.314	0.000	0.293	0.290	0.169	0.253
S_{34}	0.000	0.000	0.000	0.000	0.000	0.000	0.000	0.000	0.143	0.111	0.125	0.000	0.130	0.108	0.107
S_{41}	0.535	0.307	0.306	0.000	0.000	0.000	0.000	0.000	0.000	0.000	0.000	0.000	0.000	0.250	0.333
S_{42}	0.299	0.168	0.527	0.000	0.000	0.000	0.000	0.000	0.000	0.000	0.000	0.000	0.333	0.000	0.667
S_{43}	0.167	0.525	0.167	0.000	0.000	0.000	0.000	0.000	0.000	0.000	0.000	0.000	0.667	0.750	0.000

Table 4. The unweighted supermatrix

As mentioned before, the non-linear programming can be solved by Matlab. The optimal solutions are w_1=0.0989, w_2=0.4240, w_3=0.2544, w_4=0.2226, and λ=0.6667, which shows the experts' opinions are of good consistency, and the comparison result is acceptable, as shown in Table 3. All the local weights are acquired in the same manner.

Step 4. According to the interdependencies among dimensions and attribute-enablers, an unweighted supermatrix is built, as shown in Table 4.

Step 5. Randomize the unweighted supermatrix to derive the weighted supermatrix.

Step 6. Multiply the weighted supermatrix by itself until the values of each row converge to the same value for every column of the supermatrix. Then we choose any column from the stable limit supermatrix as the local weights of interdependency indicators, as shown in Table 5. It can be solved by Matlab, and the process of calculation is the same as Example 5 in the former section.

	S_{11}	S_{12}	S_{13}	S_{21}	S_{22}	S_{23}	S_{24}	S_{25}	S_{31}	S_{32}	S_{33}	S_{34}	S_{41}	S_{42}	S_{43}
S_{11}	0.137	0.137	0.137	0.137	0.137	0.137	0.137	0.137	0.137	0.137	0.137	0.137	0.137	0.137	0.137
S_{12}	0.106	0.106	0.106	0.106	0.106	0.106	0.106	0.106	0.106	0.106	0.106	0.106	0.106	0.106	0.106
S_{13}	0.109	0.109	0.109	0.109	0.109	0.109	0.109	0.109	0.109	0.109	0.109	0.109	0.109	0.109	0.109
S_{21}	0.123	0.123	0.123	0.123	0.123	0.123	0.123	0.123	0.123	0.123	0.123	0.123	0.123	0.123	0.123
S_{22}	0.066	0.066	0.066	0.066	0.066	0.066	0.066	0.066	0.066	0.066	0.066	0.066	0.066	0.066	0.066
S_{23}	0.059	0.059	0.059	0.059	0.059	0.059	0.059	0.059	0.059	0.059	0.059	0.059	0.059	0.059	0.059
S_{24}	0.073	0.073	0.073	0.073	0.073	0.073	0.073	0.073	0.073	0.073	0.073	0.073	0.073	0.073	0.073
S_{25}	0.033	0.033	0.033	0.033	0.033	0.033	0.033	0.033	0.033	0.033	0.033	0.033	0.033	0.033	0.033
S_{31}	0.029	0.029	0.029	0.029	0.029	0.029	0.029	0.029	0.029	0.029	0.029	0.029	0.029	0.029	0.029
S_{32}	0.048	0.048	0.048	0.048	0.048	0.048	0.048	0.048	0.048	0.048	0.048	0.048	0.048	0.048	0.048
S_{33}	0.028	0.028	0.028	0.028	0.028	0.028	0.028	0.028	0.028	0.028	0.028	0.028	0.028	0.028	0.028
S_{34}	0.013	0.013	0.013	0.013	0.013	0.013	0.013	0.013	0.013	0.013	0.013	0.013	0.013	0.013	0.013
S_{41}	0.058	0.058	0.058	0.058	0.058	0.058	0.058	0.058	0.058	0.058	0.058	0.058	0.058	0.058	0.058
S_{42}	0.059	0.059	0.059	0.059	0.059	0.059	0.059	0.059	0.059	0.059	0.059	0.059	0.059	0.059	0.059
S_{43}	0.060	0.060	0.060	0.060	0.060	0.060	0.060	0.060	0.060	0.060	0.060	0.060	0.060	0.060	0.060

Table 5. The limit supermatrix

Step 7. Calculate the comprehensive weights of each index, as shown in Table 6.

Step 8. According to equation (11), the scores of each alternative can be calculated, D_1=0.31, D_1=0.33, D_3=0.36, as shown in Table 6. Therefore, we can choose project D_3 as the best one.

6. Conclusions

Taking the interaction and feedback relationships between criteria and/or indicators into account, an evaluation index system for selecting a construction project is proposed. With the uncertain and inaccurate information during the evaluation process being considered, an evaluation and selection model based on fuzzy analytic network process method is presented. The weights of the indices, including the weights of the criterion level indicators, the weights of independent sub-indices and the weights of dependent sub-indices are determined by the fuzzy preference programming method. Meanwhile, an unweighted supermatrix based on its network structure is built for interactional indicators, and the convergent limit supermatrix is calculated after randomizing the unweighted supermatrix. Accordingly, the comprehensive weight of each index and the final score of each alternative can be calculated. Then we can choose the optimal alternative. A numerical example is given by the proposed method as well.

Two key steps in the process of decision-making with FANP are solved by Matlab. One is acquiring local weights of the fuzzy pairwise comparison matrices; the other is obtaining the limit supermatrix. Matlab is selected for its excellent performance on data processing and matrix operation. Compared with the existing research results, the proposed method fully takes into consideration the interaction and feedback relationships between the dimensions and/or attributes, and it uses triangular fuzzy numbers to represent the preference opinions of experts. It helps to make a more accurate and scientific decision.

index	P_j	A_{ij}^{I}	A_{ij}^{D}	w	w'	S_{1ij}	S_{2ij}	S_{3ij}	d_1	d_2	d_3
S_{11}	0.099	0.538	0.137	0.007	0.104	0.381	0.333	0.286	0.039	0.035	0.030
S_{12}	0.099	0.170	0.106	0.002	0.025	0.300	0.300	0.400	0.008	0.008	0.010
S_{13}	0.099	0.293	0.109	0.003	0.045	0.263	0.368	0.368	0.012	0.017	0.017
S_{21}	0.424	0.361	0.123	0.019	0.268	0.286	0.333	0.381	0.076	0.089	0.102
S_{22}	0.424	0.243	0.066	0.007	0.096	0.267	0.400	0.333	0.026	0.038	0.032
S_{23}	0.424	0.147	0.059	0.004	0.052	0.304	0.304	0.391	0.016	0.016	0.020
S_{24}	0.424	0.147	0.073	0.005	0.065	0.214	0.357	0.429	0.014	0.023	0.028
S_{25}	0.424	0.102	0.033	0.001	0.020	0.375	0.250	0.375	0.008	0.005	0.008
S_{31}	0.254	0.228	0.029	0.002	0.024	0.273	0.318	0.409	0.007	0.008	0.010
S_{32}	0.254	0.571	0.048	0.007	0.099	0.364	0.318	0.318	0.036	0.031	0.031
S_{33}	0.254	0.124	0.028	0.001	0.012	0.286	0.333	0.381	0.004	0.004	0.005
S_{34}	0.254	0.077	0.013	0.000	0.004	0.333	0.286	0.381	0.001	0.001	0.001
S_{41}	0.223	0.170	0.058	0.002	0.031	0.400	0.250	0.350	0.012	0.008	0.011
S_{42}	0.223	0.300	0.059	0.004	0.056	0.421	0.263	0.316	0.023	0.015	0.018
S_{43}	0.223	0.529	0.060	0.007	0.101	0.286	0.333	0.381	0.029	0.034	0.038
The score of alternative D_k									0.31	0.33	0.36

Table 6. The comprehensive weights and the ranking of the alternatives

Author details

Xiaoguang Zhou
Dongling School of Economics and Management, University of Science and Technology Beijing, Beijing China

Acknowledgement

The author is very grateful to the editor, Dr. Vasilios Katsikis for his valuable suggestions, and Robert Ulbrich who gives constructive comments and suggestions on English grammar, which have been very helpful in improving the book. This work was supported by "the Fundamental Research Funds for Chinese Central Universities (No. FRF-BR-11-009A)".

7. References

Amiri, Morteza Pakdin. (2010). Project selection for oil-fields development by using the AHP and fuzzy TOPSIS methods. *Expert Systems with Applications*, vol. 37, pp. 6218-6224

Aragonés-Beltrán, P.; Chaparro-González, F.; Pastor-Ferrando, J. P. & Rodríguez-Pozo, F. (2010). An ANP-based approach for the selection of photovoltaic solar power plant investment projects. *Renewable and Sustainable Energy Reviews*, vol. 14, pp. 249-264

Arunraj, N. S. & Maiti, J. (2010). Risk-based maintenance policy selection using AHP and goal programming. *Safety Science*, vol. 48, pp. 238-247

Ayağ, Z. & Özdemir, R. G. (2009). A hybrid approach to concept selection through fuzzy analytic network process. *Computers & Industrial Engineering*, vol. 56, pp. 368–379

Bhattacharyya, Rupak.; Kumar, Pankaj. & Kar, Samarjit. (2011). Fuzzy R&D portfolio selection of interdependent projects. *Computers and Mathematics with Applications*, vol. 62, pp. 3857-3870

Boran, Semra. & Goztepe, Kerim. (2010). Development of a fuzzy decision support system for commodity acquisition using fuzzy analytic network process. *Expert Systems with Applications*, vol. 37, pp. 1939-1945

Buckley, J. J. (1985). Fuzzy hierarchical analysis. *Fuzzy Sets and Systems*, vol. 17, pp. 233-247

Chang, D. Y. (1996). Applications of the extent analysis method on fuzzy AHP. *European Journal of Operational Research*, vol. 95, pp. 649-655

Chang, P. T. & Lee, J. H. (2012). A fuzzy DEA and knapsack formulation integrated model for project selection. *Computers & Operations Research*, vol. 39, pp. 112–125

Cheng, E. W. L. & Li, H. (2005). Analytic Network Process Applied to Project Selection. *Journal of Construction Engineering and Management*, vol. 131 (4), pp. 459-466.

Csutora, R. & Buckley, J. J. (2001). Fuzzy hierarchical analysis: The Lamda-Max method. *Fuzzy Sets and Systems*, vol. 120, pp. 181-195

Dağdeviren, Metin. & Yüksel, İhsan. (2010). A fuzzy analytic network process (ANP) model for measurement of the sectoral competititon level (SCL). *Expert Systems with Applications*, vol. 37, pp. 1005-1014

Dey, Prasanta Kumar. (2006). Integrated project evaluation and selection using multiple-attribute decision-making technique. *Int. J. Production Economics*, vol. 103, pp. 90–103

Ebrahimnejad, S.; Mousavi, S. M.; Tavakkoli-Moghaddam, R.; Hashemi, H. & Vahdani, B. (2011). A novel two-phase group decisionmaking approach for construction project selection in a fuzzy environment. *Applied Mathematical Modelling*. doi: 10. 1016/j. apm. 2011. 11. 050

Fang, Yong.; Chen, Lihua. & Fukushima, Masao. (2008). A mixed R&D projects and securities portfolio selection model. *European Journal of Operational Research*, vol. 185, pp. 700-715

Gabriel, Steven A.; Kumar, Satheesh.; Ordóñez, Javier. & Nasserian, Amirali. (2006). A multiobjective optimization model for project selection with probabilistic considerations. *Socio-Economic Planning Sciences*, vol. 40, pp. 297-313

Ghorbani, S. & Rabbani, M. (2009). A new multi-objective algorithm for a project selection problem. *Advances in Engineering Software*, vol. 40, pp. 9-14

Gutjahr, Walter J.; Katzensteiner, Stefan,; Reiter, Peter,; Stummer, Christian. & Denk, Michaela. (2010). Multi-objective decision analysis for competence-oriented project portfolio selection. *European Journal of Operational Research*, vol. 205, pp. 670-679

Huang, Chi-Cheng.; Chu, Pin-Yu. & Chiang, Yu-Hsiu. (2008). A fuzzy AHP application in government-sponsored R&D project selection. *Omega*, vol. 36, pp. 1038-1052

Huang, Ivy B.; Keisler, Jeffrey. & Linkov Igor. (2011). Multi-criteria decision analysis in environmental sciences- Ten years of applications and trends. *Science of the Total Environment*, vol. 409, pp. 3578-3594

Huo, Liang-an.; Lan, Jibin. & Wang, Zhongxing. (2011). New parametric prioritization methods for an analytical hierarchy process based on a pairwise comparison matrix. *Mathematical and Computer Modelling*, vol. 54, pp. 2736-2749

Ju, Yanbing.; Wang, Aihua. & Liu, Xiaoyue. (2012). Evaluating emergency response capacity by fuzzy AHP and 2-tuple fuzzy linguistic approach. *Expert Systems with Applications*, vol. 39, pp. 6972-6981

Jung, U. & Seo, D. W. (2010). An ANP approach for R&D project evaluation based on interdependencies between research objectives and evaluation criteria. *Decision Support Systems*, vol. 49, pp. 335-342

Kahraman, Cengiz.; Ertay, Tijen. & Büyüközkan, Gülçin. (2006). A fuzzy optimization model for QFD planning process using analytic network approach. *European Journal of Operational Research*, vol. 171, pp. 390-411

Kumar, D. P. (2006). Integrated project evaluation and selection using multiple-attribute decision-making technique. *International Journal of Production Economics*, vol. 103, pp. 90-103

Lee, Hakyeon.; Kim, Chulhyun.; Cho, Hyunmyung. & Park, Yongtae. (2009). An ANP-based technology network for identification of core technologies: A case of telecommunication technologies. *Expert Systems with Applications*, vol. 36: 894-908.

Liesiö, Juuso.; Mild, Pekka. & Salo, Ahti. (2007). Preference programming for robust portfolio modeling and project selection. *European Journal of Operational Research*, vol. 181, pp. 1488-1505

Lin, C. T. & Chen, Y. T. (2004). Bid/no-bid decision-making-a fuzzy linguistic approach. *International Journal of Project Management*, vol. 22, pp. 585-593

Mikhailov, L. (2003). Deriving priorities from fuzzy pairwise comparison judgements. *Fuzzy Sets and Systems*, vol. 134, pp. 365-385

Mikhailov, L. (2004). Group prioritization in the AHP by fuzzy preference programming method. *Computers & Operations Research*, vol. 31, pp. 293-301

Mohanty, R. P. (1992). Project selection by a multiple-criteria decision making method: An example from a developing country. *International Journal of Project Management*, vol. 10, pp. 31-38

Pires, Ana.; Chang, Ni-Bin. & Martinho, Graça. (2011). An AHP-based fuzzy interval TOPSIS assessment for sustainable expansion of the solid waste management system in Setúbal Peninsula, Portugal. *Resources, Conservation and Recycling*, vol. 56, pp. 7-21

Promentilla, Michael Angelo B.; Furuichi, T. ; Ishii, K. & Tanikawa, N. (2008). A fuzzy analytic network process for multi-criteria evaluation of contaminated site remedial countermeasures. *Journal of Environmental Management*, vol. 88, pp. 479–495

Saaty, T. L. (1996). *Decision-making with Dependence and Feedback: The Analytic Network Process*, RWS Publications, Pittsburgh, PA

Shakhsi-Niaei, M.; Torabi, S. A. & Iranmanesh, S. H. (2011). A comprehensive framework for project selection problem under uncertainty and real-world constraints. *Computers & Industrial Engineering*, vol. 61, pp. 226-237

Smith-Perera, Aida.; García-Melón, Mónica.; Poveda-Bautista, Rocío. & Pastor-Ferrando, Juan-Pascual. (2010). A Project Strategic Index proposal for portfolio selection in electrical company based on the Analytic Network Process. *Renewable and Sustainable Energy Reviews*, vol. 14, pp. 1569-1579

Srdjevic, Bojan. (2005). Combining different prioritization methods in the-analytic hierarchy process synthesis. *Computers & Operations Research*, vol. 32, pp. 1897-1919

Van Laarhoven, P. J. M. & Pedrycz, W. (1983). A fuzzy extension of Saaty's priority theory. *Fuzzy Sets and Systems*, vol. 11, pp. 229-241

Wang, J. & Hwang, W. L. (2007). A fuzzy set approach for R&D portfolio selection using a real option valuation model. *Omega*, vol. 35, pp. 247-57

Wang, J.; Xu,Y. J. & Li, Z. (2009). Research on project selection system of pre-evaluation of engineering design project bidding. *International Journal of Project Management*, vol. 27, pp. 584-599

Wang, Y. M.; Elhag, T. M. S. & Hua, Z. S. (2006). A modified fuzzy logarithmic least squares method for fuzzy analytic hierarchy process. *Fuzzy Sets and Systems*, vol. 157, pp. 3055-3071

Xu, R. (2000). Fuzzy least-squares priority method in the analytic hierarchy process. *Fuzzy Sets and Systems*, vol. 112, pp. 359-404

Yu, Jing-Rung. & Cheng, Sheu-Ji. (2007). An integrated approach for deriving priorities in analytic network process. *European Journal of Operational Research*, vol. 180, pp. 1427-1432

Zadeh, L. A. (1965). Fuzzy sets. *Information and Control*, vol. 8, pp. 338-353

Chapter 7

MATLAB Aided Option Replication

Vasilios N. Katsikis

Additional information is available at the end of the chapter

1. Introduction

In reality markets are incomplete in the sense that perfect replication of contingent claims using only the underlying asset and a riskless bond is impossible. In other words, that is perfect risk transfer is not possible since some payoffs cannot be replicated by trading in marketed securities. From the work of Ross in [21], it is evident that whenever the payoff of every call or put option can be replicated then the securities market is complete. In addition, an important implication of the aforementioned work of Ross, is the existence of options that cannot be replicated by the primitive securities when markets are incomplete. In [7], the authors came to the conclusion that Ross's result is, in fact, a negative result since it asserts that in an incomplete market one cannot expect to replicate the payoff of each option even if the underlying asset is traded. In the same paper, it is proved that if the number of securities is less than half the number of states of the world, then (generically) not a single option can be replicated by traded securities. In [10], the author extended the aforementioned result in [7], to accommodate cases where the condition on the number of primitive securities is not imposed. In particular, it is proved that if there exists no binary payoff vector in the asset span, then for each portfolio there exists a set of nontrivial exercise prices of full measure such that any option on the portfolio with an exercise price in this set is non-replicated. Furthermore, note that the results of Ross for two-date security markets with finitely many states holds for security markets with more than two dates, see [8, 9].

It is well accepted that the lattice theoretic ideas are the most important technical contributions of the large literature on infinite-dimensional modern mathematical finance (for example lattice theoretic ideas in general equilibrium theory). However, ordered vector spaces that are not lattice ordered arise naturally in models of portfolio trading. Moreover, if available securities have smooth payoffs, then the portfolio space is never a vector lattice. It should be pointed out that since call and put options are vector lattice operations in the space of contingent claims, their replication by available securities requires a vector lattice structure in the portfolio space. There is a large literature on vector lattice theory related to mathematical economics; see for instance [1–7, 17–20, 22, 23].

On the other hand, there is an obvious need for properly structured high performance computational methods on vector lattices. Moreover, the main concern is to describe, in computational terms, and then solve problems arising from mathematical economics such as portfolio insurance and option replication. A lot of work in this area has been done in [11, 12, 14? –16].

In this chapter, we focus to the option replication problem. We consider an incomplete market of primitive securities, meaning that some call and put options need not be marketed and our objective is to describe an efficient method for computing maximal submarkets that replicate any option. Even though, there are several important results on option replication they cannot provide a method for the determination of the replicated options. By using the theory of vector-lattices and positive bases it is provided a procedure in order to determine the set of securities with replicated options. In particular, it is shown that the union of all maximal replicated submarkets (i.e., submarkets Y, such that any option written on the elements of Y can be replicated and Y is as large as possible) defines a set of elements such that any option written on these elements is replicated.

In [11–14, 16], it was shown that it is possible to construct computational methods in order to efficiently compute vector sublattices and lattice-subspaces of $\mathbb{R}^m$ as well as in the general case of $C[a, b]$. In addition, these methods has been successfully applied in portfolio insurance and in completion of security markets.

Here we consider a two-period security market X with a finite number m of states and a finite number of primitive securities with payoffs in $\mathbb{R}^m$ and we construct computational methods in order to determine maximal replicated submarkets of X by using the theory of vector sublattices and lattice-subspaces. Moreover, in the theory of security markets it is a usual practice to take call and put options with respect to the riskless bond $\mathbf{1} = (1, 1, ..., 1)$. Then, the completion $F_1(X)$ of X by options is the subspace of $\mathbb{R}^m$ generated by all options written on the elements of $X \cup \{\mathbf{1}\}$. Since the payoff space is $\mathbb{R}^m$, which is a vector lattice, in the case where $\mathbf{1} \in X$ then $F_1(X)$ is exactly the vector sublattice generated by X. If, in addition, X is a vector sublattice of $\mathbb{R}^m$ then $F_1(X) = X$ therefore any option is replicated, unfortunately this situation is extremely rare.

A recent article, [15], provided a computationally efficient method for computing maximal submarkets that replicate any option. In particular, by using computational methods and techniques from [11–14] in order to determine vector sublattices and their positive bases, it is presented a procedure in order to calculate the set of securities with replicated options. The aforementioned article emphasizes the most important interrelationship between the theory of vector lattices, positive bases, projection bases and the problem of option replication.

The material in this chapter is spread out in 5 sections. Section 2 is divided in two subsections; in the first the fundamental properties of lattice-subspaces and vector sublattices are presented, whereas in the second we introduce the basic results for vector sublattices, positive bases and projection bases of $\mathbb{R}^k$ together with the solution to the problem of whether a finite collection of linearly independent, positive vectors of $\mathbb{R}^k$ generates a lattice-subspace or a vector sublattice. In section 3, there are three subsections where it is discussed the theoretical background for option replication. Also, section 3 emphasis the most important interrelationship between positive bases, projection bases and the problem of option replication. Section 4 presents an algorithm for calculating maximal submarkets that replicate any option followed by the corresponding computational approach. Conclusions and research directions are provided in Section 5.

In this chapter, all the numerical tasks have been performed using the Matlab 7.8 (R2009a) environment on an Intel(R) Pentium(R) Dual CPU T2310 @ 1.46 GHz 1.47 GHz 32-bit system with 2 GB of RAM memory running on the Windows Vista Home Premium Operating System.

2. Basic results in the theory of positive bases and projection bases of $\mathbb{R}^m$

In this section, a brief introduction is provided to the theory of vector lattices of $\mathbb{R}^m$. Furthermore, we present some basic results related to the theory of positive bases and projection bases of $\mathbb{R}^m$.

2.1. Preliminaries and notation

Initially, we recall some definitions and notation from the vector lattice theory. Let $\mathbb{R}^m = \{x = (x(1), x(2), ..., x(m)) | x(i) \in \mathbb{R}, \text{ for each } i\}$, where we view $\mathbb{R}^m$ as an ordered space. The *pointwise order* relation in $\mathbb{R}^m$ is defined by

$$x \leq y \text{ if and only if } x(i) \leq y(i), \text{ for each } i = 1, ..., m.$$

The positive cone of $\mathbb{R}^m$ is defined by $\mathbb{R}^m_+ = \{x \in \mathbb{R}^m | x(i) \geq 0, \text{ for each } i\}$ and if we suppose that X is a vector subspace of $\mathbb{R}^m$ then X ordered by the pointwise ordering is an *ordered subspace* of $\mathbb{R}^m$, with positive cone $X_+ = X \cap \mathbb{R}^m_+$. By $\{e_1, e_2, ..., e_m\}$ we shall denote the usual basis of $\mathbb{R}^m$. A point $x \in \mathbb{R}^m$ is an *upper bound*, (resp. *lower bound*) of a subset $S \subseteq \mathbb{R}^m$ if and only if $y \leq x$ (resp. $x \leq y$), for all $y \in S$. For a two-point set $S = \{x, y\}$, we denote by $x \vee y$ (resp. $x \wedge y$) the *supremum* of S i.e., its least upper bound (resp. the *infimum* of S i.e., its greatest lower bound). Thus, $x \vee y$ (resp. $x \wedge y$) is the componentwise maximum (resp. minimum) of x and y defined by

$$(x \vee y)(i) = \max\{x(i), y(i)\} \ ((x \wedge y)(i) = \min\{x(i), y(i)\}), \text{ for all } i = 1, ..., m.$$

For any $x = (x(1), x(2), ..., x(m)) \in \mathbb{R}^m$, the set $supp(x) = \{i | x(i) \neq 0\}$ is the *support* of x. The vectors $x, y \in \mathbb{R}^m$ have *disjoint supports* if $supp(x) \cap supp(y) = \varnothing$.

An ordered subspace Z of $\mathbb{R}^m$ is a *vector sublattice* or a *Riesz subspace* of $\mathbb{R}^m$ if for any $x, y \in Z$ the supremum and the infimum of the set $\{x, y\}$ in $\mathbb{R}^m$ belong to Z.

Assume that X is an ordered subspace of $\mathbb{R}^m$ and $B = \{b_1, b_2, ..., b_\mu\}$ is a basis for X. Then B is a *positive basis* of X if for each $x \in X$ it holds: x is positive if and only if its coefficients in the basis B are positive. In other words, B is a positive basis of X if the positive cone X_+ of X has the form,

$$X_+ = \{x = \sum_{i=1}^{\mu} \lambda_i b_i | \lambda_i \geq 0, \text{ for each } i\}.$$

Then, for any $x = \sum_{i=1}^{\mu} \lambda_i b_i$ and $y = \sum_{i=1}^{\mu} \varrho_i b_i$ we have $x \leq y$ if and only if $\lambda_i \leq \varrho_i$ for each $i = 1, 2, ..., \mu$. A positive basis $B = \{b_1, b_2, ..., b_\mu\}$ is a *partition of the unit* if the vectors b_i have disjoint supports and $\sum_{i=1}^{\mu} b_i = 1$.

Recall that a nonzero element x_0 of X_+ is an *extremal point* of X_+ if, for any $x \in X, 0 \leq x \leq x_0$ implies $x = \lambda x_0$, for a real number λ. Since each element b_i of the positive basis of X is an extremal point of X_+, a positive basis of X is unique in the sense of positive multiples.

The existence of positive bases is not always ensured, but in the case where X is a vector sublattice of $\mathbb{R}^m$ then X always has a positive basis. If $B = \{b_1, b_2, ..., b_\mu\}$ is a positive basis for a vector sublattice X the lattice operations in X, namely $x \vee y$ for the supremum and $x \wedge y$ for the infimum of the set $\{x, y\}$ in X, are given by

$$x \vee y = \sum_{i=1}^{\mu} \max\{\lambda_i, \varrho_i\} b_i \text{ and } x \wedge y = \sum_{i=1}^{\mu} \min\{\lambda_i, \varrho_i\} b_i,$$

for each $x = \sum_{i=1}^{\mu} \lambda_i b_i, y = \sum_{i=1}^{\mu} \varrho_i b_i \in X$.

Suppose that L is a finite dimensional subspace of $C(\Omega)$ generated by a set $\{z_1, z_2, ..., z_r\}$ of linearly independent positive vectors of $C(\Omega)$. If Z is the sublattice of $C(\Omega)$ generated by L and $\{b_1, ..., b_\mu\}$ is a positive basis for Z ($\mu = dim(Z)$) then, a *projection basis* $\{\tilde{b}_1, \tilde{b}_2, ..., \tilde{b}_r\}$ of Z is a basis for L such that its elements are projections of the elements of the positive basis $\{b_1, ..., b_\mu\}$. In our current work we consider that $\Omega = \{1, 2, ..., m\}$ hence $C(\Omega) = \mathbb{R}^m$.

For an extensive presentation of vector sublattices as well as for notation not defined here we refer to [11–13, 15? , 16] and the references therein.

2.2. Theoretical background

In this section we present theoretical results for positive bases and projection bases in $\mathbb{R}^m$. Given a collection $x_1, x_2, ..., x_n$ of linearly independent, positive vectors of $\mathbb{R}^m$ we define the function,

$$h : \{1, 2, ..., m\} \to \mathbb{R}^n \text{ such that } h(i) = (x_1(i), x_2(i), ..., x_n(i))$$

and the function,

$$\beta : \{1, 2, ..., m\} \to \mathbb{R}^n \text{ such that } \beta(i) = \frac{h(i)}{\|h(i)\|_1} \tag{1}$$

for each $i \in \{1, 2, ..., m\}$ with $\|h(i)\|_1 \neq 0$. We shall refer to β as the *basic function* of the vectors $x_1, x_2, ..., x_n$. The set

$$R(\beta) = \{\beta(i) | i = 1, 2, ..., m, \text{ with } \|h(i)\|_1 \neq 0\},$$

is the *range* of the basic function and the *cardinal number*, $cardR(\beta)$, of $R(\beta)$ is the number of different elements of $R(\beta)$.

Suppose that Z denotes the sublattice of $\mathbb{R}^m$ generated by $X = [x_1, x_2, ..., x_n]$. We shall denote by $P_1, P_2, ..., P_n, P_{n+1}, ..., P_\mu$ an enumeration of $R(\beta)$ such that the first n vertices $P_1, P_2, ..., P_n$ are linearly independent and $\mu = dim(Z)$. Note that such an enumeration always exists. The notation, A^T stands for the transpose of a matrix A. A procedure in order to construct the sublattice Z is given by the following theorem.

Theorem 1. *Suppose that the above assumptions are satisfied. Then,*

(i) *X is a vector sublattice of $\mathbb{R}^m$ if and only if $R(\beta)$ has exactly n points (i.e., $\mu = n$). Then a positive basis $b_1, b_2, ..., b_n$ for X is defined by the formula*

$$(b_1, b_2, ..., b_n)^T = A^{-1}(x_1, x_2, ..., x_n)^T,$$

where A is the $n \times n$ matrix whose ith column is the vector P_i, for each $i = 1, 2, ..., n$. It is clear that in such a case Z and X coincide.

(ii) Let $\mu > n$. If $I_s = \beta^{-1}(P_s)$, and

$$x_s = \sum_{i \in I_s} \|h(i)\|_1 e_i, \quad s = n+1, n+2, ..., \mu,$$

then

$$Z = [x_1, x_2, ..., x_n, x_{n+1}, ..., x_\mu],$$

is the vector sublattice generated by $x_1, x_2, ..., x_n$ and $\dim Z = \mu$.

For a positive basis $\{b_1, b_2, ..., b_\mu\}$ of Z, consider the basic function γ of $\{x_1, x_2, ..., x_\mu\}$ with range, $R(\gamma) = \{P_1', P_2', ..., P_\mu'\}$. Then, the relation

$$(b_1, b_2, ..., b_\mu)^T = B^{-1}(x_1, x_2, ..., x_\mu)^T \tag{2}$$

where B is the $\mu \times \mu$ matrix with columns the vectors $P_1', P_2', ..., P_\mu'$, defines a positive basis for Z.

The notion of the projection basis is important for our study. Furthermore, in the following, we are interested for a projection basis that corresponds to a positive basis. Let $\{z_1, z_2, ..., z_r\}$ be a set of linearly independent and positive vectors of $\mathbb{R}^m$ then by using Theorem 1 we construct the sublattice Z of $\mathbb{R}^m$ generated by these vectors. If $\dim(Z) = \mu$, by Theorem 1, a positive basis $\{b_1, b_2, ..., b_\mu\}$ of Z can be determined. The basic result for calculating the projection basis that corresponds to the positive basis $\{b_1, b_2, ..., b_\mu\}$ of Z is the following theorem.

Theorem 2. *Suppose that β is the basic function of the vectors $\{z_1, z_2, ..., z_r\}$ and $P_1, P_2, ..., P_r$, $P_{r+1}, ..., P_\mu$ is an enumeration of the range of β such that the first r vectors $P_1, P_2, ..., P_r$ are linearly independent and suppose also that $z_{r+1}, ..., z_\mu$ are the new vectors constructed in Theorem 1. If $L = [z_1, z_2, ..., z_r]$ is the subspace of $\mathbb{R}^m$ generated by the vectors $z_1, z_2, ..., z_r$ then,*

(i) $Z = L \oplus [z_{r+1}, ..., z_\mu]$,

(ii) $\{b_{r+1}, b_{r+2}, ..., b_\mu\} = \{2z_{r+1}, 2z_{r+2}, ..., 2z_\mu\}$,

(iii) *If $b_i = \tilde{b}_i + b_i'$, with $\tilde{b}_i \in L$ and $b_i' \in [z_{r+1}, ..., z_\mu]$, for each $i = 1, 2, ..., r$, then $\{\tilde{b}_1, \tilde{b}_2, ..., \tilde{b}_r\}$ is a basis for L which is given by the formula*

$$(\tilde{b}_1, \tilde{b}_2, ..., \tilde{b}_r)^T = A^{-1}(z_1, z_2, ..., z_r)^T,$$

where A is the $r \times r$ matrix whose ith column is the vector P_i, for $i = 1, 2, ..., r$. This basis, $\{\tilde{b}_1, \tilde{b}_2, ..., \tilde{b}_r\}$ is called the projection basis of L and has the property: The r first coordinates of any element $x \in L$ expressed in terms of the basis $\{b_1, b_2, ..., b_\mu\}$ coincide with the corresponding coordinates of x in the projection basis, i.e.,

$$x = \sum_{i=1}^{\mu} \lambda_i b_i \in L \Rightarrow x = \sum_{i=1}^{r} \lambda_i \tilde{b}_i$$

Suppose that Z is the sublattice generated by a collection $z_1, z_2, ..., z_r$ of linearly independent, positive vectors of $\mathbb{R}^m$ and $\{d_1, d_2, ..., d_\mu\}$ is a positive basis for Z.

Then, by Theorem 2, if

$$(\tilde{d}_1, \tilde{d}_2, ..., \tilde{d}_r)^T = A^{-1}(z_1, z_2, ..., z_r)^T,$$

where A is the $r \times r$ matrix whose ith column is the vector P_i, for $i = 1, 2, ..., r$ then $\{\tilde{d}_1, \tilde{d}_2, ..., \tilde{d}_r\}$ is the projection basis of $L = [z_1, z_2, ..., z_r]$. The projection basis $\{\tilde{d}_1, \tilde{d}_2, ..., \tilde{d}_r\}$ is called the *projection basis of X corresponding to the basis* $\{d_1, d_2, ..., d_\mu\}$. The following proposition allows us to determine a positive basis and its corresponding projection basis. Moreover, the calculated positive basis is a partition of the unit.

Proposition 1. *Suppose that* $\{d_i\}$ *is the basis of Z given by equation (2) of Theorem 1 and* $\{\tilde{d}_i\}$ *is the projection basis of* $L = [z_1, z_2, ..., z_r]$ *corresponding to the basis* $\{d_i\}$. *Then* $\{b_i = \frac{d_i}{\|d_i\|_\infty} | i = 1, 2, ..., \mu\}$ *is the positive basis of Z which is a partition of the unit and* $\{\tilde{b}_i = \frac{\tilde{d}_i}{\|d_i\|_\infty} | i = 1, 2, ..., n\}$ *is the projection basis of L corresponding to the basis* $\{b_i\}$ *of Z.*

In the following, we shall denote by $\mathbf{1}$ the vector $\mathbf{1} = (1, 1, ..., 1)$. A vector x is a *binary vector* if $x \neq \mathbf{0} = (0, 0, ..., 0)$, $x \neq \mathbf{1}$ and $x(i) = 0$ or $x(i) = 1$, for any i. Let $\{b_i | i = 1, 2, ..., \mu\}$ be a positive basis of Z which is a partition of the unit and let $\{\tilde{b}_i | i = 1, 2, ..., n\}$ be the projection basis of L corresponding to the basis $\{b_i\}$. A partition $\delta = \{\sigma_i | i = 1, 2, ..., k\}$ of $\{1, 2, ..., n\}$ is *proper* if for any $r = 1, 2, ..., k$, the vector $w_r = \sum_{i \in \sigma_r} \tilde{b}_i$ is a binary vector with $\sum_{r=1}^k w_r = \mathbf{1}$. If there is no proper partition of $\{1, 2, ..., n\}$ strictly finer than δ, then we say that δ is a *maximal proper partition* of $\{1, 2, ..., n\}$.

Example 1. Let $\{b_i | i = 1, 2, 3\}$ be a positive basis such that the corresponding projection basis is the following

$$\tilde{b}_1 = (\frac{1}{2}, 1, 0, 1, 0), \ \tilde{b}_2 = (\frac{1}{2}, 0, 0, 0, 1), \ \tilde{b}_3 = (0, 0, 1, 0, 0).$$

We calculate the partitions of $\{1, 2, 3\}$ which are the following:

$$\delta_1 = \{\sigma_1, \sigma_2\}, \ where \ \sigma_1 = \{1\}, \ \sigma_2 = \{2 \ 3\}$$
$$\delta_2 = \{\sigma_1, \sigma_2\}, \ where \ \sigma_1 = \{2\}, \ \sigma_2 = \{3 \ 4\}$$
$$\delta_3 = \{\sigma_1, \sigma_2\}, \ where \ \sigma_1 = \{3\}, \ \sigma_2 = \{1 \ 2\}$$
$$\delta_4 = \{\sigma_1, \sigma_2, \sigma_3\}, \ where \ \sigma_1 = \{1\}, \ \sigma_2 = \{2\}, \ \sigma_3 = \{3\}.$$

Then δ_1 is not a proper partition since $w_1 = \sum_{i \in \sigma_1} \tilde{b}_i = \tilde{b}_1$ and $\tilde{b}_1$ is not a binary vector. Similarly, δ_2 is not a proper partition. On the other hand δ_3 is a proper partition since $w_1 = \sum_{i \in \sigma_1} \tilde{b}_i = \tilde{b}_3$ and $\tilde{b}_3$ is a binary vector, $w_2 = \sum_{i \in \sigma_2} \tilde{b}_i = \tilde{b}_1 + \tilde{b}_2 = (1, 1, 0, 1, 1)$ which is a binary vector and $w_1 + w_2 = (1, 1, 1, 1, 1)$. Notice that δ_3 is strictly finer than δ_4, hence δ_3 is a maximal proper partition of $\{1, 2, 3\}$.

3. Option replication

In this section we shall discuss the economic model of our study. Moreover, first we discuss an inductive method for calculating the completion of security markets. So, if $\mathbf{1} \in X$ then it is possible to determine a basic set of marketed securities i.e., a set of linearly independent and positive vectors of X and the sublattice of $\mathbb{R}^m$ generated by a basic set of marketed securities is $F_1(X)$. Finally, $F_1(X)$ has a positive basis which is a partition of the unit. Under these observations we present an algorithmic procedure in order to determine maximal submarkets that replicate any option.

3.1. The economic model

In our economy there are two time periods, $t = 0, 1$, where $t = 0$ denotes the present and $t = 1$ denotes the future. We consider that at $t = 1$ we have a finite number of states indexed by $s = 1, 2, ..., m$, while at $t = 0$ the state is known to be $s = 0$.

Suppose that, agents trade $x_1, x_2, ..., x_n$ non-redundant securities in period $t = 0$, then the future payoffs of $x_1, x_2, ..., x_n$ are collected in a matrix

$$A = \left[x_i(j) \right]_{i=1,2,...n}^{j=1,2,...,m} \in \mathbb{R}^{m \times n}$$

where $x_i(j)$ is the payoff of one unit of security i in state j. In other words, A is the matrix whose columns are the non-redundant security vectors $x_1, x_2, ..., x_n$. It is clear that the matrix A is of full rank and the *asset span* is denoted by $X = Span(A)$. So, X is the vector subspace of $\mathbb{R}^m$ generated by the vectors x_i. That is, X consists of those income streams that can be generated by trading on the financial market. A *portfolio* is a column vector $\theta = (\theta_1, \theta_2, ..., \theta_n)^T$ of $\mathbb{R}^n$ and the *payoff* of a portfolio θ is the vector $x = A\theta \in \mathbb{R}^m$ which offers payoff $x(i)$ in state i, where $i = 1, ..., m$. A vector in $\mathbb{R}^m$, is said to be *marketed* or *replicated* if x is the payoff of some portfolio θ (called the *replicating portfolio* of x), or equivalently if $x \in X$. If $m = n$, then markets are said to be *complete* and the asset span coincides with the space $\mathbb{R}^m$. On the other hand, if $n < m$, the markets are *incomplete* and some state contingent claim cannot be replicated by a portfolio.

In the following, we shall denote by $\mathbf{1}$ the *riskless bond* i.e., the vector $\mathbf{1} = (1, 1, ..., 1)$. A vector x is a *binary vector* if $x \neq \mathbf{0} = (0, 0, ..., 0)$, $x \neq \mathbf{1}$ and $x(i) = 0$ or $x(i) = 1$, for any i. The *call option* written on the vector $x \in \mathbb{R}^m$ with exercise price α is the vector $c(x, a) = (x - \alpha\mathbf{1})^+ = (x - \alpha\mathbf{1}) \vee \mathbf{0}$. The *put option* written on the vector $x \in \mathbb{R}^m$ with exercise price α is the vector $p(x, a) = (\alpha\mathbf{1} - x)^+ = (\alpha\mathbf{1} - x) \vee \mathbf{0}$. If y is an element of a Riesz space then the following lattice identities hold, $y = y^+ - y^-$ and $y^- = (-y)^+$. It is clear that $x - \alpha\mathbf{1} = (x - \alpha\mathbf{1})^+ - (x - \alpha\mathbf{1})^- = (x - \alpha\mathbf{1})^+ - (\alpha\mathbf{1} - x)^+ = c(x, \alpha) - p(x, \alpha)$. Therefore we have the identity

$$x - a\mathbf{1} = c(x, a) - p(x, a),$$

which is called *put-call parity*.

If both $c(x, \alpha) > 0$ and $p(x, \alpha) > 0$, we say that the call option $c(x, \alpha)$ and the put option $p(x, \alpha)$ are *non trivial* and the exercise price α is a *non trivial exercise price* of x. If $c(x, \alpha)$ and $p(x, \alpha)$ belong to X then we say that $c(x, \alpha)$ and $p(x, \alpha)$ are *replicated*. If we suppose that $\mathbf{1} \in X$ and at least one of $c(x, a), p(x, a)$ is replicated, then both of them are replicated since, $x - \alpha\mathbf{1} = c(x, \alpha) - p(x, \alpha)$.

3.2. Completion of security markets

We shall discuss the problem of completion by options of a two-period security market in which the space of marketed securities is a subspace of $\mathbb{R}^m$. The present study involves vector sublattices generated by a subset B of $\mathbb{R}^m$ of positive, linearly independent vectors. A computational solution to this problem is provided by using the SUBlat Matlab function from [16].

Let us assume that in the beginning of a time period there are n securities traded in a market. Let $S = \{1, ..., m\}$ denote a finite set of states and $x_j \in \mathbb{R}^m_+$ be the payoff vector of security j in m states. The payoffs $x_1, x_2, ..., x_n$ are assumed linearly independent so that there are no redundant securities. If $\theta = (\theta_1, \theta_2, ..., \theta_n) \in \mathbb{R}^n$ is a non-zero portfolio then its payoff is the vector

$$T(\theta) = \sum_{i=1}^{n} \theta_i x_i.$$

The set of payoffs of all portfolios is referred as the space of *marketed securities* and it is the linear span of the payoffs vectors $x_1, x_2, ..., x_n$ in $\mathbb{R}^m$ which we shall denote it by X, i.e.,

$$X = [x_1, x_2, ... x_n].$$

For any $x, u \in \mathbb{R}^m$ and any real number a the vector $c_u(x, a) = (x - au)^+$ is the *call option* and $p_u(x, a) = (au - x)^+$ is the *put option* of x with respect to the *strike vector* u and *exercise price* a.

Let U be a fixed subspace of $\mathbb{R}^m$ which is called *strike subspace* and the elements of U are the *strike vectors*. Then, the *completion by options* of the subspace X with respect to U is the space $F_U(X)$ which is defined inductively as follows:

- X_1 is the subspace of $\mathbb{R}^m$ generated by $\mathcal{O}_1$, where $\mathcal{O}_1 = \{c_u(x, a) | x \in X, u \in U, a \in \mathbb{R}\}$, denotes the set of call options written on the elements of X,

- X_n is the subspace of $\mathbb{R}^m$ generated by $\mathcal{O}_n$, where $\mathcal{O}_n = \{c_u(x, a) | x \in X_{n-1}, u \in U, a \in \mathbb{R}\}$, denotes the set of call options written on the elements of X_{n-1},

- $F_U(X) = \cup_{n=1}^{\infty} X_n$.

The completion by options $F_U(X)$ of X with respect to U is the vector sublattice of $\mathbb{R}^m$ generated by the subspace $Y = X \cup U$. The details are presented in the next theorem,

Theorem 3. *In the above notation, we have*

(i) $Y \subseteq X_1$,

(ii) $F_U(X)$ *is the sublattice $S(Y)$ of $\mathbb{R}^m$ generated by Y, and*

(iii) *if $U \subseteq X$, then $F_U(X)$ is the sublattice of $\mathbb{R}^m$ generated by X.*

Any set $\{y_1, y_2, ..., y_r\}$ of linearly independent positive vectors of $\mathbb{R}^m$ such that $F_U(X)$ is the sublattice of $\mathbb{R}^m$ generated by $\{y_1, y_2, ..., y_r\}$ is a *basic set* of the market.

Theorem 4. *Any maximal subset $\{y_1, y_2, ..., y_r\}$ of linearly independent vectors of $\mathcal{A}$ is a basic set of the market, where $\mathcal{A} = \{x_1^+, x_1^-, ..., x_n^+, x_n^-\}$, if $U \subseteq X$ and $\mathcal{A} = \{x_1^+, x_1^-, ..., x_n^+, x_n^-, u_1^+, u_1^-, ..., u_d^+, u_d^-\}$, if $U \subsetneq X$*

The space of marketed securities X is *complete by options* with respect to U if $X = F_U(X)$.

From theorem 1 it follows,

Theorem 5. *The space X of marketed securities is complete by options with respect to U if and only if $U \subseteq X$ and $card R(\beta) = n$. In addition, the dimension of $F_U(X)$ is equal to the cardinal number of $R(\beta)$. Therefore, $F_U(X) = \mathbb{R}^k$ if and only if $card R(\beta) = k$.*

Example 2. Suppose that in a security market, the payoff space is $\mathbb{R}^{12}$ and the primitive securities are:

$$x_1 = (1,2,2,-1,1,-2,-1,-3,0,0,0,0)$$
$$x_2 = (0,2,0,0,1,2,0,3,-1,-1,-1,-2)$$
$$x_3 = (1,2,2,0,1,0,0,0,-1,-1,-1,-2)$$

and that the strike subspace is the vector subspace U generated by the vector

$$u = (1,2,2,1,1,2,1,3,-1,-1,-1,-2).$$

Then, a maximal subset of linearly independent vectors of $\{x_1^+, x_1^-, x_2^+, x_2^-, x_3^+, x_3^-, u_1^+, u_1^-\}$ can be calculated by using the following code:

```
>>XX = [max(X,zeros(size(X)));max(-X,zeros(size(X)))];
>>S = rref(XX');
>>[I,J] = find(S);
>>Linearindep = accumarray(I,J,[rank(XX),1],@min)';
>>W = XX(Linearindep,:);
```

where X denotes a matrix whose rows are the vectors x_1, x_2, x_3, u. We can determine the completion by options of X i.e., the space $F_U(X)$, with the SUBlat function from [16] by using the following code:

```
>>[VectorSublattice,Positivebasis]=SUBlat(W')
```

The results then are as follows

```
VectorSublattice =
1    2    2    0    1    0    0    0    0    0    0    0
0    2    0    0    1    2    0    3    0    0    0    0
1    2    2    1    1    2    1    3    0    0    0    0
0    0    0    0    0    0    0    0    1    1    1    2
2    0    4    0    0    0    0    0    0    0    0    0

Positivebasis =
0    0    0    0    0    0    0    0    1    1    1    2
0    0    0    1    0    0    1    0    0    0    0    0
0    0    0    0    0    4    0    6    0    0    0    0
4    0    8    0    0    0    0    0    0    0    0    0
0    6    0    0    3    0    0    0    0    0    0    0
```

3.3. Computation of maximal submarkets that replicate any option

We consider a two-period security market X with a finite number m of states and a finite number of primitive securities with payoffs in $\mathbb{R}^m$ and we construct computational methods in order to determine maximal submarkets of X that replicate any option by using the results provided in subsection 2.2. In particular, in the theory of security markets it is a usual practice to take call and put options with respect to the riskless bond $\mathbf{1} = (1, 1, ..., 1)$. Then, the completion $F_1(X)$ of X by options (see subsection 3.2) is the subspace of $\mathbb{R}^m$ generated by all options written on the elements of $X \cup \{\mathbf{1}\}$. Since the payoff space is $\mathbb{R}^m$, which is a vector lattice, in the case where $\mathbf{1} \in X$ then $F_1(X)$ is exactly the vector sublattice generated by X. If, in addition, X is a vector sublattice of $\mathbb{R}^m$ then $F_1(X) = X$ therefore any option is replicated.

A basic set of marketed securities (i.e., a set of linearly independent and positive vectors) of X always exist and the sublattice of $\mathbb{R}^m$ generated by a basic set of marketed securities is $F_1(X)$. In addition, $F_1(X)$ has a positive basis which is a partition of the unit.

Let us assume that X is generated by a basic set of marketed securities, then from Theorem 1 it is possible to determine a positive basis $\{b_1, b_2, ..., b_\mu\}$ of $F_1(X)$.

The sublattice Z, generated by a basic set of marketed securities, is exactly $F_1(X)$ and $F_1(X)$ has a positive basis which is a partition of the unit, i.e., $\sum_{i=1}^{\mu} b_i = \mathbf{1}$. This is possible since the notion of a positive basis is unique in the sense of positive multiples therefore we are able to extract from the positive basis $\{b_1, b_2, ..., b_\mu\}$ another positive basis $\{d_1, d_2, ..., d_\mu\}$ of $F_1(X)$ which is a partition of the unit. Therefore, let us denote by $\{d_1, d_2, ..., d_\mu\}$ a positive basis of $F_1(X)$ which is a partition of the unit. Then, by Theorem 2, if

$$(\tilde{d}_1, \tilde{d}_2, ..., \tilde{d}_r)^T = A^{-1}(z_1, z_2, ..., z_r)^T,$$

where A is the $r \times r$ matrix whose ith column is the vector $P_{i,}$ for $i = 1, 2, ..., r$ then $\{\tilde{d}_1, \tilde{d}_2, ..., \tilde{d}_r\}$ is a projection basis of $F_1(X)$. The projection basis $\{\tilde{d}_1, \tilde{d}_2, ..., \tilde{d}_r\}$ is the projection basis of X corresponding to the basis $\{d_1, d_2, ..., d_\mu\}$. For $Z = F_1(X)$ proposition 1 takes the following form.

Proposition 2. *Suppose that $\{d_i\}$ is the basis of $F_1(X)$ given by equation (2) of theorem 1 and $\{\tilde{d}_i\}$ is the projection basis of X corresponding to the basis $\{d_i\}$. Then $\{b_i = \frac{d_i}{\|d_i\|_\infty} | i = 1, 2, ..., \mu\}$ is the positive basis of $F_1(X)$ which is a partition of the unit and $\{\tilde{b}_i = \frac{\tilde{d}_i}{\|d_i\|_\infty} | i = 1, 2, ..., n\}$ is the projection basis of X corresponding to the basis $\{b_i\}$ of $F_1(X)$.*

Suppose that Y is a subspace of X, then if $F_1(Y) \subseteq X$ we say that Y is *replicated*. If, in addition, for any subspace Z of X with $Y \subsetneqq Z$ we have that $X \subsetneqq F_1(Z)$ then Y is a *maximal replicated subspace* or a *maximal replicated submarket* of X. Note that, the *replicated kernel of the market*, i.e., the union of all maximal replicated subspaces of the market is the set of all elements x of X so that any option written on x is replicated.

Let $\{b_i \, i = 1, 2, ..., \mu\}$ be a positive basis of $F_1(X)$ which is a partition of the unit and let $\{\tilde{b}_i \, i = 1, 2, ..., n\}$ be the projection basis of X corresponding to the basis $\{b_i\}$. Recall that, a partition $\delta = \{\sigma_i | i = 1, 2, ..., k\}$ of $\{1, 2, ..., n\}$ is *proper* if for any $r = 1, 2, ..., k$, the vector $w_r = \sum_{i \in \sigma_r} \tilde{b}_i$ is a binary vector with $\sum_{r=1}^{k} w_r = \mathbf{1}$. If there is no proper partition of $\{1, 2, ..., n\}$ strictly finer than δ, then we say that δ is a *maximal proper partition* of $\{1, 2, ..., n\}$.

The following theorem provides the development of a method in order to determine the set of securities with replicated options by using the theory of positive bases and projection bases.

Theorem 6. *Let* $\{b_i, i = 1, 2, ..., \mu\}$ *be the positive basis of* $F_1(X)$ *which is a partition of the unit and let* $\{\tilde{b}_i, i = 1, 2, ..., n\}$ *be the projection basis of* X *corresponding to the basis* $\{b_i\}$*. If* Y *is a subspace of* X*, the following are equivalent:*

(i) *Y is a maximal replicated subspace of X,*

(ii) *there exists a maximal proper partition* $\delta = \{\sigma_i | i = 1, 2, ..., k\}$ *of* $\{1, 2, ..., n\}$ *so that* Y *is the sublattice of* $\mathbb{R}^m$ *generated by* δ*.*

The set of maximal replicated submarkets of X is nonempty.

4. The computational method

We present the proposed computational method that enables us to determine maximal submarkets that replicate any option. Our numerical method is based on the introduction of the `mrsubspace` function, from [15], that allow us to perform fast testing for a variety of dimensions and subspaces.

4.1. Algorithm for calculating maximal submarkets that replicate any option

Recall that X is the security market generated by a collection $\{x_1, x_2, ..., x_n\}$ of linearly independent vectors (not necessarily positive) of $\mathbb{R}^m$. If $1 \in X$ then it is possible to determine a basic set of marketed securities i.e., a set of linearly independent and positive vectors of X. This is possible through the following easy proposition:

Proposition 3. *If* $a = \max\{\|x_i\|_\infty | i = 1, 2, ..., n\}$*, then at least one of the two sets of positive vectors of X*

$$\{y_i = a\mathbf{1} - x_i | i = 1, 2, ..., n\}, \quad \{z_i = 2a\mathbf{1} - x_i | i = 1, 2, ..., n\},$$

consists of linearly independent vectors.

The main steps of the underlying algorithmic procedure that enables us to determine maximal submarkets that replicate any option are the following:

(1) Use proposition 3 in order to determine a basic set $\{y_1, y_2, ..., y_n\}$ of marketed securities.

(2) Use Equation (1) in order to determine the basic curve β of the vectors y_i.

(3) Determine the range $R(\beta)$ of β.

(4) Use Theorem 1 in order to construct the vector sublattice generated by $y_1, y_2, ..., y_n$, which is exactly the completion by options $F_1(X)$ of X. Then, determine a positive basis $\{d_1, d_2, ..., d_\mu\}$ for $F_1(X)$.

(5) Use Theorem 2 in order to determine a projection basis $\{\tilde{d}_1, \tilde{d}_2, ..., \tilde{d}_n\}$ of X.

(6) Use Proposition 1 in order to determine a positive basis $\{b_1, b_2, ..., b_\mu\}$ of $F_1(X)$ which is a partition of the unit and the corresponding projection basis $\{\tilde{b}_1, \tilde{b}_2, ..., \tilde{b}_n\}$.

(7) Calculate all the possible proper partitions of the set $\{1, 2, ..., n\}$.

(8) Decide which of the proper partitions created in step (7) are maximal proper partitions and determine the corresponding maximal replicated submarkets.

In [15], it is presented the translation followed by the implementation of the aforementioned algorithm in $\mathbb{R}^m$ within a Matlab-based function named mrsubspace. Moreover, in the same paper, computational experiments assessing the effectiveness of this function and lead us to the conclusion that the mrsubspace function provides an important tool in order to investigate replicated subspaces.

4.2. The computational approach - Code features

We shall discuss the proposed computational method that enables us to determine maximal submarkets that replicate any option. The standard method used currently to determine the maximal replicated submarkets is based on a manual processing. From section 3, it is evident that the required number of verifications for this process can be of significant size even in a relatively low-dimensional space, thus rendering the problem too difficult to solve. Our numerical method is based on the introduction of the mrsubspace function, from [15] that allow us to perform fast testing for a variety of dimensions and subspaces.

The structure of the code ensures flexibility, meaning that it is convenient for applications as well as for research and educational purposes. The given security market X, generated by the linearly independent vectors $x_1, x_2, ..., x_n$, must be given under a matrix notation with columns the vectors $x_1, x_2, ..., x_n$. The mrsubspace function must be stored in a Matlab-accessible directory and then the input data, i.e., the matrix X, can be typed directly in the Matlab's environment. Under the following command,

```
mrsubspace(X);
```

the program solves the problem of option replication and prints out the maximal proper partitions as well as the corresponding maximal replicated subspaces. If X is a vector sublattice, then $X = F_1(X)$ and any option is replicated. In the case where the initial space X is not a vector sublattice, it is possible to produce the normalized positive basis and the corresponding projection basis with the following code,

```
[Npb,Cprb] = mrsubspace(X)
```

Inside the code there are several explanations that indicate the implemented part of the algorithm. A user proficient in Matlab can easily use the code and modify it if needed. Especially, the user can isolate a part of the code according to his/her special needs to solve different problems like

- Determine a basic set of marketed securities.
- Find the completion $F_1(X)$ of X by options in $\mathbb{R}^m$ or find the vector sublattice generated by a finite collection of linearly independent vectors of $\mathbb{R}^m$.
- Calculate a positive basis and a projection basis for a finite dimensional vector sublattice.

In the last part of the code, entitled Maximal proper partitions - Maximal replicated subspaces, the user can change the way that the mrsubspace function understands the values 0 and 1, according to his/her knowledge and needs.

Example 3. Consider the following 5 vectors $x_1, x_2, ..., x_5$ in $\mathbb{R}^{10}$,

$$\begin{bmatrix} x_1 \\ x_2 \\ x_3 \\ x_4 \\ x_5 \end{bmatrix} = \begin{bmatrix} 0 & 1 & 0 & 1 & 1 & 1 & 1 & 2 & 2 & 1 \\ 1 & 1 & 1 & 2 & 1 & 1 & 1 & 2 & 1 & 2 \\ 1 & 1 & 1 & 2 & 1 & 1 & 1 & 2 & 1 & 1 \\ 1 & 1 & 1 & 1 & 1 & 1 & 1 & 2 & 2 & 1 \\ 2 & 1 & 2 & 1 & 1 & 1 & 1 & 1 & 1 & 1 \end{bmatrix}$$

and $X = [x_1, x_2, ..., x_5]$ is the marketed space.

Note that $1 = x_5 - x_4 + x_1$. In order to determine the maximal replicated subspaces for the above collection of vectors we use the following simple code:

```
>> X = [0,1,0,1,1,1,1,2,2,1;1,1,1,2,1,1,1,2,1,2;...
1,1,1,2,1,1,1,2,1,1;1,1,1,1,1,1,1,2,2,1;2,1,2,1,1,1,1,1,1,1];
>> [Npb,Cprb] =mrsubspace(X)
```

as a result and after removing irrelevant Matlab output one gets

```
The 1 partition(s) are:
    {1} {2 3} {4} {5}

ReplicatedSubspace =

    1    0    1    0    0    0    0    0    0    0
    0    1    0    1    1    1    1    0    0    0
    0    0    0    0    0    0    0    1    1    0
    0    0    0    0    0    0    0    0    0    1

The 1 partition(s) are:
    {1} {2} {3 4} {5}

ReplicatedSubspace =

    1    0    1    0    0    0    0    0    0    0
    0    1    0    0    1    1    1    0    1    0
    0    0    0    1    0    0    0    1    0    0
    0    0    0    0    0    0    0    0    0    1

Npb =

    1    0    1    0    0    0    0    0    0    0
    0    1    0    0    1    1    1    0    0    0
    0    0    0    1    0    0    0    0    0    0
    0    0    0    0    0    0    0    1    0    0
    0    0    0    0    0    0    0    0    0    1
    0    0    0    0    0    0    0    0    1    0
```

```
Cprb =

    1      0      1      0      0      0      0      0      0      0
    0      1      0      0      1      1      1      0      1      0
    0      0      0      1      0      0      0      0     -1      0
    0      0      0      0      0      0      0      1      1      0
    0      0      0      0      0      0      0      0      0      1
```

Therefore, the marketed space X has two maximal replicated subspaces, $\{1\}$ $\{2\ 3\}$ $\{4\}$ $\{5\}$ and $\{1\}$ $\{2\}$ $\{3\ 4\}$ $\{5\}$ are maximal proper partitions with corresponding maximal replicated subspaces the subspaces

$$Y_1 = [(1,0,1,0,0,0,0,0,0,0), (0,1,0,1,1,1,1,0,0,0), (0,0,0,0,0,0,0,1,1,0),$$
$$(0,0,0,0,0,0,0,0,0,1)]$$

and

$$Y_2 = [(1,0,1,0,0,0,0,0,0,0), (0,1,0,0,1,1,1,0,1,0), (0,0,0,1,0,0,0,1,0,0),$$
$$(0,0,0,0,0,0,0,0,0,1)],$$

respectively. The replicated kernel of the market is $Y = Y_1 \cup Y_2$.

5. Conclusions

In this chapter, computational methods for option replication are presented based on vector lattice theory. It is well accepted that the lattice theoretic ideas are one of the most important technical contributions of the large literature on modern mathematical finance. In this chapter, we consider an incomplete market of primitive securities, meaning that some call and put options need not be marketed. Our objective is to describe an efficient method for computing maximal submarkets that replicate any option. Even though, there are several important results on option replication they cannot provide a method for the determination of the replicated options. By using the theory of vector-lattices and positive bases it is provided a procedure in order to determine the set of securities with replicated options. Moreover, we determine those subspaces of the marketed subspace that replicate any option by introducing a Matlab function, namely mrsubspace. The results of this work can give us an important tool in order to study the interesting problem of option replication of a two-period security market in which the space of marketed securities is a subspace of $\mathbb{R}^m$. This work is based on a recent work, [15], regarding computational methods for option replication.

Author details

Vasilios N. Katsikis
General Department of Mathematics, Technological Education Institute of Piraeus, 12244 Athens, Greece

6. References

[1] Aliprantis, C.D. & Brown, D.J. (1983). Equilibria in markets with a Riesz space of commodities, *J. Math. Econom.*, 11, pp. 189–207.

[2] Aliprantis, C.D., Brown, D.J. & Burkinshaw, O. (1987a). Edgeworth equilibria, *Econometrica*, 55, pp. 1109–1137.

[3] Aliprantis, C.D., Brown, D.J. & Burkinshaw, O. (1987b). Edgeworth equilibria in production economies, *J. Econom. Theory*, 43, pp. 253–291.

[4] Aliprantis, C.D., Brown, D.J. & Burkinshaw, O. (1990). Existence and optimally of competitive equilibria, *Springer–Verlag*.

[5] Aliprantis, C.D. & Burkinshaw, O. (1991). When is the core equivalence theorem valid?, *Econom. Theory*, 1, pp. 169–182.

[6] Aliprantis, C.D., Tourky, R. & Yannelis, N. C. (2001). A theory of value with non–linear prices. Equilibrium analysis beyond vector lattices, *J. Econom. Theory*, 100, pp. 22–72.

[7] Aliprantis, C.D. & Tourky, R. (2002). Markets that don't replicate any option, *Economics Letter*, 76, pp.443–447.

[8] Baptista A.M. (2003). Spanning with american options, *Journal of Economic Theory*, 110, pp.264-289.

[9] Baptista A.M. (2005). Options and efficiency in multidate security markets, *Mathematical Fi- nance*, 15, No.4, pp.569-587.

[10] Baptista A.M. (2007). On the non-existence of redundant options, *Economic Theory*, 31, pp.205-212.

[11] Katsikis, V.N. (2007). Computational methods in portfolio insurance, *Applied Mathematics and Computation*, 189, pp.9-22.

[12] Katsikis, V.N. (2008). Computational methods in lattice-subspaces of $C[a,b]$ with applications in portfolio insurance, *Applied Mathematics and Computation*, 200, pp.204-219.

[13] Katsikis, V.N. (2009). A Matlab-based rapid method for computing lattice-subspaces and vector sublattices of $\mathbb{R}^n$: Applications in portfolio insurance, *Applied Mathematics and Computation*, 215, pp.961-972.

[14] Katsikis, V.N. (2010). Computational and Mathematical Methods in Portfolio Insurance. A MATLAB-Based Approach., Matlab - Modelling, Programming and Simulations, Emilson Pereira Leite(Ed.), ISBN: 978-953-307-125-1, InTech, Available from: http://www.intechopen.com/articles/show/title/computational-and-mathematical-methods-in-portfolio-insurance-a-matlab-based-approach-

[15] Katsikis, V.N. (2011). Computational methods for option replication, *International Journal of Computer Mathematics*, 88, No. 13, pp. 2752-2769.

[16] Katsikis V.N. & Polyrakis I. (2012). Computation of vector sublattices and minimal lattice-subspaces. Applications in finance, *Applied Mathematics and Computation*, 218, pp.6860–6873.

[17] Mas-Colell, A. (1986). The price equilibrium existence problem in topological vector lattices, *Econometrica*, 54, pp. 1039–1053.

[18] Mas-Colell, A. & Richard, S.F. (1991). A new approach to the existence of equilibrium in vector lattices, *J. Econom. Theory*, 53, pp. 1–11.

[19] Podczeck, K. (1996). Equilibria in vector lattices without ordered preferences or uniform properness, *J. Math. Econom.*, 25, pp. 465–484.

[20] Richard, S.F. (1989). A new approach to production equilibria in vector lattices, *J. Math. Econom.*, 18, pp. 231–247.
[21] Ross, S.A. (1976). Options and efficiency, *Quaterly Journal of Economics*, 90, pp.75-89.
[22] Tourky, R. (1998). A new approach to the limit theorem on the core of an economy in vector lattices, *J. Econom. Theory*, 78, pp. 321–328.
[23] Yannelis, N.C. & Zame, W.R. (1986). Equilibria in Banach lattices without ordered preferences, *J. Math. Econom.*, 15, pp. 85–110.

Chapter 8

Fractal Dimension Estimation Methods for Biomedical Images

Antonio Napolitano, Sara Ungania and Vittorio Cannata

Additional information is available at the end of the chapter

1. Introduction

The use of medical images has its main aim in the detection of potential abnormalities. This goal is accurately achieved with the synergy between the ability in recognizing unique image patterns and finding the relationship between them and possible diagnoses. One of the methods used to aid this process is the extrapolation of important features from the images called texture; texture is an important source of visual information and is a key component in image analysis.

The current evolution of both texture analysis algorithms and computer technology made boosted development of new algorithms to quantify the textural properties of an image and for medical imaging in recent years. Promising results have shown the ability of texture analysis methods to extract diagnostically meaningful information from medical images that were obtained with various imaging modalities such as positron emission tomography (PET) and magnetic resonance imaging (MRI). Among the texture analysis techniques, fractal geometry has become a tool in medical image analysis. In fact, the concept of fractal dimension can be used in a large number of applications, such as shape analysis[1] and image segmentation[2]. Interestingly, even though the fact that self-similarity can hardly be verified in biological objects imaged with a finite resolution, certain similarities at different spatial scales are quite evident. Precisely, the fractal dimension offers the ability to describe and to characterize the complexity of the images or more precisely of their texture composition.

2. Fractals

2.1. Fractal geometry

A fractal is a geometrical object characterized by two fundamental properties: *Self-similarity* and *Hausdorff Besicovich dimension*. A self-similar object is exactly or approximately similar to a part of itself and that can be continuously subdivided in parts each of which is (at least approximately) a reduced-scale copy of the whole. Furthermore, a fractal generally shows irregular shapes that cannot be simply described by Euclidian dimension, but, fractal dimension (fd) has to be introduced to extend the concept of dimension to these objects. However, unlike topological dimensions the fd can take non-integer values, meaning that the way a fractal set fills its space is qualitatively and quantitatively different from how an ordinary geometrical set does.

Nature presents a large variety of fractal forms, including trees, rocks, mountains, clouds, biological structures, water courses, coast lines, galaxies[3]. Moreover, it is possible to construct mathematical objects which satisfy the condition of self-similarity and that present fd (Figure 1).

Figure 1. Sierpinski triangle: starting with a simple initial configuration of units or with a geometrical object then the simple seed configuration is repeatedly added to itself in such way that the seed configuration is regarded as a unit and in the new structure these units are arranged with respect to each other according to the same symmetry as the original units in the seed configuration. And so on.

The objects in Figure 1 are self-similar since a part of the object is similar to the whole and the fractal dimension can be calculated by the equation:

$$D = \frac{\log N}{\log S} \tag{1}$$

where N is the number of the auto-similar parts in which an object can be subdivided and S is the scaling, that is, the factor needed to observe N auto-similar parts. According to the Eq.1, the following values are obtained for the Koch fractal and the Sierpinski triangle:

$$D_{Koch} = \frac{\log 4}{\log 3} \approx 1.26 \qquad D_{Sierpinski} = \frac{\log 3}{\log 3} \approx 1.58 \tag{2}$$

In mathematics, no universal definition of fd exists and the several definitions of fd may lead to different results for the same object. Among the wide variety of fd definitions that have been introduced, the Hausdorff dimension D_H is surely the most important and the most widely used[4]. Such definition can be theoretically applied to every fractal set but has the disadvantage it cannot always be easily determined by computational methods.

2.2. Hausdorff dimension D_H

Hausdorff dimension D_H was introduced in 1918 by mathematical Felix Hausdorff [3]. Since many of the technical developments used to compute the Hausdorff dimension for highly irregular sets were obtained by Abram Samoilovitch Besicovitch, D_H is sometimes called Hausdorff-Besicovitch dimension.

Hausdorff formulation[3] is based on the construction of a particular measure, H^D_δ, representing the uniform density of the fractal object.

Intuitively we can sum up the construction as follows: let be A a fractal and $C(r, A) = \{B_1....B_k\}$ a complete coverage of A consisting of spheres of diameter smaller than a given r that approximate A, so $\delta_i = \delta_i(B_i) < r$.

We define the Hausdorff measure as the function H^D_δ that identifies the smallest of all the covering spheres for A with $\delta < r$:

$$H^D_\delta(A) = \omega_D \lim_{r \to 0} \{inf \sum_i \delta_i^D\} \tag{3}$$

with ω_D volume of the unit sphere in R^D for integer D.

We obtain an approximate measurement of A, the so-called *course-grained volume*[4].

In the one-dimensional case ($D = 1$), H^D_δ supplies the length of set A measured with a ruler of length r. The shorter the ruler, the longer the length measured, a paradox known as the *coastline paradox*[3].

Hence, when $r \to 0$ the effective length of A is well approximated. Limit for small r calculated for other values of D, however, lead to a degenerate H^D_δ:

$$\mathcal{H}^D_\delta \to 0 \quad \text{and} \quad \mathcal{H}^D_\delta \to \infty \tag{4}$$

Therefore, D_H can be defined as the transition point for the function H^D_δ monotonically decreasing with D:

$$D_H(A) = inf_{D>0} \{H^D_\delta(A) = 0\} \tag{5}$$

with H^D_δ the D-dimensional Hausdorff measure given by Eq. 3.

The *course-grained volume* defined by Eq. 3 normally presents a scaling like:

$$H^D_\delta \sim r^{(D-D_H)} \tag{6}$$

that provides a method to estimate the dimension D_H.

In the uni-dimensional case $D = 1$ we can easily obtain:

$$L^D_\delta \sim r^{(1-D_H)} \qquad \text{with } L^D_\delta = measured\ length \tag{7}$$

from which we derive D_H.

3. Methods

Although the definition of Hausdorff dimension is particularly useful to operatively define the fd, that presents difficulties when implementing it. In fact, determining the lower bound value of all coverings, as defined in Eq. 5, can be quite complex. For example, let's consider the uni-dimensional case, in which we want to compute the fd of a coastline (Koch Curve). According to Eq. 3 in the case of $D = 1$ the coastline length is measured by a ruler of length r. Accuracy of the measure increase with decreasing r. For $r \to 0$ the coastline will have infinite length. Similar arguments can be applied to $D = 2$; for $r \to 0$ the measure of $H^D_\delta \to 0$.

This discussion implies that our coastline (ex. Koch Curve) will have a fd value more than one-dimensional and less than two- dimensional. For this reason, the fd is considered as the transition point (the lower bound value in Eq. 5) between $H_\delta^D \to 0$ and $H_\delta^D \to \infty$.

Several computational approaches have been developed to avoid the need of defining the lower bound at issue. Therefore many strategies accomplished the fd computation by retrieving it from the scaling of the object's bulk with its size. In fact, object's bulk and its size have a linear relationship in a logarithmic scale so that the slope of the best fitting line may provide an accurate estimation of this relationship. By using this log-log graph, called *Richardson's plot*, the requirement of knowing the infimum over all coverings is relaxed.

Several approaches have been developed to estimate fractal dimension of images. In particular, this section will introduce two fractal analysis strategies: the *Box Counting Method* and the *Hand and Dividers Method*.

These methods overcome the problem by choosing as covering a simple rectangle fixed grid in order to obtain an upper bound on D_H.

Five algorithms for a practical fd calculation based on these methods will also be presented.

3.1. Box counting method

The most popular method using the best fitting procedure is the so-called *Box Counting Method*[5][6]. Given a fractal structure A embedded in a d-dimensional volume the box-counting method basically consists of partitioning the structure space with a d-dimensional fixed-grid of square boxes of equal size r.

The number $N(r)$ of nonempty boxes of size r needed to cover the fractal structure depends on r:

$$N(r) \sim r^{-D} \tag{8}$$

The box counting algorithm hence counts the number $N(r)$ for different values of r and plot the log of the number $N(r)$ versus the log of the actual box size r. The value of the box-counting dimension D is estimated from the Richardson's plot best fitting curve slope.

$$-D = \lim_{r \to 0} \frac{\log N(r)}{\log r} \tag{9}$$

Figure 2 shows the Box counting method for the Koch Curve.

Several algorithms[7][8][9] based on box counting method have been developed and widely used for fd estimation, as it can be applied to sets with or without self-similarity. However, in computing fd with this method, one either counts or does not count a box according to whether there are no points or some points in the box. No provision is made for weighting the box according to the number of points belonging to the fractal and inside the current box.

3.2. Hand and dividers method

Useful features and information can be deducted from the contours of structures belonging to an image and there is a number of techniques that can be used when estimating the boundary fractal dimension.

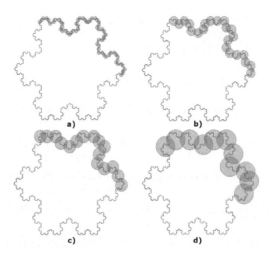

Figure 2. The Box-counting method applied to the Koch Curve with box size r = 0.4 (a); r = 1 (b); r = 1.4 (c); r= 2 (d)

The most popular methods are all based on the *Hand and Divers Method* which was originally introduced by Richardson[10] and successively developed by Mandelbrot[11].

The Richardson method employs the so-called *walking technique* consisting of "walking" around the boundary of the structure with a given step length.

The actual structure boundary is so approximated by a polygon whose length is equal to:

$$l(\epsilon) = \epsilon\, n(\epsilon) \tag{10}$$

In a nutshell, it corresponds to the length of the single step multiplied by the number of steps needed to complete the walk.

The process is then reiterated for different step lengths:

$$P_i = l(\epsilon_i) = \epsilon_i\, n(\epsilon_i) \tag{11}$$

With P_i the perimeter calculated with steps of length ϵ_i.

The object's boundary fd D is finally estimate from:

$$D = 1 - m \tag{12}$$

where m is the slope of the Richardson's plot.

The perimeter length of the boundary depends on the step length used so that a large step provides a rough estimation of the perimeter whereas a smaller step can take into account finer details of the contour.

Consequently, if the step length ϵ decreases the perimeter P increases.

In practice, the perimeter length is obtained by constructing a generally irregular polygon which approximate the border. Let δB be the set of coordinates of object boundary and let be

ϵ a fixed step length. Given a starting point, an arbitrary contour point (x_s, y_s), the next point on the boundary (x_{s_2}, y_{s_2}) in a fixed direction (e.g. clockwise) is the point that has a distance

$$d_i = \sqrt{(x_s - x_{s_2})^2 + (y_s - y_{s_2})^2} \qquad (13)$$

as close as possible to ϵ.

The reached point then becomes the new starting point and is used to locate the next point on the boundary that satisfies the previous condition. This process is repeated until the initial starting point is reached.

The sum of all distances dj corresponds to the irregular polygon perimeter (Figure3).

A number of different perimeters for each polygon at each fixed step length are used to build the Richardson's plot and the slope of its best linear fit is exploited to estimate the fd.

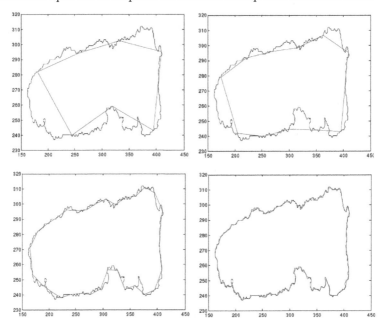

Figure 3. Walking technique applied to a coastline with different step lengths.

4. Algorithms

All Hand and dividers techniques rely on the same identical principle that attempt to approximate the border perimeter with a different polygons. However, since the point coordinates belonging to border set are discrete, all the implemented methods differ in the choice of which point in the set has a distance that better approximate the step length.

The following two methods are the implementations of two different choices about how to overcome this particular issue.

4.1. HYBRID algorithm

The HYBRID algorithm is a computer implementation of Hand and Dividers method developed by Clark[12]. Let δB be the boundary of the object whose fd we wish to compute. The main part of the method focuses on the perimeter estimation and the corresponding Richardson's plot is then attained by reiterating this hard core part at different step size. Figure 4 shows the flow chart of the method.

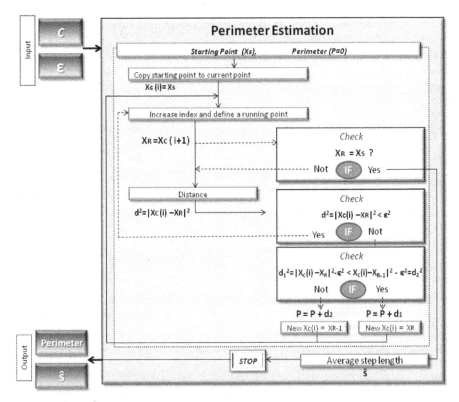

Figure 4. Perimeter estimation by HYBRID method flowchart: an arbitrary *starting point* S (x_S, y_S) on the boundary line is chosen and copied in a new variable, which is called *current point* C $(x_C(i), y_C(i))$. The index i runs through the total number of coordinate points and is iteratively increased defining the *running point* R with coordinates (x_R, y_R). The distance d between S and R is calculated and a check on d when smaller than a fixed step length ϵ is done. The process is repeated until a boundary point whose distance from (x_S, y_S) is larger than the step ϵ is reached. The next pivot point on the boundary line is determined by choosing between the two points the closest to the step length. The distance is then stored and this point becomes the new starting point in order to calculate the next pivot point and so on, until the initial starting point S is reached.

Given an arbitrary *starting point* S and its coordinates (x_S, y_S) on the boundary, the algorithm searches for the next pivot point. In particular the starting point is copied into a *current point*,

$C\ (x_C, y_C)$, which identifies all points having a mutual distance of about ϵ. The actual point running through the entire border is indicated as *running point* $R\ (x_R, y_R)$.

Therefore the program searches for a specific running point having a distance from C as near as possible to the step ϵ. In particular, in the HYBRID method the real step may be chosen to be longer or shorter than the fixed step depending on the minimum deviation from it. Similarly once the running point hits a contour point having a distance from the actual current one bigger than the size step, the choice is made between that point and the preceding one.

Afterward, the computed distance between these two points R and C is stored and the running point becomes the new current point.

The procedure continues until the initial starting point is reached. Obviously it is likely that after a complete walking the starting point S may be reached before having hit the following current point C. In other words, there may not be a multiple of step size ϵ so that the final incomplete step length r is added to the others stored distances, whose sum represent the boundary's perimeter. Since the fixed step length is adapted every time during the perimeter computation, its averaged value is then computed and used in the Richardson's plot.

4.2. EXACT algorithm

The EXACT algorithm was proposed for the first time by Clark in 1986[12]. As it will be shown, this method requires a longer computational time by providing a simpler solution to the choice of the best current points.

Similarly to the previous method the entire perimeter estimation is displayed in the flow chart of Figure 5.

The procedure is very similar to the one used for the previous method. As before (see Figure 5), the end of the step may not coincide with the digitized coordinates of the boundary.

The way the EXACT method attempts to overcome this problem relies on the assumption of piecewise linearity, meaning that all the points on the contour can be joined by a series of straight line[13, 14] (see Figure 6 (a)).

The location of the next current point C on the boundary from the one previously determined is schematically illustrated in Figure 6 (b).

The procedure starts from an arbitrary starting point (x_S, y_S) and the algorithm searches for the next pivot point. In particular the starting point is copied into a *current point*, $C\ (x_C, y_C)$, which identifies all points having a mutual distance of about ϵ. The actual point running through the entire border is indicated as *running point* $R\ (x_R, y_R)$.

The distance from the current point to each point on the contour line is then calculated until the step length ϵ falls between two consecutive boundary points, (x_R, y_R) and (x_{R+1}, y_{R+1}) for which:

$$\sqrt{(x_R - x_C)^2 + (y_R - y_C)^2} < \epsilon < \sqrt{(x_{R+1} - x_C)^2 + (y_{R+1} - y_C)^2} \tag{14}$$

The exact position of the point N with coordinates (x, y) is deduced by a process of geometric interpolation between the two consecutive running points (x_R, y_R) and (x_{R+1}, y_{R+1}). This point then becomes the new current point and is used to calculate the next boundary point and so on.

The process is stopped when we come back to the initial starting point (x_s, y_s) in order to obtain a polygon as is shown in Figure 8.

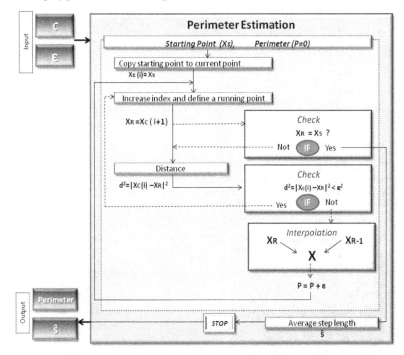

Figure 5. Perimeter estimation by EXACT method flowchart: an arbitrary *starting point* S (x_s, y_s) on the boundary line is chosen and copied in a new variable, which is called *current point* C $(x_c(i), y_c(i))$. The index i runs through the total number of coordinate points and is iteratively increased defining the *running point* R with coordinates (x_R, y_R). The distance d between S and R is calculated and a check on d when smaller than a fixed step length ϵ is done. The process is repeated until a boundary point whose distance from (x_s, y_s) is larger than the step ϵ is reached. The exact position of the next pivot point (x, y) on the boundary line is determined by interpolating the two consecutivepoints (x_R, y_R) and (x_{R+1}, y_{R+1}).
The point (x, y) becomes the new starting point in order to calculate the next pivot point and so on, until the initial starting point S is reached.

The perimeter length of the polygon is found by adding the final incomplete step length to the sum of the other step lengths needed to entirely cover the boundary.

The procedure is then repeated for different step lengths[15].

The results, i.e., perimeter lengths versus step lengths, are plotted on a log-log Richardson's Plot. From the slope of the fitting line on the Richardson's plot we obtain the fd of the examined boundary[1, 4, 12, 16–21]

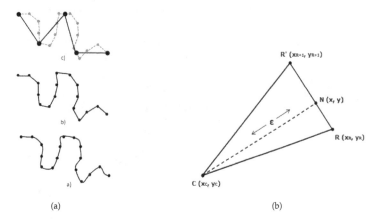

(a)   (b)

Figure 6. a) The piece-wise linear assumption (a) (b) and the EXACT algorithm (c); b)Geometric EXACT interpolation scheme, with S starting point given by (x_C, y_C) coordinates, R and R' two consecutive boundary running points respectly given by (x_R, y_R) and (x_{R+1}, y_{R+1}) coordinates, N new current point obtained by the interpolation between R and R' and ϵ a fixed step length.

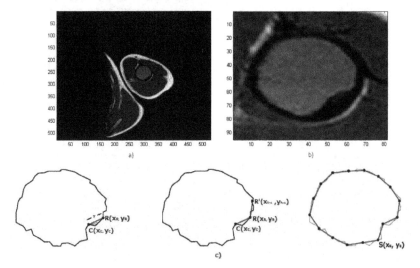

Figure 7. MRI image of an aneurismatic bone cyst (a), (b). Walking technique applied to an aneurysmatic bone cyst boundary (c).

4.3. Box-counting algorithm

The Box-counting algorithm implementation of box-counting method relies on the basic idea of covering a given digital binary image with a set of measuring boxes of sizes S and then to count the number of boxes which actually contain the image.

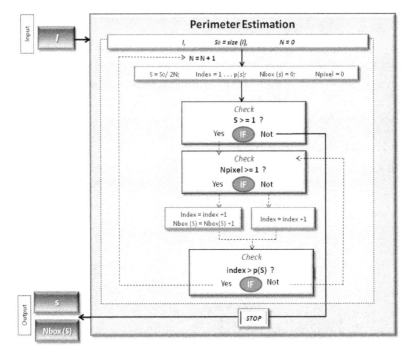

Figure 8. The Box-counting algorithm flowchart: given an image I, its size, S_0, is set as the maximum size from which the computer program starts to calculate the others decreasing box-sizes according to $S = S_0/2^N$. The S value has minimum value which is equal to the pixel size. The number p indicates the total number of box size S. The next step is a check on whether at least one pixel is in the box: if the box is non-empty, the check is stopped when one pixel is found. The procedure continues until the maximum index $p(s)$ is reached. Then the number $Nboxes(S)$ for a given size S is stored and the process restarts with a different box size. When the minimum box size is reached the program stops and gives the output variables of $Nboxes$ and the size value. Using the Eq. 8 the fractal dimension D can be estimate, from the least square linear fit.

Figure 8 shows the flow chart for box-counting fd estimation and for different box sizes. Moreover, since the procedure of size scaling ($S = S_0/2^N$ with N number of iterations) may be not always applicable to any image matrix size, image padding with background pixels is performed.

Therefore the final image I has a dimension that is a power of 2. This can be easily implemented by using *padarray* matlab function.

4.4. Differential Box-counting algorithm (DBC)

The box counting method is an extremely powerful tool for fd computation; in fact, it is easy to implement as well as flexible and robust.

However, a major limitation lies on the fact that the counting process of nonempty boxes implies its use only for binary images rather than gray scale ones. An extension of the standard approach to gray scale images is called the *Differential Box Counting (DBC)* and has been proposed in 1994 by N. Sarkar and Chaudhuri[8].

In the DBC method, a gray level image I is considered as a 3-D spatial surface with (x, y) denoting the pixels spatial coordinates and the third axis z the pixels gray level.

As for the standard box counting, the $M \times M$ image matrix is partitioned into non-overlapping $s \times s$-sized boxes, where s is an integer falling in the interval $[M/2, 1]$.

Then, the scale of each block is $r = s$. On each block there is a column of boxes of size $s \times s \times s'$, with s' denoting the height of a single box. Named G the total number of gray levels in I, hence s' is defined by the relationship $G/s' = M/s$[7].

Let numbers $1, 2, 3...$ be assigned to the boxes so to group the gray levels. Let the minimum and the maximum gray level of the image in the $(i, j)th$ grid fall in box number k and l, respectively.

The number of boxes covering this block is calculated as:

$$n_r(i, j) = l - k + 1 \tag{15}$$

In Figure 9 for example $s = s' = 3$, hence $n_r = 3 - 1 + 1$. Extending to the contribution from

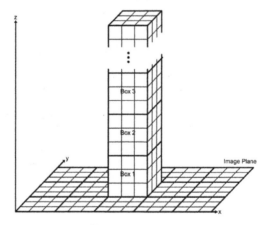

Figure 9. Example of DBC method application for determining the number of boxes of size $s \times s \times s$, when $s = 3$.

all blocks:

$$N_r = \sum_{i,j} n_r(i, j) \tag{16}$$

The Eq. 16 is computed for different box size s (so for different r) and the values of N_r are plotted versus the values of r in a log-log plot.

A matlab implementation of DBC can make use of functions such as *blockproc* or *colfilt* in order to make the box partitioning and apply the Eq. 15.

The DBC procedure has some weak points in the method used to select an appropriate box height[7], since the values of s is limited to the image size and s' is limited by the number of blocks of size $s \times s$ in which the image is divided.

Secondly, the box number calculation may lead to overestimate the number of boxes needed to cover the surface. Let A and B be the pixels associated with the minimum and the maximum gray level of the block respectively, as is illustrated in Figure 10.

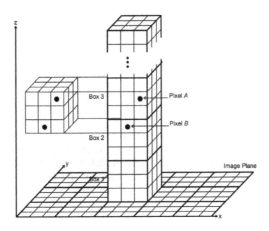

Figure 10. Example of DBC method application with boxes of $s \times s \times s$, when $s = 3$. The two pixels A and B, denoting the maximum and the minimum gray levels of the block, are assigned in two differents boxes, having distance in eight direction smaller than the box size $s = 3$.

According to DBC procedure, the two pixels are assigned in boxes 2 and boxes 3. The distance between A and B is smaller than 3, which is the size of the box.

Hence, when calculating Eq. 15, the block can be covered by a single box but its pixels with minimum and maximum gray levels fall into two different boxes.

To solve the aforementioned problems some modifications was proposed by J. Li, Q. Du and C. Sun[7]. Given a digital image I of size $M \times M$, a new scale r is defined instead of r, i.e. $r' = r/c$ where $c1$ is a positive real number.

In particular, let μ and σ be the mean and the standard deviation of I respectively. Hence, if the greater part of image pixels fall into the interval of gray level within $[\mu - a\sigma, \mu + a\sigma]$, where a is a positive integer, the height of the boxes is given by:

$$r' = \frac{r}{1 + 2a\sigma} \qquad (17)$$

If dz is the height of the boxes in the direction of z, the number of the column of boxes on a single image block correspond to the integer part of $(dz/r' + 1)$ instead of $(dz/r + 1)$ as in the original DBC method. Thus, since $r' < r$, the residual part of dz/r' is smaller than that of dz/r.

As a result, the errors introduced using r' are smaller than in the original DBC method. A box with smaller height is chosen when a higher intensity variation is present on the image surface. So the improved method uses, in general, finer scales to count[7].

Moreover, the use of dz instead of z to count the number of boxes leads to the following modification of Eq. 15:

$$n_r = \begin{cases} ceil(\frac{l-k}{r}), & \\ 1, & l = k \end{cases} \tag{18}$$

with ceil(.) denoting the function rounds the elements of the quantity into (.) to the nearest integers greater or equal to it.

Eq. 18 relies a new way to count the number of boxes that cover the $(i, j)th$ block surface in which the boxes are assigned to the minimum gray level to the block rather than gray level 0[7].

As an example, suppose that the $(i, j)th$ block is covered by a column boxes with the size 3x3x3. If the pixels A and B represent the maximum and the minimum gray levels of the block, the two pixels will be assigned as in Figure 10.

According to Eq. 18 the number of counted boxes is $n_r = 1$, which is exactly the number of boxes covering the block.

As in standard box counting method, after having determined the number nr(i,j) for each block, the total number of boxes N_r covering the full image surface is computed for different scales r. Plotting the linear fit of log N_r versus the log r (Richardson's plot) the fd is finally estimated.

5. Applications and discussion

Each described method has been implemented in Matlab 2010a and applied to either well-known fractals or biomedical images.

The results on the hand and dividers methods are shown in the table 1. The computed values are also compared to the theoretical fd values. The computational time for a 2.50 GHz 5i CPU is also shown.

The value ranges for the step size are not displayed but they were automatically chosen based upon the computation of the structure's maximum caliber diameter which is defined as the major axis of an ellipse in which the structure can be embedded. The range was then running from the 40% of the maximum caliber diameter to the minimum step defined as the maximum distance between any two contiguous border points.

In practice, both EXACT and HYBRID methods computed the different step sizes by scaling each time the maximum step by a^k with k the number of the iteration. The chosen value of $a = 1.2$ is a compromise between a sufficient number of fitting points and the need to avoid too small variations of the step size so to duplicate perimeter estimation. The latter usually occurs in HYBRID method for it hits the same current points if the step does not vary enough in two consecutive iterations.

The parameter's estimation uncertainty is also shown in the table 1; that is calculated from the fitting accuracy based upon standard linear regression.

The number of data points used in the Richardson's plot was about 60 and two examples of that computation using EXACT and HYBRID are shown in Figure 12.

On the table 2 the computation results for the box counting method are also shown. The type of the displayed values are similar to the previous ones with the exception of Box counting uncertainty. In fact, the way an image can be partitioned into several boxes may affect the final computation of the number of nonempty boxes.

To investigate the variability of the fd for different box partitioning layouts, random box subdivisions have been applied. Therefore, the results on the table 2 show the standard deviation of the different computed fds and the mean values for each fractal at issue. In general, that variability is more pronounced in images having rougher resolution.

Fractal	fd_{theo}	fd_{exp}	Time (sec)	BC error	Image size
Apollonian Gasket	1.3057	1.408	1.5	0.001	2000 × 2000
Sierpinski	1.5849	1.587	0.3	0.005	1000 × 1000
Dragon	2.0000	1.747	7.2	0.006	3670 × 3978
Hexaflake	1.7719	1.640	1.6	0.011	1050 × 1050

Table 1. Tabular of results for box counting method application.

Fractal	fd_{theo}	fd_{exp}	Time (sec)	BC error	Vector size
Twin Dragon Hybrid	1.5236	1.466	8.6	0.006	117005
Twin Dragon Exact	1.5236	1.465	11.5	0.006	117005
Dragon Hybrid	1.5236	1.474	11.1	0.005	115665
Dragon Exact	1.5236	1.462	12.8	0.004	115665
Koch Hybrid	1.2619	1.276	31.2	0.004	786433
Koch Exact	1.2619	1.260	154.9	0.003	786433
Gosper Hybrid	1.1292	1.133	3.8	0.001	23280
Gosper Exact	1.1292	1.128	4.7	0.001	23280

Table 2. Tabular of results for walking-based methods application.

In general, the EXACT and the HYBRID methods appeared to be more precise than the box counting method but on the other hand they have a less wide range of applicability. However, this is also the reason of the fortune of the box counting methods compared to the others. Also, HYBRID technique is computationally less expensive than EXACT especially when the number of border points is quite large. The use of a variable step length which can be shorter or longer than the fixed step size leads to a larger variability and so to a Richardson's plot having a less accurate fitting. That has effects on the uncertainties of the parameter to estimate. Because of that, a more careful choice of the step size range is needed in the case of HYBRID method.

Importantly, it is quite clear that the choice of the starting point may also affect the perimeter value as the following currents points will depend upon this. A test on 80 random starting points for the Gosper Island fractal revealed that the fd computation performed with the HYBRID method appeared to be more stable than the one with EXACT.

As for walking method, in box counting the process of scaling from the maximum box size is limited by the pixel size so in principle a gross resolution might be the reason of a bad estimate of fd. It is noteworthy that the tests performed do not show any correlation between resolution and fd accuracy; that may be also caused by the fact that some fractals such as dragon does not reproduce the real fractal at small scales.

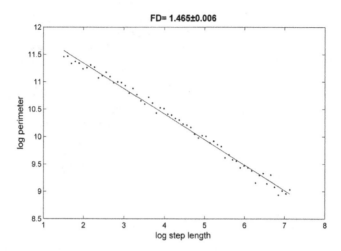

Figure 11. EXACT method apllied to the twin dragon fractal: Richardson's Plot.

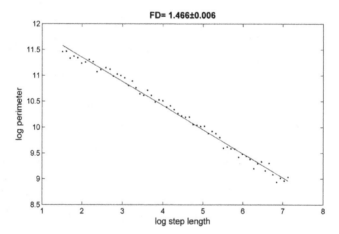

Figure 12. HYBRID method apllied to the twin dragon fractal: Richardson's Plot.

An application of the DBC method on a x-ray image is also shown in Figure 13 where breast cancer mammography image has been processed. The method uses a sliding technique as implemented in *blockproc* or *colfilt* matlab functions so to produce an image rather than a single fd value as previously described.

The second DBC method shows higher contrast in the area of the cancer and consequently lower fd values. Due to the enormous amount of linear fitting performed for an image size of 3450×3100 the computational time reached 15 minutes.

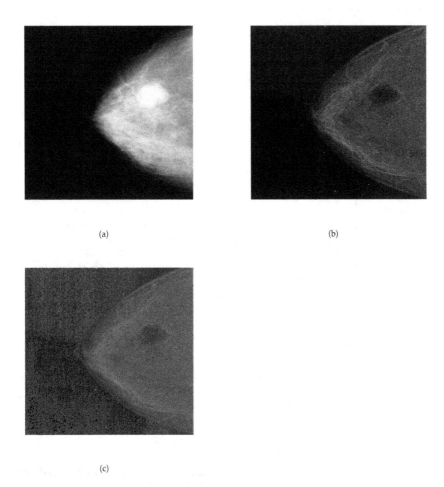

(a)   (b)

(c)

Figure 13. High resolution mammography image (a); fd recostruction image by standard Differential Box Counting (DBC) (b); fd reconstruction image by modified DBC (c).

6. Conclusions

In this chapter some of the most widely used and robust methods for fractal dimension estimation as well as their performances have been described. For few of them a detailed description of the algorithm has been also reported to make much easier for a beginner to start and implement his own Matlab code. Computational time is not excessively long to necessitate compiled functions such as C-mex files but that can be an advantage when using very high resolution images. The use of the described algorithms is obviously not restricted to the sole field of the image processing but it can be applied with some changes to any data analysis.

Author details

Antonio Napolitano, Sara Ungania and Vittorio Cannata
Department of Occupational Health and Safety, Medical Physics, Bambino Gesù Children's Hospital, Rome, Italy

7. References

[1] J. Orford and W. Whalley, *The use of the fractal dimension to quantify the morphology of irregular-shaped particles*, [Sedimentology, 30, 655-668], (1983).

[2] J. Keller et al., *Texture description and segmentation through fractal geometry*, [Computer Vision, Graphics and Image Processing, 45, 150-166], (1989).

[3] F. Hausdorff, *Dimension und ausseres Mass*, [Math. Annalen 79, 157] (1919).

[4] J. Theiler, *Estimating fractal dimension*, [7, 6/June 1990/J. Opt. Soc. Am. A] (1989).

[5] B. Mandelbrot, *The Fractal Geometry of Nature*, W.H.Freeman and Company, New York, (1983).

[6] S. Deepa,T. Tessamma *Fractal Features based on Differential Box Counting Method for the Categoritazion of Digital Mammograms*, [International Journal of Computer Information System and Industrial Management Applications, 2, 011-019], (2010).

[7] J. Li, Q. Du, *An improved box-counting method for image fractal dimension estimation*, [Pattern Recognition, 42, 2460-2469], (2009).

[8] N. Sarker, B. B. Chaudhuri, *An efficient differential box-counting approach to compute fractal dimension of image*, [IEEE Transaction on Systems, Man, and Cybernetics, 24, 115-120], (1994).

[9] A. P. Pentland, *Fractal-based description of natural scenes*, [IEEE Transaction on Pattern Analysis and Machine Intelligence, 6, 661-674], (1984).

[10] L. F. Richardson, *Fractal growth phenomena*, [Ann. Arbor, Mich. : The Society 6, 139] (1961).

[11] B. Mandelbrot, *How long is the coast of Britain? Statistical self-similarity and fractional dimension*, [Science 155, 636-638] (1967).

[12] N. Clark, *Three techiques for implementing digital fractal analysis of particle shape*, [Powder Technology 46, 45] (1986).

[13] M. Allen, G. J. Brown, N. J. Miles, *Measurement of boundary fractal dimensions: review of current techinques*, University of Nottingham , UK (1994).

[14] M. Allen, *Ph.D. Thesis*, University of Nottingham , UK (1994).

[15] P. Podsiadlo, G. W. Stachowiak, *Evaluation of boundary fractal methods for the characterization of wear particles*, [Wear 217(1) , 24-34] (1998).

[16] J. D. Farmer, E. Ott. and J. A. Yorke, *The dimension of chaotic attractors*, [Physica 7D, 153] (1983).

[17] B. Kaye, *A Random Walk Through Fractal Dimension*, [VCH Verlagsgesellschaft] (1986)

[18] L. Niemeyer, L. Pietronero and H. J. Wiesmann, *Fractals dimension of dielectric breakdown*, [Phys. Rev. Lett. 52, 1033] (1984).

[19] H. Schwarz and E. Exner, *The implementation of the concept of fractal dimension on semi-automatic image analyzer*, [Powder Technology, 27, 207-213], (1980).

[20] J. Russ, *Fractals surfaces*, [Plenum Press] (1994).

[21] H. von Koch, *Sur une courbe continue sans tangente, obtenue par une construction geometrique elementaire*, Archiv for Matemat., [Astron. och Fys. 1, 681-702] (1904).

Chapter 9

Convolution Kernel for Fast CPU/GPU Computation of 2D/3D Isotropic Gradients on a Square/Cubic Lattice

Sébastien Leclaire, Maud El-Hachem and Marcelo Reggio

Additional information is available at the end of the chapter

1. Introduction

The design of discrete operators or filters for the calculation of gradients is a classical topic in scientific computing. Typical applications are gradient reconstruction in computational fluid dynamics, edge detection in computer graphics and biomedical imaging, and phase boundary definition in the modeling of multiphase flows.

Edge detection, which is widely performed in image analysis, is an operation that requires gradient calculation. Commonly used edge detection methods are *Canny, Prewitt, Roberts* and *Sobel*, which can be found in MATLAB's platform. In this field, edge detection techniques rely on the application of convolution masks to provide a filter or kernel to calculate gradients in two perpendicular directions. A threshold is then applied to obtain an edge shape.

For multiphase flows, an edge or contour corresponds to the interface between the fluids. In this respect, traditional gradient calculation methods based on 1D edge detection are not necessarily suited for the underlying physics, because there is no direction in which the gradients of the phase contours tend to evolve over time. As a result, definition of the geometric progress of the interface requires many gradient estimation computations, as is the case in moving and deforming bubbles or droplets, for example. Although it can still be a viable tool, it is clear that the 1D-based method is becoming less useful for simulating these phenomena, which are not, in general, biased toward any particular direction.

To address this issue, we present an efficient computational method for obtaining discrete isotropic gradients that was previously applied to simulate two-phase flows within the lattice Boltzman framework [1, 2]. This "omnidirectional" approach makes it possible to improve the limitations inherent in handling high density ratios between the phases and to significantly reduce spurious currents at the interface. The method is based on a filter which is generally not split along any direction, and there is no need to make the assumption of a continuous filter to reach isotropy, as done by [3]. We also believe that optimal or maximal isotropy can only be reached with a discrete filter when the error terms of Taylor's series expansion are isotropic, as explained in detail by [1, 2].

Below, we describe isotropic and anisotropic discretizations that will and will not conserve the isotropic property of the differentiated function respectively. This is followed by a description of how convolution can be used to reduce computer time in the gradient calculation. We then present details of the MATLAB implementation of these ideas, along with speedup comparisons of convolution performed on a single core of an Intel® Core i7-970 processor and on an Nvidia® GeForce GTX 580 GPU using the Jacket plugin for MATLAB developed by AccelerEyes®. The GPU with the Jacket plugin for MATLAB speeds up gradient computation by a factor of up to $138x$ in the more challenging case. Our study ends with an example of multiphase flow simulation conducted using the lattice Boltzmann method. Finally, we provide useful stencils and weights (or kernels) to yield isotropic gradients in two and three dimensions.

2. Gradient discretization

Let us define the real scalar function $F(x,y) \in \Re$. There are various methods for calculating the derivative of a function, and one way of doing so is to apply a finite difference approximation. If both the horizontal and vertical lattice spacings are h in length, a simple procedure for evaluating the gradient of this function is as follows:

$$\frac{\partial F}{\partial x} \approx \frac{1}{6h^2} \sum_i F(x + c_i^x, y + c_i^y)c_i^x \tag{1}$$

$$\frac{\partial F}{\partial y} \approx \frac{1}{6h^2} \sum_i F(x + c_i^x, y + c_i^y)c_i^y \tag{2}$$

with

$$c^x = [0, h, h, h, 0, -h, -h, -h] \tag{3}$$

$$c^y = [h, h, 0, -h, -h, -h, 0, h] \tag{4}$$

This finite difference discretization is very similar to Prewitt's operator/kernel [4], which is used in image processing. Note that $h = 1$ in this field, and that the application of Prewitt's operator results in a vector that points in the same direction as the finite difference gradient, but with a norm 6 times larger. The application of Prewitt's operator to an image can be computed very quickly using a convolution product. We address the topic of convolution product later in section (3), but first, let us analyze the isotropy property of the previous gradient discretization.

2.1. Anisotropic discretization

As in Ref. [2] and without loss of generality, the function F is expressed using a 2D Taylor series expansion around the zero vector:

$$F(x,y) = F(0,0) + x\frac{\partial F}{\partial x}\Big|_{(0,0)} + y\frac{\partial F}{\partial y}\Big|_{(0,0)} + \frac{1}{2}x^2\frac{\partial^2 F}{\partial x^2}\Big|_{(0,0)} + xy\frac{\partial^2 F}{\partial x\partial y}\Big|_{(0,0)}$$

$$+ \frac{1}{2}y^2\frac{\partial^2 F}{\partial y^2}\Big|_{(0,0)} + \frac{1}{6}x^3\frac{\partial^3 F}{\partial x^3}\Big|_{(0,0)} + \frac{1}{2}x^2y\frac{\partial^3 F}{\partial x^2\partial y}\Big|_{(0,0)}$$

$$+ \frac{1}{2}xy^2\frac{\partial^3 F}{\partial x\partial y^2}\Big|_{(0,0)} + \frac{1}{6}y^3\frac{\partial^3 F}{\partial y^3}\Big|_{(0,0)} + O(x^n y^m)$$

with $n + m > 3$.

To calculate the gradient in the x direction, the following stencil values can be taken: $F(h,h)$, $F(h,0)$, $F(h,-h)$, $F(-h,-h)$, $F(-h,0)$, and $F(-h,h)$. When these stencil values are combined, as in the case of the gradient approximation in Eqs. (1) and (2), an exact expression for the gradient in the x direction at $(0,0)$ is obtained:

$$\frac{\partial F}{\partial x}\Big|_{(0,0)} = \frac{1}{6h}\Big(F(h,h) + F(h,0) + F(h,-h) - F(-h,-h) - F(-h,0) - F(-h,h)\Big)$$

$$- \frac{h^2}{6}\frac{\partial^3 F}{\partial x^3}\Big|_{(0,0)} - \frac{h^2}{3}\frac{\partial^3 F}{\partial x^2\partial y}\Big|_{(0,0)} + O(h^3) \tag{5}$$

A similar expression is found for the y direction:

$$\frac{\partial F}{\partial y}\Big|_{(0,0)} = \frac{1}{6h}\Big(F(-h,h) + F(0,h) + F(h,h) - F(h,-h) - F(0,-h) - F(-h,-h)\Big)$$

$$- \frac{h^2}{6}\frac{\partial^3 F}{\partial y^3}\Big|_{(0,0)} - \frac{h^2}{3}\frac{\partial^3 F}{\partial x\partial y^2}\Big|_{(0,0)} + O(h^3) \tag{6}$$

In the gradients of Eqs. (5) and (6), the leading $O(h^2)$ differential operator of the error term can be written in vector form:

$$\vec{E}^{(2)} = -\frac{h^2}{6}\left[\frac{\partial^3}{\partial x^3} + 2\frac{\partial^3}{\partial x^2\partial y}, \frac{\partial^3}{\partial y^3} + 2\frac{\partial^3}{\partial x\partial y^2}\right] \tag{7}$$

Using the following transformation from a Cartesian to a polar partial derivative operator:

$$\frac{\partial}{\partial x} = \cos(\theta)\frac{\partial}{\partial r} - \frac{1}{r}\sin(\theta)\frac{\partial}{\partial \theta} \tag{8}$$

$$\frac{\partial}{\partial y} = \sin(\theta)\frac{\partial}{\partial r} + \frac{1}{r}\cos(\theta)\frac{\partial}{\partial \theta} \tag{9}$$

And, by supposing that $F = F(r)$ is rotationally invariant, it is possible to show (after a lengthy algebraic manipulation) that the vector that results when the differential operator $\vec{E}^{(2)}$ is applied to $F(r)$ will have a Euclidean norm that is a function of θ and r, except if $F(r)$ is a constant. This result, that is, the norm $\|\vec{E}^{(2)}F(r)\| \equiv f(r,\theta)$, is an equation that takes up almost a page, and so is not presented here. Let us note, however, that this expression can easily be obtained using symbolic mathematics software. For a vector function to be rotationally invariant, it must have an Euclidean norm that is a function of the radius only. Therefore, this gradient approximation is not isotropic to the second order in space, but anisotropic. It is worth noting that the calculated derivatives have a leading error term that is not isotropic, even if the function F is isotropic, i.e. $F = F(r)$ around $(0,0)$. This means that the discrete gradient will not conserve the isotropic property of the differentiated function when the gradient is approximated with this finite difference stencil.

2.2. Isotropic discretization

Taking into consideration the previous anisotropy problem, it is possible to change the weights of the grid points when computing the gradients to make them isotropic, up to the second order in space, by defining gradients in the x and y directions, as follows:

$$
\left.\frac{\partial F}{\partial x}\right|_{(0,0)} = \frac{1}{12h}\Big(F(h,h) + 4F(h,0) + F(h,-h) - F(-h,-h) - 4F(-h,0) - F(-h,h) \Big)
$$

$$
- \frac{h^2}{6}\frac{\partial}{\partial x}\left(\frac{\partial^2 F}{\partial x^2} + \frac{\partial^2 F}{\partial y^2}\right)\bigg|_{(0,0)} - \frac{h^4}{72}\frac{\partial}{\partial x}\left(\frac{\partial^4 F}{\partial x^4} + 2\frac{\partial^4 F}{\partial x^2 \partial y^2} + \frac{\partial^4 F}{\partial y^4}\right)\bigg|_{(0,0)}
$$

$$
- \frac{h^4}{180}\frac{\partial^5 F}{\partial x^5}\bigg|_{(0,0)} + O(h^5) \tag{10}
$$

$$
\left.\frac{\partial F}{\partial y}\right|_{(0,0)} = \frac{1}{12h}\Big(F(-h,h) + 4F(0,h) + F(h,h) - F(h,-h) - 4F(0,-h) - F(-h,-h) \Big)
$$

$$
- \frac{h^2}{6}\frac{\partial}{\partial y}\left(\frac{\partial^2 F}{\partial x^2} + \frac{\partial^2 F}{\partial y^2}\right)\bigg|_{(0,0)} - \frac{h^4}{72}\frac{\partial}{\partial y}\left(\frac{\partial^4 F}{\partial y^4} + 2\frac{\partial^4 F}{\partial x^2 \partial y^2} + \frac{\partial^4 F}{\partial x^4}\right)\bigg|_{(0,0)}
$$

$$
- \frac{h^4}{180}\frac{\partial^5 F}{\partial y^5}\bigg|_{(0,0)} + O(h^5) \tag{11}
$$

With this new discretization, the dominant differential operator of the second order error term takes the form:

$$
\vec{E}^{(2)} = [E_x^{(2)}, E_y^{(2)}] = -\frac{h^2}{6}\left[\frac{\partial}{\partial x}\left(\frac{\partial^2}{\partial x^2} + \frac{\partial^2}{\partial y^2}\right), \frac{\partial}{\partial y}\left(\frac{\partial^2}{\partial x^2} + \frac{\partial^2}{\partial y^2}\right)\right] \tag{12}
$$

If a gradient has a small dependence on direction, this would imply that the dominant error term has only an axial dependence when the function being derived also only depends on the radius. That is, the operator in Eq. (12) applied on $F(r)$ would lead to a function that depends only on the radius:

$$
\vec{E}^{(2)}F(r) \equiv \vec{e}_r f(r) \tag{13}
$$

with $\vec{e}_r = [\cos(\theta), \sin(\theta)]$ being the unit radial vector. Using the partial derivative operator transformation of Eqs. (8) and (9), and supposing that $F = F(r)$ around $(0,0)$, the components $E_x^{(2)}F(r)$ and $E_y^{(2)}F(r)$ are:

$$E_x^{(2)}F(r) = \frac{h^2\cos(\theta)}{6r^2}\left(-\frac{\partial F(r)}{\partial r} + r\frac{\partial^2 F(r)}{\partial r^2} + r^2\frac{\partial^3 F(r)}{\partial r^3}\right) \tag{14}$$

$$E_y^{(2)}F(r) = \frac{h^2\sin(\theta)}{6r^2}\left(-\frac{\partial F(r)}{\partial r} + r\frac{\partial^2 F(r)}{\partial r^2} + r^2\frac{\partial^3 F(r)}{\partial r^3}\right) \tag{15}$$

which can be rewritten in the same form as Eq. (13). Similarly, the first differential operator of the fourth order error term in Eqs. (10) and (11) takes the form:

$$\vec{E}_{iso}^{(4)} = [E_{x,iso}^{(4)}, E_{y,iso}^{(4)}] = -\frac{h^4}{72}\left[\frac{\partial}{\partial x}\left(\frac{\partial^4}{\partial x^4} + 2\frac{\partial^4}{\partial x^2\partial y^2} + \frac{\partial^4}{\partial y^4}\right), \frac{\partial}{\partial y}\left(\frac{\partial^4}{\partial y^4} + 2\frac{\partial^4}{\partial x^2\partial y^2} + \frac{\partial^4}{\partial x^4}\right)\right] \tag{16}$$

and the associated components in polar coordinates, when applied to a rotationally invariant function $F(r)$ around $(0,0)$, are given by:

$$E_{x,iso}^{(4)}F(r) = \frac{h^4\cos(\theta)}{72}\left(3\frac{\partial F(r)}{\partial r} - 3r\frac{\partial^2 F(r)}{\partial r^2} + 3r^2\frac{\partial^3 F(r)}{\partial r^3} - 2r^3\frac{\partial^4 F(r)}{\partial r^4} - r^4\frac{\partial^5 F(r)}{\partial r^5}\right) \tag{17}$$

$$E_{y,iso}^{(4)}F(r) = \frac{h^4\sin(\theta)}{72}\left(3\frac{\partial F(r)}{\partial r} - 3r\frac{\partial^2 F(r)}{\partial r^2} + 3r^2\frac{\partial^3 F(r)}{\partial r^3} - 2r^3\frac{\partial^4 F(r)}{\partial r^4} - r^4\frac{\partial^5 F(r)}{\partial r^5}\right) \tag{18}$$

which again meets the rotational invariance requirement, and can be rewritten in the same form as given in Eq. (13). The last differential error operator of the fourth order error term in Eqs. (10) and (11) is:

$$\vec{E}_{ani}^{(4)} = -\frac{h^4}{180}\left[\frac{\partial^5}{\partial x^5}, \frac{\partial^5}{\partial y^5}\right] \tag{19}$$

and can be shown to be anisotropic (i.e. f in Eq. 13 would also be a function of θ). Therefore, the error associated with the anisotropy is lower by two orders when compared to the main second order leading term. It is important to point out that both gradient approximations presented so far are second order approximations in space, but only the latter is a second order approximation in space for the isotropy.

In this work, we only consider the gradient approximation of scalar functions over a square or cubic lattice of unit spacing, so we need to take $h = 1$ from now on. In a more general way, the stencil points with the corresponding weights needed to obtain 2D and 3D isotropic gradients was generalized by [1].

3. Convolution

Here, we present the mathematical and computational aspects of convolution. As finite difference discretization and edge detection kernels are very similar, let us return to the mathematical foundations of these techniques. We often give examples involving 2D images, but we could give the same examples and talk about 2D discrete functions. We don't know the exact coding in the MATLAB and Jacket libraries, as they are under license, but we do have a general idea about function algorithms, which is given in the next section.

3.1. Frequential and spatial filtering

The convolution product of two functions $f(x)$ and $g(x)$, defined by Eq. (20), calculates an average function by sliding g all over f. In common language, we say that the function $g(x)$ acts as a filter of the function $f(x)$.

$$(f * g)(x) = \int_{-\infty}^{\infty} f(x)g(x - s)ds \tag{20}$$

If Eq. (20) defines the convolution of two functions in the space domain, it is also equivalent to the point wise product of these functions in the frequency domain. In mathematics, the convolution theorem for Fourier transforms [5, chap. 4] is formalized by the following equation, where $\mathcal{F}$ corresponds to the Fourier transform applied on a function:

$$\mathcal{F}\{f * g\} = \mathcal{F}\{f\} \cdot \mathcal{F}\{g\} \tag{21}$$

The Fourier transform of a function generates the frequency spectrum of a function. This representation can easily be extended to two dimensions, which is more suitable to image or spatial analysis if the image is a function of two spatial variables. In our case, the output of the Fourier transform will generate a 2D function in the frequency domain from the 2D spatial domain. High frequencies will correspond to information varying rapidly in the original function, while low frequencies correspond to slow variations.

By applying the inverse Fourier Transform to both sides of Eq. (21), we obtain a method for calculating the convolution of two functions:

$$f * g = \mathcal{F}^{-1}\{\mathcal{F}\{f\} \cdot \mathcal{F}\{g\}\} \tag{22}$$

Therefore, there are two possible ways of convoluting two functions: the Fourier transform pipeline in three steps (Fourier transform, frequency spectrum filtering, and Fourier inverse transform), or the application of a stencil in the spatial domain. Indeed, edge detection kernels acts as high pass filters, accentuating high frequency contributions to the image or to the 2D function in the form of edges and details.

3.2. Discrete circular convolution

Knowing that the properties of the Fourier transform also work for a sampled signal, we present the definition of the 2D discrete Fourier transform (2D DFT), where M and N represent the number of samples in each dimension, x and y are the discrete spatial variables, and u and v are the transform or frequency variables:

$$\mathcal{F}\{u,v\} = \frac{1}{MN} \sum_{x=0}^{N-1} \sum_{y=0}^{M-1} f(x,y)e^{-2\pi j(\frac{ux}{N} + \frac{vy}{M})} \tag{23}$$

In addition to having the same properties as the continuous Fourier transform, which are outside the scope of this presentation and can be found in [6], there are two more in 2D DFT that are important: periodicity and separability. Since the discrete signal is sampled from the finite length sequences, its frequency spectrum will be periodic. In the spatial domain, this property allows us to slide the filter from one frontier to the opposite one, and then start again at the frontier where we began. Moreover, its Fourier transform is separable. The 2D DFT can be processed in two steps: applying 1D DFT on the lines, and then applying 1D DFT on the resulting columns. In the spatial domain, a 2D filter represented by K_1-by-K_2 matrix is separable if it can be obtained by the outer product of two vectors of size K_1 and K_2, knowing that DFT separability does not imply that the matrix kernel is always separable.

As an example, let us take kernelX, the 2D separable kernel in section (4.2):

$$\frac{1}{6}\begin{bmatrix} 3 \\ 0 \\ -3 \end{bmatrix} \otimes \frac{1}{6}\begin{bmatrix} 1 \\ 4 \\ 1 \end{bmatrix} = \frac{1}{36}\begin{bmatrix} 3 \\ 0 \\ -3 \end{bmatrix}\begin{bmatrix} 1 & 4 & 1 \end{bmatrix} = \begin{bmatrix} \frac{1}{12} & \frac{1}{3} & \frac{1}{12} \\ 0 & 0 & 0 \\ -\frac{1}{12} & -\frac{1}{3} & -\frac{1}{12} \end{bmatrix} \tag{24}$$

We can easily deduce the main functionality of the 2D kernel, the gradient component in x that approximates the derivative in x, by calculating the difference between the first and third rows in the neighborhood of a point, instead of the first and third columns, because of the rotation of our axis system. The separated 1D filters give us further information about the kernel function: a smoothing mask is applied on the differentiating mask, in order to reduce noise that could be exaggerated by the first filter.

Now, to explain how to apply a circular convolution mask in the spatial domain, we go back to the definition of convolution for discrete functions, presented in 2D and 3D in Eqs. (25) and (26) respectively, where A is the image and B is the mask. Processing a convolution filter consists of computing the scalar product of the filter weights with the input values within a window of the filter dimensions surrounding each of the output values, after flipping the mask in each dimension, as described in [7, chap. 4].

$$(A * B)(x, y) = \sum_i \sum_j A(i, j)B(x - i, y - j) \tag{25}$$

$$(A * B)(x, y, z) = \sum_i \sum_j \sum_k A(i, j, k)B(x - i, y - j, z - k) \tag{26}$$

In circular convolution, the equation is slightly modified to model periodic shifting. Here we consider a square image N by N:

$$(A \circledast B)(x, y) = \sum_i \sum_j A(i, j)B[(x - i) \mod N, (y - j) \mod N] \tag{27}$$

The values on the image we see in the window of the K-by-K filter are distributed on a periodic surface. The 2D filter is rolled up in the opposite direction and will turn in a clockwise direction. For each output value, the stencil is lined up on the input values, the scalar product is applied, and then the stencil rotates to shift to the next position to compute. Therefore, in the spatial domain, an N-by-N image convoluted with a K-by-K filter requires N^2K^2 multiplications and nearly N^2K^2 additions. The K^2 multiplications or additions can be reduced to $2K$ if the filter is separable, resulting in a total complexity of $O(N^2K)$ for spatial convolution with a separable filter.

In the frequency domain, the 2D discrete Fourier transform and its inverse are computed using the divide-and-conquer algorithm of the Fast Fourier Transform (FFT and IFFT), which reduces the complexity from N^3 multiplications and N^3 additions to $2N^2 \log_2(N)$ operations. The same order of complexity is required to compute the FFT of the K-by-K filter: $2K^2 \log_2(K)$.

To those computational complexities, the product cost of two complex numbers, which is six operations, has to be added N^2 times. In the frequency domain, the resulting computational complexity of convoluting an N-by-N image by a K-by-K filter would equal $2N^2 \log_2(N) + K^2 \log_2(K) + 6N^2$, or $O(N^2 \log_2(N))$ if $N \gg K$. Furthermore, the separability property could be used to implement a 2D FFT by the application of 1D FFT along each direction, in turn, with a global transpose between each of the 1D transform, which computationnal complexity is $O(N \log_2(N))$. To decide whether to use the FFT algorithm or spatial convolution, the two complexity functions should be compared to verify that convolution in the spatial domain performs better than FFT for small kernels only.

4. MATLAB

In this section, we present a systematic method that can be applied in MATLAB to calculate the gradient of scalar functions on a square lattice, or in 2D, which is simply the gradient of the images. The 3D case is a straightforward extension of the 2D case. First, let us define a function with which it is possible to test the gradient discretization previously defined in section (2.2):

$$F(x,y) = Ne^{-30\left(\left(\frac{x}{N}-\frac{1}{2}\right)^2+\left(\frac{y}{N}-\frac{1}{2}\right)^2\right)} \tag{28}$$

For the purpose of this test and for simplicity, we consider only a square image N in width. The exponential function is multiplied by N to make sure that the scaling ratio of the function F is always the same, whatever the value of N. In MATLAB m-code, this function can be defined as:

```
N=256+1;Nx=N;Ny=N;
[X,Y]=ind2sub([Nx Ny],1:Nx*Ny);
X=reshape(X,Nx,Ny)-1;Y=reshape(Y,Nx,Ny)-1;
F=N*exp(-30*(((X)/N-0.5).^2+((Y)/N-0.5).^2));
```

Figures 1(a) and 1(b) show the surface shape and contour of this function.

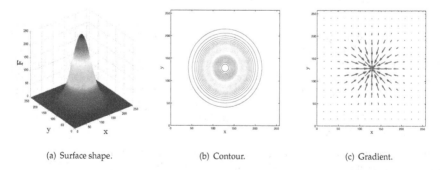

| (a) Surface shape. | (b) Contour. | (c) Gradient. |

Figure 1. Characteristics of the function $F(x,y)$.

4.1. Naive computation of the gradient

When the gradient of a function needs to be computed, it may be tempting to apply Eqs. (10)
and (11) directly. This is quite a simple approach, and in MATLAB can be applied as follows:

```
% Stencils and weights

w1=1/3;w2=1/12;
xi=[w1*ones(1,4),w2*ones(1,4)];
d=unique([perms([1 0]);perms([-1 0])],'rows');
d=[d;unique([perms([1 1]);perms([-1 1]);perms([-1 -1])],'rows')];
dxX=(d(d(:,1)~=0,1));dyX=(d(d(:,1)~=0,2));
dxY=(d(d(:,2)~=0,1));dyY=(d(d(:,2)~=0,2));
xiX=(xi(d(:,1)~=0));xiY=(xi(d(:,2)~=0));

% Periodic padding

nPad=max(dxX);
Fpad=padarray(F,[nPad nPad],'circular');

% Naive computation of the gradient

gradFX=0;
for i=1:numel(dxX)
    gradFX=gradFX+xiX(i)*dxX(i).*Fpad(nPad+(1:Nx)+dxX(i),nPad+(1:Ny)+dyX(i));
end

gradFY=0;
for i=1:numel(dyY)
    gradFY=gradFY+xiY(i)*dyY(i).*Fpad(nPad+(1:Nx)+dxY(i),nPad+(1:Ny)+dyY(i));
end
```

However, this is rather a naive and slow implementation for MATLAB. It is far more efficient
to evaluate the gradient by using a convolution product, as presented in section (4.2).

4.2. Techniques for calculating the gradient with convolution

Instead of calculating the gradient as previously shown, the use of a convolution product
between the functions to differentiate them, and a kernel representing the weights and stencils
of the finite difference approximation is more beneficial. For the isotropic discretization of Eqs.
(10) and (11), this computation can be performed in MATLAB as follows:

```
% 2D kernel

w1=1/3;w2=1/12;
c01=1*[w2;w1;w2];
kernelX=[-c01,zeros(3,1),c01];
kernelX=-kernelX';
kernelY=kernelX';

% Periodic padding

nPad=(numel(kernelX(:,1))-1)/2;
Fpad=padarray(F,[nPad nPad],'circular');
```

```
% Fast convolution for computing the gradient

gradFX=conv2(Fpad,kernelX,'valid');
gradFY=conv2(Fpad,kernelY,'valid');
```

A useful list of 2D and 3D kernels for calculating isotropic gradients is available in sections (6.1) and (6.2).

4.3. Separable kernel

Sometimes the kernel is separable, which means that, instead of applying an nD convolution, we can apply an 1D convolution n times to obtain the same result with much less computational effort. The previous kernel for computing a 2D isotropic gradient with only the nearest neighbors is, fortunately, separable, and in MATLAB the evaluation takes place as follows:

```
% 1D kernels

kernelXsep10=[3 0 -3]'/6;kernelXsep01=[1 4 1]/6;
kernelYsep10=[1 4 1]'/6;kernelYsep01=[3 0 -3]/6;

% Faster separable convolution for computing the gradient

gradFXconvSep=conv2(kernelXsep10,kernelXsep01,Fpad,'valid');
gradFYconvSep=conv2(kernelYsep10,kernelYsep01,Fpad,'valid');
```

Note that in the work of [1], one of the most important 3D isotropic kernels, which is the one that uses the nearest neighbors only, was not presented. In this work, two variants of this kernel were obtained, one using only 10 nearest neighbors and the other using only 18 nearest neighbors, and their MATLAB form are given in section (6.2). Moreover, the 3D kernel using 18 nearest neighbors has the advantage of being separable, which means that we should expect to be able to rapidly compute a 3D gradient of low isotropic order using the knowledge presented in this chapter. Also note that the higher isotropic order (>2nd) kernels given in sections (6.1) and (6.2) are not separable.

4.4. Accuracy

In this work, the order accuracy is defined by n, the value in h^n in Taylor's series expansion for which the space or the isotropic order is achieved. Therefore, the space and isotropic order may be different. Although this may not have been explicitly stated by [1, 2], all isotropic gradients found in sections (6.1) and (6.2) are of second order accuracy in space, i.e. if the lattice size doubles, the error on the gradient is divided approximately by four. This can be demonstrated numerically, or analytically by means of the expression $E_x^{(2)}F(r)$ and $E_y^{(2)}F(r)$ in polar coordinates, as in Eqs. (14) and (15). These expressions are non zero for every isotropic gradient presented in this work.

The main point about the kernel that we make in this study is that, as its size increases, it becomes possible to set isotropic the higher order error term in the Taylor series expansion at fixed space second order accuracy. It is therefore important to be careful not to confuse space order accuracy and isotropic order accuracy. We believe that, based on this result, future research could provide other kernels (perhaps of similar size) for which the leading space order accuracy would be the same as the leading isotropic order accuracy. For some applications, finding such kernels could be a significant step forward. In fact, achieving leading higher space order accuracy with equal leading isotropic order accuracy might have greater impact than achieving leading low space order with very high isotropic order accuracy, as is currently the case. However, higher space order gradient discretizations may suffer from another non physical numerical artifacts, known as spurious oscillations.

4.5. Performance

As previously indicated, computation of the gradient by applying convolution is faster than using a simpler, more straightforward method, but a naive one. We present some numerical results in this section that will show that this is indeed true. We also show that using a GPU instead of a CPU significantly reduces computation time.

First, all performance testing consists in evaluating gradients of random 2D and 3D double precision images. Note that we suppose a periodic padding for these images. All these image gradients are computed using MATLAB with the -singleCompThread startup option. This is done for benchmarking purposes, because the reference case should be computed using a sequential algorithm, that is, with a single core only. The CPU used in this work is an Intel® Core i7-970 processor, while the GPU is an Nvidia® GeForce GTX 580. All computations on the GPU are performed in MATLAB via the Jacket plugin developed by AccelerEyes®. The version of MATLAB is R2010b, and the Jacket version is 2.0 (build a15607c).

The timing method on the CPU is the usual MATLAB tic; m-code; toc; procedure. However, this method is not suited for timing m-code on the GPU. For this, we refer the reader to the method proposed by [8]. In Figures 2-5, the time taken for one simulation "dot" or result "dot" is the average of a hundred simulations.

To test performance, five different algorithms are considered for computing the gradient:

1. MATLAB singlethread naive (section 4.1)
2. MATLAB singlethread convolution (section 4.2) [REFERENCE CASE]
3. MATLAB Jacket naive
4. MATLAB Jacket convolution
5. MATLAB Jacket GFOR + convolution

Note that all results differ with respect to machine accuracy in double precision, and that the padding of the images is computed on the fly to save computer memory. This is because padding is very cheap in terms of computing cost, when compared to the cost of evaluating the gradient.

Case (4), MATLAB Jacket convolution, is the GPU equivalent of reference case (2) with a CPU. Case (3) is the GPU equivalent of case (1) with a CPU. The last case (5), MATLAB Jacket GFOR + convolution, is a special case that is not available on the CPU. To explain this, let us suppose that the user wishes to evaluate the gradient of N different images simultaneously. Using MATLAB, this is not possible without parfor , which is only available with the Parallel

Computing Toolbox. Also note that `parfor` is usually used for coarse-grained parallelism, while `gfor` can be used for fine-grained parallelism. Without `parfor`, an `for` loop is required to evaluate the gradients of the images sequentially, and to store the results in one large matrix by subassignment. With Jacket, it is possible to perform these N convolutions in parallel on the GPU using an `gfor` loop. Usually, this significantly reduces computation time, compared to the sequential `for` loop. More details on the functionality and limitations of the `gfor` loop can be found in [8]. In order to be able to compare the `gfor` loop case to the other cases, all performance tests have been conducted with $N = 3$, unless otherwise stated, i.e. it is supposed the user needs to evaluate three image gradients simultaneously at a given time.

In all the figures showing performance behavior, the y-axis is in log scale. Figures 2(a) and 2(b) show the performance speedup with the 2D 2nd and 14th order isotropic gradients as a function of image size. For large images, speedups of $31x$ to $39x$ can be achieved.

Figures 3(a) and 3(b) show the same situation, but with the 3D 2nd and 8th order isotropic gradients. For large images, a speedup of $34x$ to $124x$ can be achieved. These results indicate an important speedup and show the usefulness of Jacket for MATLAB.

Figures 4(a) and 4(b) show the speedup with the 2D and 3D isotropic gradient as function of the isotropy order at a fixed image size. In 2D, images are 992x992, and in 3D they are 110x110x110. For high isotropy, speedups of $49x$ to $124x$ can be achieved.

Figure 5 shows the speedup with the 3D 8th order isotropic gradient as a function of N, the number of images to be evaluated simultaneously at a fixed image size of 110x110x110. Speedups of $86x$ to $138x$ can be achieved, depending on the value of N.

For both 2D and 3D cases, as the isotropy order or the number of images to evaluate simultaneously increases, the speedup that can be achieved using the GPU also increases. This is to be expected, since the computational complexity increases. Nevertheless, the chances of obtaining a speedup of $86x$ to $138x$ for the more challenging case were much better than we had anticipated. In fact, the Jacket plugin allowed us to tackle problems that would not have been possible to deal with without using a low level programming language.

We must remember that the speedups were computed with the reference case, which uses convolution. It is important to note that a speedup of $280x$ may be achieved for the most computationally expensive test (Fig. 5) when comparing the two following cases: Jacket GFOR + convolution, and MATLAB singlethread naive. Thus, depending on how the gradient evaluations are implemented, a huge difference in computational time may be reached. Note that Jacket code does not currently take advantage of the zero entry in the kernel, and that the convolutions are performed in the spatial domain only for 9x9 kernels in 2D and 3x3x3 kernels in 3D. The naive implementation always takes advantage of the zero entry in the kernel, which means that the zero entry could yield an additional speedup, because some kernels are sparse. For example, 2D kernels have 26% to 68% zeros, while in 3D, this number varies from 33% to 84%. The 3x3 kernel contains 33% zeros while the 3x3x3 kernels contain 67% or 33% zeros.

5. Scientific application: lattice Boltzmann method

The lattice Boltzmann method is a computational approach that is mainly used for fluid flow simulation with its roots in the field of cellular automata [9]. This method is particularly useful for solving complex flow systems, such as multiphase flows, in porous media where classical

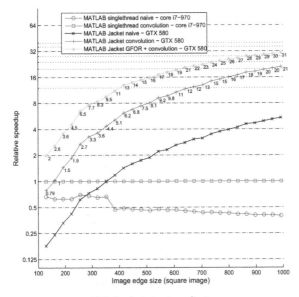

(a) 2nd order isotropic gradient.

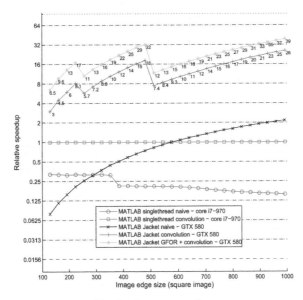

(b) 14th order isotropic gradient.

Figure 2. Speedup as a function of image size (2D isotropic gradient).

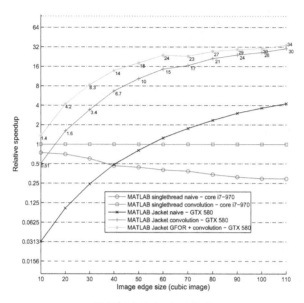

(a) 2nd order isotropic gradient.

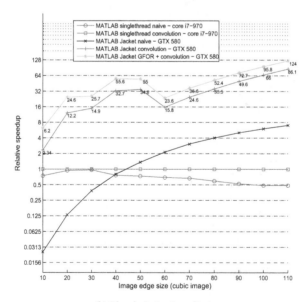

(b) 8th order isotropic gradient.

Figure 3. Speedup as a function of image size (3D isotropic gradient).

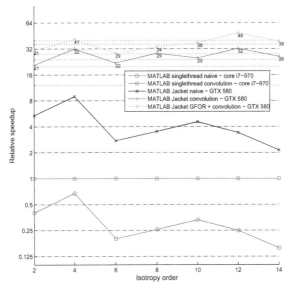

(a) Square image (992x992).

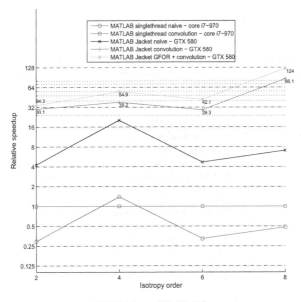

(b) Cubic image (110x110x110).

Figure 4. Speedup as a function of the gradient isotropy order.

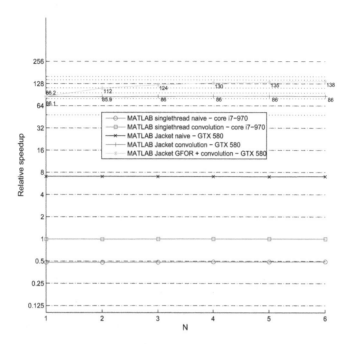

Figure 5. Speedup as a function of the number of cubic images (110x110x110) to be evaluated simultaneously using the 3D 8th order isotropic gradient.

approaches based on the Navier-Stokes equations, like finite volumes or finite elements, encounter some difficulties. The method we use is based on the original Ph.D. thesis of [10]. Since then, there have been several improvements. However, these enhancements are outside the scope of this chapter, and will not be described.

The isotropic gradients we present here are useful for simulating immiscible multiphase flows, where the orientation of the various fluid interfaces has to be computed very frequently. The gradients of the density of each fluid color (phase) define the normal orientation of the interface, and special operators are used to keep the different interfaces between the fluids defined. Moreover, the norm of these gradients serves as a means to introduce a certain amount of surface tension between the fluids.

Suppose we wish to simulate the behavior of three fluids. At a certain point in the algorithm, three image gradients need to be computed, corresponding to the interface normal of each fluid density. Here is where the methods presented in this chapter become useful, a situation described in section (4.5) with $N = 3$. It is important to point out that the isotropy of the gradient helps to reduce some of the computational artifacts that appear at the interface [1, 2]. These are called spurious currents in the lattice Boltzmann community, and are non-physical.

In multiphase flow simulation, calculation of a high order isotropic gradient is the most expensive part of the method, and the use of Jacket, has enabled us to reduce the computational cost by an astonishing amount. This type of calculation would not have been possible, in a reasonable time, by applying plain MATLAB.

We end this section with a simulation example that shows the spinodal decomposition of a three phase flow. This flow consists of an initial random mixture, where each phase self-agglomerates until a steady state is achieved. Figure 6 shows the spinodal decomposition at various times (in lattice Boltzmann units). Note that this simulation is given for illustration purposes only, and that spinodal decomposition has been quantitatively studied by [11].

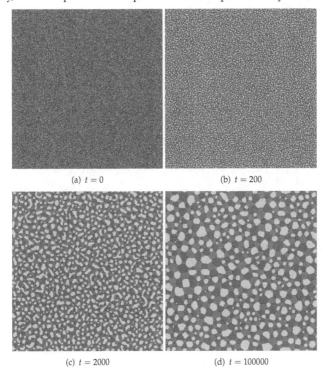

(a) $t = 0$ (b) $t = 200$

(c) $t = 2000$ (d) $t = 100000$

Figure 6. Random spinodal decomposition of a three phase flow.

6. Convolution kernel for discrete gradient approximation

In this section, we give several convolution kernels in the form of MATLAB m-code, which is very useful for calculating 2D/3D isotropic gradients on a square or cubic lattice. Most of the weights were taken from Ref. [1].

6.1. Convolution kernel for a 2D isotropic gradient

```
% 2D isotropy up to 2nd order
% This approximation use nearest neighbors only
```

```
w1=1/3;w2=1/12;
c01=1*[w2;w1;w2];
kernel=[-c01,zeros(3,1),c01];

% 2D isotropy up to 2nd order
% This approximation use nearest neighbors only (separable version)

kernelXsep10=[-3 0 3]'/6;kernelXsep01=[-1 -4 -1]/6;
kernelYsep10=[-1 -4 -1]'/6;kernelYsep01=[-3 0 3]/6;

% 2D isotropy up to 4th order

w1=4/15;w2=1/10;w4=1/120;
c01=1*[0;w2;w1;w2;0];c02=2*[0;0;w4;0;0];
kernel=[-c02,-c01,zeros(5,1),c01,c02];

% 2D isotropy up to 6th order

w1=4/21;w2=4/45;w4=1/60;w5=2/315;w8=1/5040;
c01=1*[w5;w2;w1;w2;w5];c02=2*[w8;w5;w4;w5;w8];
kernel=[-c02,-c01,zeros(5,1),c01,c02];

% 2D isotropy up to 8th order

w1=262/1785;w2=93/1190;w4=7/340;w5=6/595;
w8=9/9520;w9=2/5355;w10=1/7140;
c01=1*[w10;w5;w2;w1;w2;w5;w10];
c02=2*[0;w8;w5;w4;w5;w8;0];
c03=3*[0;0;w10;w9;w10;0;0];
kernel=[-c03,-c02,-c01,zeros(7,1),c01,c02,c03];

% 2D isotropy up to 10th order

w1=68/585;w2=68/1001;w4=1/45;w5=62/5005;w8=1/520;
w9=4/4095;w10=2/4095;w13=2/45045;w16=1/480480;
c01=1*[0;w10;w5;w2;w1;w2;w5;w10;0];
c02=2*[0;w13;w8;w5;w4;w5;w8;w13;0];
c03=3*[0;0;w13;w10;w9;w10;w13;0;0];
c04=4*[0;0;0;0;w16;0;0;0;0];
kernel=[-c04,-c03,-c02,-c01,zeros(9,1),c01,c02,c03,c04];

% 2D isotropy up to 12th order

w1=19414/228375;w2=549797/10048500;w4=175729/7917000;w5=50728/3628625;
w8=3029/913500;w9=15181/7536375;w10=221/182700;w13=68/279125;
w16=1139/26796000;w17=68/2968875;w18=17/1425060;w20=17/5742000;
w25_50=1/32657625;w25_34=1/32657625;
c01=1*[0;w17;w10;w5;w2;w1;w2;w5;w10;w17;0];
c02=2*[0;w20;w13;w8;w5;w4;w5;w8;w13;w20;0];
c03=3*[0;w25_34;w18;w13;w10;w9;w10;w13;w18;w25_34;0];
c04=4*[0;0;w25_34;w20;w17;w16;w17;w20;w25_34;0;0];
c05=5*[0;0;0;0;0;w25_50;0;0;0;0;0];
kernel=[-c05,-c04,-c03,-c02,-c01,zeros(11,1),c01,c02,c03,c04,c05];

% 2D isotropy up to 14th order

w1=285860656/3979934595;w2=2113732952/43779280545;w4=940787801/43779280545;
w5=124525000/8755856109;w8=15841927/3979934595;w9=2046152/795986919;
w10=14436304/8755856109;w13=18185828/43779280545;w16=13537939/140093697744;
w17=231568/3979934595;w18=1516472/43779280545;w20=18769/1591973838;
```

```
w25_50=184/315867825;w25_34=464/795986919;w26=1448/4864364505;
w29=148/4864364505;w32=629/400267707840;
c01=1*[w26;w17;w10;w5;w2;w1;w2;w5;w10;w17;w26];
c02=2*[w29;w20;w13;w8;w5;w4;w5;w8;w13;w20;w29];
c03=3*[0;w25_34;w18;w13;w10;w9;w10;w13;w18;w25_34;0];
c04=4*[0;w32;w25_34;w20;w17;w16;w17;w20;w25_34;w32;0];
c05=5*[0;0;0;w29;w26;w25_50;w26;w29;0;0;0];
kernel=[-c05,-c04,-c03,-c02,-c01,zeros(11,1),c01,c02,c03,c04,c05];

%%%%%%%%%%%%%%%%%%%%%%%%%%%%%%%%%%%%%%%%%%%%%%%%%%%%%%%
% Final 2D kernels for gradient approximation %
%%%%%%%%%%%%%%%%%%%%%%%%%%%%%%%%%%%%%%%%%%%%%%%%%%%%%%%

kernelX=-kernel';
kernelY=permute(kernelX,[2 1]);
```

6.2. Convolution kernel for a 3D isotropic gradient

```
% 3D isotropy up to 2nd order
% This approximation use only 10 nearest neighbors
% Note that this kernel IS NOT separable

w1=1/6;w2=1/12;w3=0;
c01=1*[w2;w1;w2];c11=1*[w3;w2;w3];
kernel(:,:,1)=[-c11,zeros(3,1),c11];
kernel(:,:,2)=[-c01,zeros(3,1),c01];
kernel(:,:,3)=kernel(:,:,1);

% 3D isotropy up to 2nd order
% This approximation use only 18 nearest neighbors
% Note that this kernel IS separable

w1=2/9;w2=1/18;w3=1/72;
c01=1*[w2;w1;w2];c11=1*[w3;w2;w3];
kernel(:,:,1)=[-c11,zeros(3,1),c11];
kernel(:,:,2)=[-c01,zeros(3,1),c01];
kernel(:,:,3)=kernel(:,:,1);

% 3D isotropy up to 4th order

w1=2/15;w2=1/15;w3=1/60;w4=1/120;
c01=1*[0;w2;w1;w2;0];c02=2*[0;0;w4;0;0];c11=1*[0;w3;w2;w3;0];
c12=2*[0;0;0;0;0];c21=1*[0;0;w4;0;0];c22=2*[0;0;0;0;0];
kernel(:,:,1)=[-c22,-c21,zeros(5,1),c21,c22];
kernel(:,:,2)=[-c12,-c11,zeros(5,1),c11,c12];
kernel(:,:,3)=[-c02,-c01,zeros(5,1),c01,c02];
kernel(:,:,4:5)=kernel(:,:,2:-1:1);

% 3D isotropy up to 6th order

w1=4/45;w2=1/21;w3=2/105;w4=5/504;w5=1/315;w6=1/630;w8=1/5040;
c01=1*[w5;w2;w1;w2;w5];c02=2*[w8;w5;w4;w5;w8];c11=1*[w6;w3;w2;w3;w6];
c12=2*[0;w6;w5;w6;0];c21=1*[0;w6;w5;w6;0];c22=2*[0;0;w8;0;0];
kernel(:,:,1)=[-c22,-c21,zeros(5,1),c21,c22];
kernel(:,:,2)=[-c12,-c11,zeros(5,1),c11,c12];
kernel(:,:,3)=[-c02,-c01,zeros(5,1),c01,c02];
kernel(:,:,4:5)=kernel(:,:,2:-1:1);
```

```
% 3D isotropy up to 8th order

w1=352/5355;w2=38/1071;w3=271/14280;w4=139/14280;w5=53/10710;w6=5/2142;
w8=41/85680;w9_221=1/4284;w9_300=1/5355;w10=1/10710;w11=1/42840;
c01=1*[w10;w5;w2;w1;w2;w5;w10];c02=2*[0;w8;w5;w4;w5;w8;0];
c03=3*[0;0;w10;w9_300;w10;0;0];c11=1*[w11;w6;w3;w2;w3;w6;w11];
c12=2*[0;w9_221;w6;w5;w6;w9_221;0];c13=3*[0;0;w11;w10;w11;0;0];
c21=1*[0;w9_221;w6;w5;w6;w9_221;0];c22=2*[0;0;w9_221;w8;w9_221;0;0];
c23=3*[0;0;0;0;0;0;0];c31=1*[0;0;w11;w10;w11;0;0];
c32=2*[0;0;0;0;0;0;0];c33=3*[0;0;0;0;0;0;0];
kernel(:,:,1)=[-c33,-c32,-c31,zeros(7,1),c31,c32,c33];
kernel(:,:,2)=[-c23,-c22,-c21,zeros(7,1),c21,c22,c23];
kernel(:,:,3)=[-c13,-c12,-c11,zeros(7,1),c11,c12,c13];
kernel(:,:,4)=[-c03,-c02,-c01,zeros(7,1),c01,c02,c03];
kernel(:,:,5:7)=kernel(:,:,3:-1:1);

%%%%%%%%%%%%%%%%%%%%%%%%%%%%%%%%%%%%%%%%%%%%%%%%%%%%
% Final 3D kernels for gradient approximation %
%%%%%%%%%%%%%%%%%%%%%%%%%%%%%%%%%%%%%%%%%%%%%%%%%%%%

kernelX=-permute(kernel,[2 1 3]);
kernelY=permute(kernelX,[2 1 3]);
kernelZ=permute(kernelX,[3 2 1]);
```

6.3. Convolution kernel for 2D anisotropic edge detection

```
% 2D Prewitt kernel

w1=1;w2=1;
c01=1*[w2;w1;w2];
kernel=[-c01,zeros(3,1),c01];

% 2D Sobel kernel

w1=2;w2=1;
c01=1*[w2;w1;w2];
kernel=[-c01,zeros(3,1),c01];

% 2D Scharr kernel

w1=3;w2=10;
c01=1*[w2;w1;w2];
kernel=[-c01,zeros(3,1),c01];

%%%%%%%%%%%%%%%%%%%%%%%%%%%%%%%%%%%%%%%%%%%%%%%%%%%%
% Final 2D kernels for gradient approximation %
%%%%%%%%%%%%%%%%%%%%%%%%%%%%%%%%%%%%%%%%%%%%%%%%%%%%

kernelX=-kernel';
kernelY=permute(kernelX,[2 1]);
```

7. Conclusion

In this work, a detailed description of isotropic gradient discretizations and convolution products has been presented. These isotropic gradients are useful, and superior to anisotropic discretizations. This is especially true in the field of flow simulation, when the lattice Boltzmann method is used. However, high order isotropic gradients are computationally expensive. To address this issue, we combined the convolution product with the Jacket plugin in MATLAB and GPU hardware, which enabled us to achieve high computational speedups (up to $138x$), compared to plain MATLAB computations using a CPU. We end this chapter with one final note. While we have provided a useful list of MATLAB m-code defining the kernels needed for evaluating 2D and 3D isotropic gradients, these kernels only lead to second order space accuracy with high isotropic order. The development of kernels that would lead to high order space accuracy combined with high isotropic order could generate significant benefits, particularly for the lattice Boltzmann community addressing multiphase flows. However, the benefits may not be straightforward, because the higher space order gradient discretization may lead to another unwanted numerical artifacts, such as spurious oscillations in regions separating two phases.

Acknowledgments

We extend our special thanks to Pavan Yalamanchili from AccelerEyes for his quick response to our queries and his generous support. We applied the sequence-determines-credit (SDC) approach to our listing of authors [12]. This work was supported by a grant from the NSERC (Natural Sciences and Engineering Research Council of Canada).

Author details

Sébastien Leclaire, Maud El-Hachem and Marcelo Reggio
Department of Mechanical Engineering, École Polytechnique de Montréal, Canada

8. References

[1] M. Sbragaglia, R. Benzi, L. Biferale, S. Succi, K. Sugiyama, and F. Toschi. Generalized lattice boltzmann method with multirange pseudopotential. *Physical Review E*, 75(2):026702, 2007.

[2] Sébastien Leclaire, Marcelo Reggio, and Jean-Yves Trépanier. Isotropic color gradient for simulating very high-density ratios with a two-phase flow lattice boltzmann model. *Computers & Fluids*, 48(1):98–112, 2011.

[3] Sayed Kamaledin Ghiasi Shirazi and Reza Safabakhsh. Omnidirectional edge detection. *Computer Vision and Image Understanding*, 113(4):556 – 564, 2009.

[4] M.K. Ray, D. Mitra, and S. Saha. Simplified novel method for edge detection in digital images. In *Signal Processing, Communication, Computing and Networking Technologies (ICSCCN), 2011 International Conference on*, pages 197–202, july 2011.

[5] T.L. Chow. *Mathematical methods for physicists: a concise introduction*. Cambridge University Press, 2000.

[6] E. Oran Brigham. *The fast Fourier transform and its applications*. Prentice-Hall, Inc., Upper Saddle River, NJ, USA, 1988.

[7] Rafael C. Gonzalez and Richard E. Woods. *Digital Image Processing (3rd Edition)*. Prentice-Hall, Inc., Upper Saddle River, NJ, USA, 2006.

[8] Accelereyes website, 2012.

[9] Hasslacher B. Frish U and Y. Pomeau. *Phys. Rev. Lett.*, 56(14):1505, 1986.

[10] Andrew K. Gunstensen. *Lattice-Boltzmann Studies of Multiphase Flow Through Porous Media*. PhD thesis, 1992.

[11] F. J. Alexander, S. Chen, and D. W. Grunau. Hydrodynamic spinodal decomposition: Growth kinetics and scaling functions. *Physical Review B*, 48(1):634, 1993.

[12] Teja Tscharntke, Michael E. Hochberg, Tatyana A. Rand, Vincent H. Resh, and Jochen Krauss. Author sequence and credit for contributions in multiauthored publications. *PLoS Biol*, 5(1):e18, 2007.

Permissions

The contributors of this book come from diverse backgrounds, making this book a truly international effort. This book will bring forth new frontiers with its revolutionizing research information and detailed analysis of the nascent developments around the world.

We would like to thank Vasilios N. Katsikis, for lending his expertise to make the book truly unique. He has played a crucial role in the development of this book. Without his invaluable contribution this book wouldn't have been possible. He has made vital efforts to compile up to date information on the varied aspects of this subject to make this book a valuable addition to the collection of many professionals and students.

This book was conceptualized with the vision of imparting up-to-date information and advanced data in this field. To ensure the same, a matchless editorial board was set up. Every individual on the board went through rigorous rounds of assessment to prove their worth. After which they invested a large part of their time researching and compiling the most relevant data for our readers. Conferences and sessions were held from time to time between the editorial board and the contributing authors to present the data in the most comprehensible form. The editorial team has worked tirelessly to provide valuable and valid information to help people across the globe.

Every chapter published in this book has been scrutinized by our experts. Their significance has been extensively debated. The topics covered herein carry significant findings which will fuel the growth of the discipline. They may even be implemented as practical applications or may be referred to as a beginning point for another development. Chapters in this book were first published by InTech; hereby published with permission under the Creative Commons Attribution License or equivalent.

The editorial board has been involved in producing this book since its inception. They have spent rigorous hours researching and exploring the diverse topics which have resulted in the successful publishing of this book. They have passed on their knowledge of decades through this book. To expedite this challenging task, the publisher supported the team at every step. A small team of assistant editors was also appointed to further simplify the editing procedure and attain best results for the readers.

Our editorial team has been hand-picked from every corner of the world. Their multi-ethnicity adds dynamic inputs to the discussions which result in innovative outcomes. These outcomes are then further discussed with the researchers and contributors who give their valuable feedback and opinion regarding the same. The feedback is then collaborated with the researches and they are edited in a comprehensive manner to aid the understanding of the subject.

Apart from the editorial board, the designing team has also invested a significant amount of their time in understanding the subject and creating the most relevant covers. They scrutinized every image to scout for the most suitable representation of the subject and create an appropriate cover for the book.

The publishing team has been involved in this book since its early stages. They were actively engaged in every process, be it collecting the data, connecting with the contributors or procuring relevant information. The team has been an ardent support to the editorial, designing and production team. Their endless efforts to recruit the best for this project, has resulted in the accomplishment of this book. They are a veteran in the field of academics and their pool of knowledge is as vast as their experience in printing. Their expertise and guidance has proved useful at every step. Their uncompromising quality standards have made this book an exceptional effort. Their encouragement from time to time has been an inspiration for everyone.

The publisher and the editorial board hope that this book will prove to be a valuable piece of knowledge for researchers, students, practitioners and scholars across the globe.

Ocular Diseases

List of Contributors

Fatima El Guezar
ESSI & ERMAGIM, Ibn Zohr University, EST, PO Box 32/S, Agadir, Morocco

Hassane Bouzahir
ESSI & ERMAGIM, Ibn Zohr University, EST, PO Box 32/S, Agadir, Morocco
Faculty of Engineering, AlHosn University, PO Box 38772, Abu Dhabi, United Arab Emirates

Hassan Al-Haj Ibrahim
Department of Chemical Engineering, Al-Baath University, Homs, Syria

Cyril Belavý, Gabriel Hulkó and Karol Ondrejkovič
Institute of Automation, Measurement and Applied Informatics, Faculty of Mechanical Engineering, Center for Control of Distributed Parameter Systems, Slovak University of Technology in Bratislava, Slovak Republic

Bhar K. Aliyu, Charles A. Osheku, Lanre M.A. Adetoro and Aliyu A. Funmilayo
Federal Ministry of Science and Technology (FMST), National Space Research & Development Agency (NASRDA), Center For Space Transport & Propulsion (CSTP) Epe, Lagos, Nigeria

Charis Harley
Faculty of Science, University of the Witwatersrand, School of Computational and Applied Mathematics, Centre for Differential Equations, Continuum Mechanics and Applications, South Africa

Xiaoguang Zhou
Dongling School of Economics and Management, University of Science and Technology Beijing, Beijing, China

Vasilios N. Katsikis
General Department of Mathematics, Technological Education Institute of Piraeus, 12244 Athens, Greece

Antonio Napolitano, Sara Ungania and Vittorio Cannata
Department of Occupational Health and Safety, Medical Physics, Bambino Gesù Children's Hospital, Rome, Italy

Sébastien Leclaire, Maud El-Hachem and Marcelo Reggio
Department of Mechanical Engineering, École Polytechnique de Montréal, Canada

Printed in the USA
CPSIA information can be obtained
at www.ICGtesting.com
JSHW011413221024
72173JS00004B/537

9 781632 401922